# Designing
# Software
# Architectures

# Designing Software Architectures

## A Practical Approach

Humberto Cervantes
Rick Kazman

♦♦Addison-Wesley

Boston • Columbus • Indianapolis • New York • San Francisco • Amsterdam • Cape Town
Dubai • London • Madrid • Milan • Munich • Paris • Montreal • Toronto • Delhi • Mexico City
São Paulo • Sidney • Hong Kong • Seoul • Singapore • Taipei • Tokyo

The SEI Series in Software Engineering

For information about buying this title in bulk quantities, or for special sales opportunities (which may include electronic versions; custom cover designs; and content particular to your business, training goals, marketing focus, or branding interests), please contact our corporate sales department at corpsales@pearsoned.com or (800) 382-3419.

For government sales inquiries, please contact governmentsales@pearsoned.com.

For questions about sales outside the United States, please contact intlcs@pearson.com.

Visit us on the Web: informit.com/aw

*Library of Congress Cataloging-in-Publication Data*

Names: Cervantes, Humberto, 1974- author. I Kazman, Rick, author.
Title: Designing software architectures : a practical approach / Humberto
    Cervantes, Rick Kazman.
Description: Boston : Addison-Wesley, [2016] I Series: The SEI series in
    software engineering I Includes bibliographical references and index.
Identifiers: LCCN 2016005436I ISBN 9780134390789 (hardcover : alk. paper) I
    ISBN 0134390784 (hardcover : alk. paper)
Subjects: LCSH: Software architecture. I Big data.
Classification: LCC QA76.758 .C44 2016 I DDC 005.1/2—dc23
LC record available at https://lccn.loc.gov/2016005436

ISBN-13: 978-013-439078-9
ISBN-10: 0-13-439078-4

Text printed in the United States on recycled paper at RR Donnelley in Crawfordsville, Indiana.
8 2020

# Contents

*I dedicate this book to my parents, Ilse and Humberto; to my wife, Gabriela; and to my sons, Julian and Alexis. Thank you for all your love, support, and inspiration.*

H. C.

*I dedicate this book to my wife, for her loving support, and to my Grandmasters, Hee Il Cho and Philip Ameris, for the examples that they set, leading me to always strive to be my best.*

R. K.

# Preface

When asked about software architecture, people think frequently about models—that is, the representations of the structures that constitute the architecture. Less frequently, people think about the thought processes that produce these structures—that is, the *process of design*. Design is a complex activity to perform and a complex topic to write about, as it involves making a myriad of decisions that take into account many aspects of a system. These aspects are oftentimes hard to express, particularly when they originate from experience and knowledge that is hard-earned in the "battlefield" of previous software development projects. Nevertheless, the activity of design is the basis of software architecture and, as such, it begs to be explained. Although experience can hardly be communicated through a book, what *can* be shared is a method that can help you perform the process of design in a systematic way.

This book is about that design process and about one particular design method, called Attribute-Driven Design (ADD). We believe that this method is a powerful tool that will help you perform design in a principled, disciplined, and repeatable way. In this book, employing ADD and several examples of ADD's use in the real world, we show you how to perform architectural design. Even though you may not currently possess sufficient design experience, we illustrate how the method promotes reusing *design concepts*—that is, proven solutions that embody the experience of others.

Although ADD has existed for more than a decade, relatively little has been written about it and few examples have been provided to explain how it is performed. This lack of published information has made it difficult for people to adopt the method or to teach others about it. Furthermore, the documentation that has been published about ADD is somewhat "high level" and can be hard to relate to the concepts, practices, and technologies that architects use in their day-to-day activities.

We have been working with practicing architects for several years, coaching them on how to perform design, and learning in the process. We have learned, for example, that practicing architects take technologies into consideration *early* in the design process and this is something that was not part of the original version of ADD. For this reason, the method felt "disconnected" from reality for many practitioners. In this book, we provide a revised version of ADD in which we have tried to bridge the gap between theory and practice.

We have also been teaching software architecture and software design for many years. Along the way, we realized how hard it is for people without any experience to perform design. This understanding motivated us to create a roadmap for design that, we believe, is helpful in guiding people to perform the design process. We also created a game that is useful in teaching about software design; it can be considered a companion to this book.

The target audience for this book is anyone interested in the design of software architectures. We believe it will be particularly useful for practitioners who must perform this task but who currently perform it in an ad hoc way. Experienced practitioners who already perform design following an established method will also find new ideas—for example, how to track design progress using a Kanban board, how to analyze a design using tactics-based questionnaires, and how to incorporate a design method for early estimation. Finally, people who are already familiar with the other architecture methods from the Software Engineering Institute will find information about the ways to connect ADD to methods such as the Quality Attribute Workshop (QAW), the Architecture Tradeoff Analysis Method (ATAM), and the Cost Benefit Analysis Method (CBAM). This book will also be useful to students and teachers of computer science or software engineering programs. We believe that the case studies included here will help them understand how to perform the design process more easily. Certainly, we have been using similar examples in our courses with great success. As Albert Einstein said, "Example isn't another way to teach; it is the *only* way to teach."

Our hope is that this book will help you in understanding that design can be performed following a method, and that this realization will help you produce better software systems in the future.

The book is structured as follows.

- In Chapter 1, we briefly introduce software architecture and the Attribute-Driven Design method.
- In Chapter 2, we discuss architecture design in more detail, along with the main inputs to the design process—what we call *architectural drivers,* plus the design concepts that will help you satisfy these drivers using proven solutions.
- Chapter 3 presents the ADD method in detail. We discuss each of the steps of the method along with various techniques that can be used to perform these steps appropriately.
- Chapter 4 is our first case study, which illustrates the development of a greenfield system. For this case study, we have made an effort to show how a majority of the concepts described in Chapter 3 are used in the design process, so you can think of this case study as being more "academic" in nature (although it is derived from a real-world system).
- Chapter 5 presents our second case study, which was co-written with practicing software architects and as such is much more technical and detailed

in nature. It will show you the nitty-gritty details of how ADD is used in the design of a Big Data system that involves many different technologies. This example illustrates the development of a system in what we consider to be a "novel" domain, as opposed to the more traditional domain used in Chapter 4.

- Chapter 6 is a shorter case study that illustrates the use of ADD in the design of an extension of a legacy (or brownfield) system, which is a common situation. This example demonstrates that architectural design is not something that is performed only once, when the first version of the system is developed, but rather is an activity that can be performed at different moments of the development process.
- Chapter 7 presents other design methods. In our revision of ADD, we adopted ideas from other authors who have also investigated the process of design, and here we briefly summarize their approaches both as an homage to their work and as a means to compare ADD to these methods.
- Chapter 8 discusses the topic of analysis in depth, even though this is a book on design. Analysis is naturally performed as part of design, so here we describe techniques that can be used both during the design process or after a portion of the design has been completed. In particular, we introduce the use of tactics-based questionnaires, which are helpful in understanding, in a time-efficient and simple manner, the decisions made in the design process.
- Chapter 9 describes how the design process fits at an organizational level. For instance, performing some amount of architectural design at the earliest moments of the project's life is useful for estimation purposes. We also show how ADD can be associated with different software development approaches.
- Chapter 10 concludes the book.

We also include two appendixes. Appendix A presents *A Design Concepts Catalog*, which, as its name suggests, is a catalog of different types of design concepts that can be used to design for a particular application domain. This catalog includes design concepts that we have gathered from different sources, reflecting how experienced and disciplined architects work in the real world. In this case, our catalog contains a sample of the design concepts used in the case study presented in Chapter 4. Appendix B provides a set of tactics-based questionnaires (as introduced in Chapter 8) for the seven most common quality attributes and an additional questionnaire for DevOps.

---

Register your copy of *Designing Software Architectures* at informit.com for convenient access to downloads, updates, and corrections as they become available. To start the registration process, go to informit.com/register and log in or create an account. Enter the product ISBN (9780134390789) and click Submit. Once the process is complete, you will find any available bonus content under "Registered Products."

# Acknowledgments

The authors wish to acknowledge our reviewers—Marty Barrett, Roger Champagne, Siva Muthu, Robert Nord, Vishal Prabhu, Andriy Shapochka, David Sisk, Perla Velasco-Elizondo, and Olaf Zimmermann—for their generosity in providing both opinions and comments. We also wish to thank Serge Haziyev and Olha Hrytsay for their contributions to Chapter 5. In addition, we would be remiss if we did not thank the many architects at Softserve—Serge, Olha, and Andriy included—for their overall strong support of our work.

Humberto wishes to thank the directors and the group of architects at Quarksoft; many ideas for the revision of ADD and one of the case studies presented in this book originated from putting the method into practice at this company. Thank you to the architects and developers in other companies with whom I have had the opportunity to collaborate and exchange ideas—I have learned a lot from them. I also wish to thank the people at the Software Engineering Institute, who have welcomed me and other academics for many years at the ACE Educators Workshop. I also want to give recognition to my university, Universidad Autónoma Metropolitana Iztapalapa, as it has always supported my work. Thanks to my colleagues Perla Velasco-Elizondo and Luis Castro, who have accompanied me for several years in this architectural journey. Thank you to Alonso Leal, who gave me the opportunity to become a practicing architect many years ago. Thanks to Richard S. Hall, who taught me many skills that have proved invaluable in writing this book. Finally, I wish to thank my coauthor Rick, for being such a nice person and colleague; it is always a pleasure to work and exchange opinions with him.

Rick wishes to thank James Ivers and his research group at the Software Engineering Institute. In particular, I would like to thank Rod Nord, for his careful and insightful review comments and suggestions. I would also like to thank my long-time collaborator and mentor Len Bass, who got me started on this software architecture journey many years ago. Without Len, who knows where I would be today. In addition, I would like to thank Linda Northrop, who vigorously supported my research for many years and provided many wonderful "opportunities to excel." Finally, I would like to thank my coauthor Humberto, who has always been energetic, positive, and a true pleasure to work with.

# 1

# Introduction

In this chapter we provide an introduction to the topic of software architecture. We briefly discuss what architecture is and why it is fundamental to take it into account when developing software systems. We also discuss the different activities that are associated with the development of software architecture so that architectural design—which is the primary topic of this book—can be understood in the context of these activities. We also briefly discuss the role of the architect, who is the person responsible for creating the design. Finally, we introduce the Attribute-Driven Design (ADD) method, the architecture design method that we will discuss extensively in this book.

## 1.1 Motivations

Our goal in this book is to teach you how to design software architecture in a systematic, predictable, repeatable, and cost-effective way. If you are reading this book, then presumably you already have an interest in architecture and aspire to be an architect. The good news is that this goal is within your grasp. To convince you of that point, we will spend a few moments talking about the idea of design—the design of anything—and we will see how and why architectural design is not so different. In most fields, "design" involves the same sorts of challenges and considerations—meeting stakeholder needs, adhering to budgets and schedules, dealing with constraints, and so forth. While the primitives and tools of design may vary from field to field, the goals and steps of design do not.

This is encouraging news, because it means that design is not the sole province of wizards. That is, design can be taught, and it can be learned. Most design, particularly in engineering, consists of putting known design primitives together in (sometimes innovative) ways that achieve predictable outcomes. Of course, the devil is in the details, but that is why we have methods. It may seem difficult at first to imagine that a creative endeavor such as design can be captured in a step-by-step method; this, however, is not only possible but also valuable, as Parnas and Clements have discussed in their paper "A Rational Design Process: How and Why to Fake It". Of course, not everyone can be a great designer, just as not everyone can be a Thomas Edison or a LeBron James or a Ronaldo. What we do claim is that everyone can be a much *better* designer, and that structured methods supported by reusable chunks of design knowledge, which we provide in this book, can help pave the road from mediocrity to excellence.

Why are we writing a book on software architecture design? While much has been written about design in general, and while there have been some writings on software architecture design, there is no existing book dedicated solely to architecture design. Moreover, most of what has been written on architecture design is relatively abstract.

Our goal in writing this book was to provide a practical method that can be enacted by any competent software engineer, and also (and just as important) to provide a set of rich case studies that realize the method. Albert Einstein was reputed to have said, "Example isn't another way to teach, it is the only way to teach". We firmly believe that. Most of us learn better from examples than from sets of rules or steps or principles. Of course, we need the steps and rules and principles to structure what we do and to create the examples, but the examples speak to our day-to-day concerns and help us by making the steps concrete.

This is not to say that architecture design will ever be simple. If you are building a complex system, then chances are that you are trying to balance many competing forces—things like time to market, cost, performance, evolvability, usability, availability, and so on. If you are pushing the boundaries in any of these dimensions, then your job as an architect will be even more complex. This is true in any engineering discipline, not just software. If you examine the history of building large ships or skyscrapers or any other complex "system", you will see how the architects of those systems struggled with making the appropriate decisions and tradeoffs. No, architecture design may never be *easy*, but our purpose is to make it tractable and achievable by well-trained, well-educated software engineers.

## 1.2  Software Architecture

Much has been written on what *software architecture* is. We adopt the definition of software architecture from *Software Architecture in Practice* (third edition):

> The software architecture of a system is the set of structures needed to reason about the system, which comprise software elements, relations among them, and properties of both.

As you will see, our design method embodies this definition and helps to guide the designer in creating an architecture that has the *desired* properties.

### 1.2.1  The Importance of Software Architecture

Much has also been written on why *architecture* is important. Again, following *Software Architecture in Practice*, we note that architecture is important for a wide variety of reasons, and a similarly wide variety of consequences stem from those reasons:

- An architecture will inhibit or enable a system's driving quality attributes.
- The decisions made in an architecture allow you to reason about and manage change as the system evolves.
- The analysis of an architecture enables early prediction of a system's qualities.
- A documented architecture enhances communication among stakeholders.
- The architecture is a carrier of the earliest and hence most fundamental, hardest-to-change design decisions.
- An architecture defines a set of constraints on subsequent implementation.
- The architecture influences the structure of an organization, and vice versa.
- An architecture can provide the basis for evolutionary, or even throwaway, prototyping.
- An architecture is the key artifact that allows the architect and the project manager to reason about cost and schedule.
- An architecture can be created as a transferable, reusable model that forms the heart of a product line.
- Architecture-based development focuses attention on the assembly of components, rather than simply on their creation.
- By restricting design alternatives, architecture channels the creativity of developers, reducing design and system complexity.
- An architecture can be the foundation for training a new team member.

If an architecture is important for all of these reasons—if it affects the structure of the organization, and the qualities of the system, and the people involved in its creation and evolution—then surely great care must be taken in designing this crucial artifact. Sadly, that is most often not the case. Architectures often "evolve" or "emerge". While we have nothing against evolution or emergence, and while we emphatically are not arguing for "big design up front", doing no architecture at all is often too risky for anything but the simplest projects. Would you want to drive over a bridge or ride in a jet that had not been carefully designed? Of course not. But you use software every day that is buggy, costly, insecure, unreliable, fault prone, and slow—and many of these undesirable characteristics can be avoided!

The core message of this book is that architecture design does not need to be difficult or scary; it is not the sole province of wizards; and it does not have to be costly and all done up front. Our job is to show you how and convince you that it is within your reach.

### 1.2.2   Life-Cycle Activities

Software architecture design is one of the software architecture life-cycle activities (Figure 1.1). As in any software project life cycle, this activity is concerned with the translation of requirements into a design into an implementation. Specifically, the architect needs to worry about the following issues:

- *Architectural requirements.* Among all the requirements, a few will have a particular importance with respect to the software architecture. These *architecturally significant requirements (ASRs)* include not only the most important functionality of the system and the constraints that need to be taken into account, but also—and most importantly—quality attributes such as high performance, high availability, ease of evolution, and iron-clad security. These requirements, along with a clear design purpose and other architectural concerns that may never be written down or may be invisible to external stakeholders, will guide you to choose one set of architectural structures and components over another. We will refer to these ASRs and concerns as *drivers*, as they can be said to drive the design.
- *Architectural design.* Design is a translation, from the world of needs (requirements) to the world of solutions, in terms of structures composed of code, frameworks, and components. A good design is one that *satisfies* the drivers. Architectural design is the focus of this book.

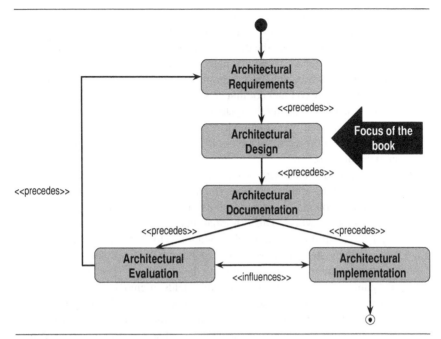

**FIGURE 1.1**  Software architecture life-cycle activities

- *Architectural documentation.* Some level of preliminary documentation (or *sketches*) of the structures should be created as part of architectural design. This activity, however, refers to the creation of a more formal document from these sketches. If the project is small and has a precedent, then architecture documentation may be minimal. In contrast, if the project is large, if distributed teams are collaborating, or if significant technical challenges exist, then architectural documentation will repay the effort invested in this activity. While documentation is often avoided and derided by programmers, it is a standard, non-negotiable deliverable in almost every other engineering discipline. If your system is big enough and if it is mission critical, it should be documented. In other engineering disciplines, a "blueprint"— some sort of documented design—is an absolutely essential step in moving toward implementation and the commitment of resources.

- *Architectural evaluation.* As with documentation, if your project is non-trivial, then you owe it to yourself and to your stakeholders to evaluate it—that is, to ensure that the decisions made are appropriate to address the critical requirements. Would you deliver code without testing it? Of course not. Similarly, why would you commit enormous resources to fleshing out an architecture if you had not first "tested" the design? You might want to do this when first creating the system or when putting it through a major refactoring. Typically evaluation is done informally and internally, but for truly important projects it is advisable to have a formal evaluation done by an external team.
- *Architectural implementation/conformance checking.* Finally, you need to implement the architecture that you have created (and evaluated). As an architect, you may need to tweak the design as the system grows and as requirements evolve. This is normal. In addition to this tweaking, your major responsibility during implementation is to ensure conformance of the code to the design. If developers are not faithfully implementing the architecture, they may be undermining the qualities that you have designed in. Again, consider what is done in other fields of engineering. When a concrete foundation for a new building is poured, the building that rests on top of that foundation is not constructed until the foundation has first been tested, typically via a core sample, to ensure that it is strong enough, dense enough, sufficiently impermeable to water and gases, and so forth. Without conformance checking, we have no way of ensuring the quality of what is being subsequently constructed.

Note that we are not proposing a specific life-cycle methodology in Figure 1.1. The stereotype <<precedes>> simply means that some effort in an activity must be performed, and hence precede, effort in a later activity. For example, you cannot perform design activities if you have no idea about the requirements, and you cannot evaluate an architecture if you have not first made some design decisions.

Today most commercial software is developed using some form of Agile methodology. None of these architecture activities is incompatible with Agile practices. The question for a software architect is not "Should I do Agile or architecture?", but rather "How much architecture should I do up front versus how much should I defer until the project's requirements have solidified somewhat?" and "How much of the architecture should I formally document, and when?" Agile and architecture are happy companions for many software projects.

We will discuss the relationship between architecture design and various software life-cycle methods and process models, including iterative development, in Chapter 9.

## 1.3 The Role of the Architect

An architect is much more than "just" a designer. This role, which may be played by one or more individuals, has a long list of duties, skills, and knowledge that must be satisfied if it is to be successful. These prerequisites include the following:

- *Leadership:* mentoring, team-building, establishing a vision, coaching
- *Communication:* both technical and nontechnical, encouraging collaboration
- *Negotiation:* dealing with internal and external stakeholders and their conflicting needs and expectations
- *Technical skills:* life-cycle skills, expertise with technologies, continuous learning, coding
- *Project skills:* budgeting, personnel, schedule management, risk management
- *Analytical skills:* architectural analysis, general analysis mindset for project management and measurement (see the sidebar "The Meaning of Analysis")

A successful design is not a static document that is "thrown over the wall". That is, architects must not only design well, but must also be intimately involved in every aspect of the project, from conception and business justification to design and creation, through to operation, maintenance, and eventually retirement.

---

The Meaning of Analysis

In the *Merriam-Webster Dictionary*, the word *analysis* is defined as follows:

- The careful study of something to learn about its parts, what they do, and how they are related to each other
- An explanation of the nature and meaning of something

In this book we use the word *analysis* for different purposes, and both of these definitions apply. For instance, as part of the architectural evaluation activity, an existing architecture is analyzed to gauge if it is appropriate to satisfy its associated drivers. During the design process, the inputs are analyzed to make design decisions. The creation of prototypes is also a form of analysis. In fact, analysis is so important to the design process that we devote Chapter 8 to just this topic. Here we also discuss, in more detail, the relationship between analysis and evaluation. In this book, we focus primarily on the design activity, its associated technical skills, and its integration into the development life cycle. For a fuller treatment of the other aspects of an architect's life, we invite you to read a more general book on software architecture, such as *Software Architecture in Practice* or *Just Enough Software Architecture*.

---

## 1.4 A Brief History of ADD

While an architect has many duties and responsibilities, in this book we focus on what is arguably the single most important skill that a software engineer must master to be called "architect": the process of design. To make architectural design more tractable and repeatable, in this book we focus most of our attention on the Attribute-Driven Design (ADD) method, which provides step-by-step guidance on how to iteratively perform the design activity shown in Figure 1.1. Chapter 3 describes the most recent version of ADD, version 3.0, in detail, so here we provide a bit of background for those who are familiar with previous versions of ADD. The first version of ADD (ADD 1.0, originally called ABD, for "Architecture-Based Design") was published in January 2000, and the second version (ADD 2.0) was published in November 2006. The third edition of the book *Software Architecture in Practice* presents this method with a reduced number of steps. This discussion, however, does not introduce a new version of ADD, but rather a repackaged version that summarizes the actual steps of the method.

ADD is, to our knowledge, the most comprehensive and most widely used documented architecture design method. (We provide an overview of a number of alternative design methods in Chapter 7.) When ADD appeared, it was the first design method to focus specifically on quality attributes and their achievement through the creation of architectural structures and their representation through views. Another important contribution of ADD is that it includes architecture analysis and documentation as an integral part of the design process. In ADD, design activities include refining the sketches created during early design iterations to produce a more detailed architecture, and continuously evaluating the design.

While ADD 2.0 was useful for linking quality attributes to design choices, it had several shortcomings that needed to be addressed:

- ADD 2.0 guides the architect to use and combine tactics and patterns to achieve the satisfaction of quality attribute scenarios. Patterns and tactics are abstractions, however, and the method did not explain how to map these abstractions to concrete implementation technologies.
- ADD 2.0 was invented before Agile methods became widely adopted and, therefore, did not offer guidance for architecture design in an Agile setting.
- ADD 2.0 provided no guidance on how to begin the design process. While this omission enhanced its generalizability, it presented difficulties for novice designers, who often do not know where to begin. Specifically, ADD 2.0 did not explicitly promote the (re)use of reference architectures, which are an ideal starting point for many architects, as we will discuss later in this book.
- ADD 2.0 did not explicitly consider different design purposes. For example, one might be doing design as part of a pre-sales process or as part of

"standard" design for construction. These are very different purposes and will result in different uses of ADD.

- ADD 2.0 did not consider that design requires some architectural concerns (i.e., internal requirements) to be addressed whether or not they are expressed in the list of "traditional" drivers (requirements and constraints). It is a rare user who will ask that a system be "testable" or will require that the system provide special testing interfaces, but a wise architect might choose to include such an infrastructure, particularly if the system is complex and used in contexts that are difficult to control and replicate.
- ADD 2.0 iterations are always driven by the selection and decomposition of architectural elements. This occurs because ADD 2.0 instructs that first an element to decompose must be chosen, and then the drivers must be identified. In ADD 3.0, we recognize that sometimes a design step is driven by the critical architectural requirements, which guides the selection and decomposition of elements.
- ADD 2.0 includes (initial) documentation and analysis, but they are not explicit steps of the design process.

ADD 3.0 addresses all of these shortcomings. To be sure, ADD 3.0 is evolutionary, not revolutionary. It was catalyzed by the creation of ADD 2.5,[1] which was itself a reaction to attempting to use ADD in the real world, in many different contexts.

We published ADD 2.5 in 2013. In that work, we advocated the use of application frameworks such as JSF, Spring, or Hibernate as first-class design concepts. This change was intended to address ADD 2.0's shortcoming of being too abstract to apply easily. ADD starts with drivers, systematically links them to design decisions, and then links those decisions to the available implementation options, including externally developed components. For Agile development, ADD 3.0 promotes quick design iterations in which a small number of design decisions are made, potentially followed by an implementation spike. In addition, ADD 3.0 explicitly promotes the (re)use of reference architectures and is paired with a "design concepts catalog", which includes a broad selection of tactics, patterns, frameworks, reference architectures, and technologies (see Appendix A).

## 1.5 Summary

Having covered our motivations and background, we now move on to the heart and soul of this book. In the next few chapters, we describe what we mean by design and by architectural design in particular, we discuss ADD, and we provide three case studies showing in detail how ADD can be used in the real world. We

---

1. This is our own coding notation; the 2.5 number is not used elsewhere.

also discuss the critical role that analysis plays in the design process and provide examples of how analysis can be performed on design artifacts.

---

## 1.6   Further Reading

Fred Brooks has written a thoughtful series of essays on the nature of design, reflecting his 50 years of experience as a designer and researcher: F. P. Brooks, Jr. *The Design of Design: Essays from a Computer Scientist.* Addison-Wesley, 2010.

The usefulness of having a documented process for design and other development activities is discussed in D. Parnas and P. Clements, "A Rational Design Process: How and Why to Fake It", *IEEE Transactions on Software Engineering*, SE-12, 2, February 1986.

The definition of software architecture used here, as well as the arguments for the importance of architecture and the role of the architect, all derive from L. Bass, P. Clements, and R. Kazman, *Software Architecture in Practice*, 3rd ed., Addison-Wesley, 2012.

Several books cover the different activities of the architecture development life cycle, including G. Fairbanks, *Just Enough Software Architecture: A Risk Driven Approach*, Marshall & Brainerd, 2010, and the ones whose design approaches are described in Chapter 7.

An early reference for the first version of ADD can be found in F. Bachmann, L. Bass, G. Chastek, P. Donohoe, and F. Peruzzi, *The Architecture Based Design Method*, CMU/SEI-2000-TR-001. The second version of ADD was described in R. Wojcik, F. Bachmann, L. Bass, P. Clements, P. Merson, R. Nord, and W. Wood, *Attribute-Driven Design (ADD), Version 2.0*, CMU/SEI-2006-TR-023. The version of ADD that we have referred to here as ADD 2.5 was published in H. Cervantes, P. Velasco-Elizondo, and R. Kazman, "A Principled Way of Using Frameworks in Architectural Design", *IEEE Software*, 46–53, March/April 2013.

# 2

# Architectural Design

We now dive into the process of architecture design: what it is, why it is important, how it works (at an abstract level). and which major concepts and activities it involves. We first discuss architectural drivers: the various factors that "drive" design decisions, some of which are documented as requirements, but many of which are not. In addition, we provide an overview of design concepts—the major building blocks that you will select, combine, instantiate, analyze, and document as part of your design process.

## 2.1  Design in General

*Design* is both a verb and a noun. Design is a process, an activity, and hence a verb. The process results in the creation of a design—a description of a desired end state. Thus the output of the design process is the thing, the noun, the artifact that you will eventually implement. Designing means making decisions to achieve goals and satisfy requirements and constraints. The outputs of the design process are a direct reflection of those goals, requirements, and constraints. Think about houses, for example. Why do traditional houses in China look different from those in Switzerland or Algeria? Why does a yurt look like a yurt, which is different from an igloo or a chalet or a longhouse?

The architectures of these styles of houses have evolved over the centuries to reflect their unique sets of goals, requirements, and constraints. Houses in

China feature symmetric enclosures, sky wells to increase ventilation, south-facing courtyards to collect sunlight and provide protection from cold north winds, and so forth. A-frame houses have steep pitched roofs that extend to the ground, meaning minimal painting and protection from heavy snow loads (which just slide off to the ground). Igloos are built of ice, reflecting the availability of ice, the relative poverty of other building materials, and the constraints of time (a small one can be built in an hour).

In each case, the process of design involved the selection and adaptation of a number of solution approaches. Even igloo designs can vary. Some are small and meant for a temporary travel shelter. Others are large, often connecting several structures, meant for entire communities to meet. Some are simple unadorned snow huts. Others are lined with furs, with ice "windows", and doors made of animal skin.

The process of design, in each case, balances the various "forces" facing the designer. Some designs require considerable skill to execute (such as carving and stacking snow blocks in such a way that they produce a self-supporting dome). Others require relatively little skill—a lean-to can be constructed from branches and bark by almost anyone. But the qualities that these structures exhibit may also vary considerably. Lean-tos provide little protection from the elements and are easily destroyed, whereas an igloo can withstand Arctic storms and support the weight of a person standing on the roof.

Is design "hard"? Well, yes and no. *Novel* design is hard. It is pretty clear how to design a conventional bicycle, but the design for the Segway broke new ground. Fortunately, most design is not novel, because most of the time our requirements are not novel. Most people want a bicycle that will reliably convey them from place to place. The same holds true in every domain. Consider houses, for example. Most people living in Phoenix want a house that can be easily and economically kept cool, whereas most people in Edmonton are primarily concerned with a house that can be kept warm. In contrast, people living in Japan and Los Angeles are concerned with buildings that can withstand earthquakes.

The good news for you, the architect, is that there are ample proven designs and design fragments, or building blocks that we call *design concepts*, that can be reused and combined to reliably achieve these goals. If your design is truly novel—if you are designing the next Sydney Opera House—then the design process will likely be "hard". The Sydney Opera House, for example, cost 14 times its original budget estimate and was delivered ten years late. So, too, with the design of software architectures.

## 2.2   Design in Software Architecture

Architectural design for software systems is no different than design in general: It involves making decisions, working with available skills and materials, to satisfy requirements and constraints. In architectural design, we make decisions to transform our design purpose, requirements, constraints, and architectural concerns—what we call the architectural *drivers*—into structures, as shown in Figure 2.1. These structures are then used to guide the project. They guide analysis and construction, and serve as the foundation for educating a new project member. They also guide cost and schedule estimation, team formation, risk analysis and mitigation, and, of course, implementation.

Architectural design is, therefore, a key step to achieving your product and project goals. Some of these goals are technical (e.g., achieving low and predictable latency in a video game or an e-commerce website), and some are nontechnical (e.g., keeping the workforce employed, entering a new market, meeting a deadline). The decisions that you, as an architect, make will have implications for the achievement of these goals and may, in some cases, be in conflict. The choice

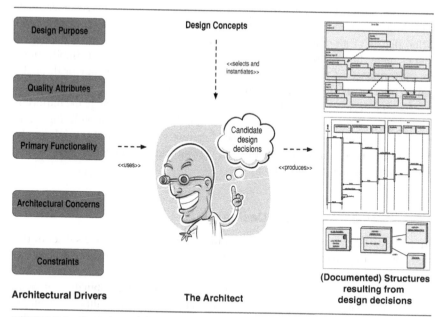

**FIGURE 2.1**   Overview of the architecture design activity
(Architect image © Brett Lamb I Dreamstime.com)

of a particular reference architecture (e.g., the Rich Client Application) may provide a good foundation for achieving your latency goals and will keep your workforce employed because they are already familiar with that reference architecture and its supporting technology stack. But this choice may not help you enter a new market—mobile games, for example.

In general, when designing, a change in some structure to achieve one quality attribute will have negative effects on other quality attributes. These tradeoffs are a fact of life for every practicing architect in every domain. We will see this over and over again in the examples and case studies provided in this book. Thus the architect's job is not one of finding an *optimal* solution, but rather one of *satisficing*—searching through a potentially large space of design alternatives and decisions until an acceptable solution is found.

### 2.2.1   Architectural Design

Grady Booch has said, "All architecture is design, but not all design is architecture". What makes a decision "architectural"? A decision is architectural if it has non-local consequences *and* those consequences matter to the achievement of an architectural driver. No decision is, therefore, inherently architectural or non-architectural. The choice of a buffering strategy within a single element may have little effect on the rest of the system, in which case it is an implementation detail that is of no concern to anyone except the implementer or maintainer of that element. In contrast, the buffering strategy may have enormous implications for performance (if the buffering affects the achievement of latency or throughput or jitter goals) or availability (if the buffers might not be large enough and information gets lost) or modifiability (if we wish to flexibly change the buffering strategy in different deployments or contexts). The choice of a buffering strategy, like most design choices, is neither inherently architectural nor inherently non-architectural. Instead, this distinction is completely dependent on the current and anticipated architectural drivers.

### 2.2.2   Element Interaction Design

Architectural design generally results in the identification of only a subset of the elements that are part of the system's structure. This is to be expected because, during initial architectural design, the architect will focus on the primary functionality of the system. What makes a use case primary? A combination of business importance, risk, and complexity considerations feed into this designation. Of course, to your users, everything is urgent and top priority. More realistically, a small number of use cases provide the most fundamental business value or represent the greatest risk (if they are done wrong), so these are deemed primary.

Every system has many more use cases, beyond the primary ones, that need to be satisfied. The elements that support these nonprimary use cases and their interfaces are identified as part of what we call *element interaction design*. This level of design usually follows architectural design. The location and relationships of these elements, however, are constrained by the decisions that were made during architectural design. These elements can be units of work (i.e., modules) assigned to an individual or to a team, so this level of design is important for defining not only how nonprimary functionality is allocated, but also for planning purposes (e.g., team formation and communication, budgeting, outsourcing, release planning, unit and integration test planning).

Depending on the scale and complexity of the system, the architect should be involved in element interaction design, either directly or in an auditing role. This involvement ensures that the system's important quality attributes are not compromised—for example, if the elements are not defined, located, and connected correctly. It will also help the architect spot opportunities for generalization.

### 2.2.3  Element Internals Design

A third level of design follows element interaction design, which we call *element internals design*. In this level of design, which is usually conducted as part of the element development activities, the internals of the elements identified in the previous design level are established, so as to satisfy the element's interface.

Architectural decisions can and do occur at the three levels of design. Moreover, during architectural design, the architect may need to delve as deeply as element internals design to achieve a particular architectural driver. An example of this is the selection of a buffering strategy that was previously discussed. In this sense, architectural design can involve considerable detail, which explains why we do not like to think about it in terms of "high-level design" or "detailed design" (see the sidebar "Detailed Design?").

Architectural design precedes element interaction design, which precedes element internals design. This is logically necessary: One cannot design an element's internals until the elements themselves have been defined, and one cannot reason about interaction until several elements and some patterns of interactions among them have been defined. But as projects grow and evolve, there is, in practice, considerable iteration between these activities.

---

Detailed Design?

The term "detailed design" is often used to refer to the design of the internals of modules. Although it is widely used, we really don't like this term, which is presented as somehow in opposition to "high-level design". We prefer the more precise terms "architectural design", "element interaction design", and "element internals design".

After all, architectural design may be quite detailed, if your system is complex. And some design "details" will turn out to be architectural. For the same reason, we also don't like the terms "high-level design" and "low-level design". Who can really know what these terms actually mean? Clearly, "high-level design" should be somehow "higher" or more abstract, and cover more of the architectural landscape than "low-level design", but beyond that we are at a loss to imbue these terms with any precise meaning.

So here is what we recommend: Just avoid using terms such as "high", "low", or "detailed" altogether. There is always a better, more precise choice, such as "architectural", "element interaction", or "element internals" design!

Think carefully about the impact of the decisions you are making, the information that you are trying to convey in your design documentation, and the likely audience for that information, and then give that process an appropriate, meaningful name.

## 2.3   Why Is Architectural Design So Important?

There is a very high cost to a project of *not* making certain design decisions, or of not making them early enough. This manifests itself in many different ways. Early on, an initial architecture is critical for project proposals (or, as it is sometimes called in the consulting world, the *pre-sales process*). Without doing some architectural thinking and some early design work, you cannot confidently predict project cost, schedule, and quality. Even at this early stage, an architecture will determine the key approaches for achieving architectural drivers, the gross work-breakdown structure, and the choices of tools, skills, and technologies needed to realize the system.

In addition, architecture is a key enabler of agility, as we will discuss in Chapter 9. Whether your organization has embraced Agile processes or not, it is difficult to imagine anyone who would willingly choose an architecture that is brittle and hard to change or extend or tune—and yet it happens all the time. This so-called *technical debt* occurs for a variety of reasons, but paramount among these is the combination of a focus on features—typically driven by stakeholder demands—and the inability of architects and project managers to measure the return on investment of good architectural practices. Features provide immediate benefit. Architectural improvement provides immediate costs and long-term benefits. Put this way, why would anyone ever "invest" in architecture? The answer is simple: Without architecture, the benefits that the system is supposed to bring will be far harder to realize.

Simply put, if you do not make some key architectural decisions early and if you allow your architecture to degrade, you will be unable to maintain sprint velocity, because you cannot easily respond to change requests. However, we vehemently disagree with what the original creators of the Agile Manifesto claimed: "The best architectures, requirements, and designs emerge from self-organizing teams". Indeed, our demurral with this point is precisely why we have written this book. Good architectural design is difficult (and still rare), and it does not just "emerge". This opinion mirrors a growing consensus within the Agile community. More and more, we see techniques such as "disciplined agility at scale", the "walking skeleton", and the "scaled Agile framework" embraced by Agile thought leaders and practitioners alike. Each of these techniques advocates some architectural thinking and design prior to much, if any, development. To reiterate, architecture enables agility, and not the other way around.

Furthermore, the architecture will influence, but not determine, other decisions that are not in and of themselves design decisions. These decisions do not influence the achievement of quality attributes directly, but they may still need to be made by the architect. For example, such decisions may include selection of tools; structuring the development environment; supporting releases, deployment, and operations; and making work assignments.

Finally, a well-designed, properly communicated architecture is key to achieving *agreements* that will guide the team. The most important kinds to make are agreements on interfaces and on shared resources. Agreeing on interfaces early is important for component-based development, and critically important for distributed development. These decisions *will* be made sooner or later. If you don't make the decisions early, the system will be much more difficult to integrate. In Section 3.6, we will discuss how to define interfaces as part of architectural design—both the external interfaces to other systems and the internal interfaces that mediate your element interactions.

## 2.4 Architectural Drivers

Before commencing design with ADD (or with any other design method, for that matter), you need to think about what you are doing and why. While this statement may seem blindingly obvious, the devil is, as usual, in the details. We categorize these "what" and "why" questions as architectural drivers. As shown in Figure 2.1, these drivers include a design purpose, quality attributes, primary functionality, architectural concerns, and constraints. These considerations are critical to the success of the system and, as such, they *drive* and shape the architecture.

As with any other important requirements, architectural drivers need to be baselined and managed throughout the development life cycle.

### 2.4.1   Design Purpose

First, you need to be clear about the purpose of the design that you want to achieve. When and why are you doing this architecture design? Which business goals is the organization most concerned about at this time?

1. You may be doing architecture design as part of a project proposal (for the pre-sales process in a consulting organization, or for internal project selection and prioritization in a company, as discussed in Section 9.1.1). It is not uncommon that, as part of determining project feasibility, schedule, and budget, an initial architecture is created. Such an architecture would not be very detailed; its purpose is to understand and break down the architecture in sufficient detail that the units of work are understood and hence may be estimated.
2. You may be doing architecture design as part of the process of creating an exploratory prototype. In this case, the purpose of the architecture design process is not so much to create a releasable or reusable system, but rather to explore the domain, to explore new technology, to place something executable in front of a customer to elicit rapid feedback, or to explore some quality attribute (such as performance scalability or failover for availability).
3. You may be designing your architecture during development. This could be for an entire new system, for a substantial portion of a new system, or for a portion of an existing system that is being refactored or replaced. In this case, the purpose is to do enough design work to satisfy requirements, guide system construction and work assignments, and prepare for an eventual release.

These purposes may be interpreted and realized differently for greenfield systems in mature domains, for greenfield systems in novel domains, and for existing systems. In a mature domain, the pre-sales process, for example, might be relatively straightforward; the architect can reuse existing systems as examples and confidently make estimates based on analogy. In novel domains, the pre-sales estimation process will be far more complex and risky, and may have highly variable results. In these circumstances, a prototype of the system, or a key part of the system, may need to be created to mitigate risk and reduce uncertainty. In many cases, this architecture may also need to be quickly adapted as new requirements are learned and embraced. In brownfield systems, while the requirements are better understood, the existing system is itself a complex object that must be well understood for planning to be accurate.

Finally, the development organization's goals during development or maintenance may affect the architecture design process. For example, the organization might be interested in designing for reuse, designing for future extension or subsetting, designing for scalability, designing for continuous delivery, designing to best utilize existing project capabilities and team member skills, and so forth. Or the organization might have a strategic relationship with a vendor. Or the CIO might have a specific like or dislike and wants to impose it on your project.

Why do we bother to list these considerations? Because they *will* affect both the process of design and the outputs of design. Architectures exist to help achieve business goals. The architect should be clear about these goals and should communicate them (and negotiate them!) and establish a clear design purpose *before* beginning the design process.

### 2.4.2  Quality Attributes

In the book *Software Architecture in Practice*, *quality attributes* are defined as being measurable or testable properties of a system that are used to indicate how well the system satisfies the needs of its stakeholders. Because quality tends to be a subjective concept in itself, these properties allow quality to be expressed succinctly and objectively.

Among the drivers, quality attributes are the ones that shape the architecture the most significantly. The critical choices that you make when you are doing architectural design determine, in large part, the ways that your system will or will not meet these driving quality attribute goals.

Given their importance, you must worry about eliciting, specifying, prioritizing, and validating quality attributes. Given that so much depends on getting these drivers right, this sounds like a daunting task. Fortunately, a number of well-understood, widely disseminated techniques can help you here (see sidebar "The Quality Attribute Workshop and the Utility Tree"):

- Quality Attribute Workshop (QAW) is a facilitated brainstorming session involving a group of system stakeholders that covers the bulk of the activities of eliciting, specifying, prioritizing, and achieving consensus on quality attributes.
- Mission Thread Workshop serves the same purpose as QAW, but for a system of systems.
- The Utility Tree can be used by the architect to prioritize quality attribute requirements according to their technical difficulty and risk.

We believe that the best way to discuss, document, and prioritize quality attribute requirements is as a set of scenarios. A *scenario*, in its most basic form, describes the system's response to some stimulus. Why are scenarios the best approach? Because all other approaches are worse! Endless time may be wasted in defining terms such as "performance" or "modifiability" or "configurability", as these discussions tend to shed little light on the real system. It is meaningless to say that a system will be "modifiable", because every system is modifiable with respect to some changes and not modifiable with respect to others. One can, however, specify the modifiability response measure you would like to achieve (say, elapsed time or effort) in response to a specific change request. For example, you might want to specify that "a change to update shipping rates on the e-commerce website is completed and tested in less than 1 person-day of effort"—an unambiguous criterion.

The heart of a quality attribute scenario, therefore, is the pairing of a stimulus with a response. Suppose that you are building a video game and you have a functional requirement like this: "The game shall change view modes when the user presses the <C> button". This functional requirement, if it is important, needs to be associated with quality attribute requirements. For example:

- How fast should the function be?
- How secure should the function be?
- How modifiable should the function be?

To address this problem, we use a scenario to describe a quality attribute requirement. A quality attribute scenario is a short description of how a system is required to respond to some stimulus. For example, we might annotate the functional requirement given earlier as follows: "The game shall change view modes in < 500 ms when the user presses the <C> button". A scenario associates a stimulus (in this case, the pressing of the <C> button) with a response (changing the view mode) that is measured using a response measure (< 500 ms). A complete quality attribute scenario adds three other parts: the source of the stimulus (in this case, the user), the artifact affected (in this case, because we are dealing with end-to-end latency, the artifact is the entire system) and the environment (are we in normal operation, startup, degraded mode, or some other mode?). In total, then, there are six parts of a completely well-specified scenario, as shown in Figure 2.2.

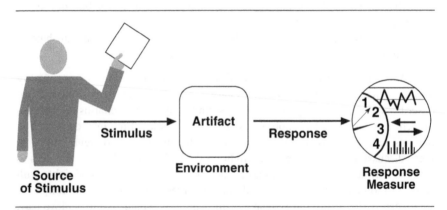

**FIGURE 2.2**   The six parts of a quality attribute scenario

Scenarios are testable, *falsifiable hypotheses* about the quality attribute behavior of the system under consideration. Because they have explicit stimuli and responses, we can evaluate a design in terms of how likely it is to support the scenario, and we can take measurements and test a prototype or fully fleshed-out system for whether it satisfies the scenario in practice. If the analysis (or prototyping results) indicates that the scenario's response goal cannot be met, then the hypothesis is deemed falsified.

As with other requirements, scenarios should be prioritized. This can be achieved by considering two dimensions that are associated with each scenario and that are assigned a rank of importance:

- The first dimension corresponds to the importance of the scenario with respect to the success of the system. This is ranked by the customer.
- The second dimension corresponds to the degree of technical risk associated with the scenario. This is ranked by the architect.

A low/medium/high (L/M/H) scale is used to rank both dimensions. Once the dimensions have been ranked, scenarios are prioritized by selecting those that have a combination of (H, H), (H, M), or (M, H) rankings.

In addition, some traditional requirements elicitation techniques can be modified slightly to focus on quality attribute requirements, such as Joint Requirements Planning (JRP), Joint Application Design (JAD), discovery prototyping, and accelerated systems analysis.

But whatever technique you use, *do not* start design without a prioritized list of measurable quality attributes! While stakeholders might plead ignorance ("I don't know how fast it needs to be; just make it fast!"), you can almost always elicit at least a range of possible responses. Instead of saying the system should be "fast", ask the stakeholder if a 10-second response time is acceptable. If that is unacceptable, ask if 5 seconds is OK, or 1 second. You will find that, in most cases, users know more than they realize about their requirements, and you can at least "box them in" to a range.

---

### The Quality Attribute Workshop and the Utility Tree

#### The Quality Attribute Workshop (QAW)

The QAW is a facilitated, stakeholder-focused method to generate, prioritize, and refine quality attribute scenarios. A QAW meeting is ideally enacted before the software architecture has been defined although, in practice, we have seen the QAW being used at all points in the software development life cycle. The QAW is focused on system-level concerns and specifically the role that software will play in the system. The steps of the QAW are as follows:

1. QAW Presentation and Introductions

   The QAW facilitators describe the motivation for the QAW and explain each step of the method.

2. Business Goals Presentation

   A stakeholder representing the project's business concerns presents the system's business context, broad functional requirements, constraints, and known quality attribute requirements. The quality attributes that will be refined in later QAW steps will be derived from, and should be traceable to, the business goals presented in this step. For this reason, these business goals must be prioritized.

3. Architectural Plan Presentation

   The architect presents the system architectural plans as they currently exist. Although the architecture has frequently not been defined yet (particularly for greenfield systems), the architect often knows quite a lot about it even at this early stage. For example, the architect might already know about technologies that are mandated, other systems that this system must interact with, standards that must be followed, subsystems or components that could be reused, and so forth.

4. Identification of Architectural Drivers

   The facilitators share their list of key architectural drivers that they assembled during steps 2 and 3 and ask the stakeholders for clarifications, additions, deletions, and corrections. The idea here is to reach a consensus on a distilled list of architectural drivers that covers major functional requirements, business drivers, constraints, and quality attributes.

5. Scenario Brainstorming

   Given this context, each stakeholder now has the opportunity to express a scenario representing that stakeholder's needs and desires with respect to the system. The facilitators ensure that each scenario has an explicit stimulus and response. The facilitators also ensure traceability and completeness: At least one representative scenario should exist for each architectural driver listed in step 4 and should cover all the business goals listed in step 2.

6. Scenario Consolidation

   Similar scenarios are consolidated where reasonable. In step 7, the stakeholders vote for their favorite scenarios, and consolidation helps to prevent votes from being spread across several scenarios that are expressing essentially the same concern.

7. Scenario Prioritization

   Prioritization of the scenarios is accomplished by allocating to each stakeholder a number of votes equal to 30 percent of the total number of scenarios. The stakeholders can distribute these votes to any scenario or scenarios. Once all the stakeholders have voted, the results are tallied and the scenarios are sorted in order of popularity.

8. Scenario Refinement

The highest-priority scenarios are refined and elaborated. The facilitators help the stakeholders express these in the form of six-part scenarios: source, stimulus, artifact, environment, response, and response measure.

The output of the QAW is therefore a prioritized list of scenarios, aligned with business goals, where the highest-priority scenarios have been explored and refined. A QAW can be conducted in as little as 2–3 hours for a simple system or as part of an iteration, and as much as 2 days for a complex system where requirements completeness is a goal.

## Utility Tree

If no stakeholders are readily available to consult, you still need to decide what to do and how to prioritize the many challenges facing the system. One way to organize your thoughts is to create a Utility Tree. The Utility Tree, such as the one shown in the following figure, helps to articulate your quality attribute goals in detail, and then to prioritize them.

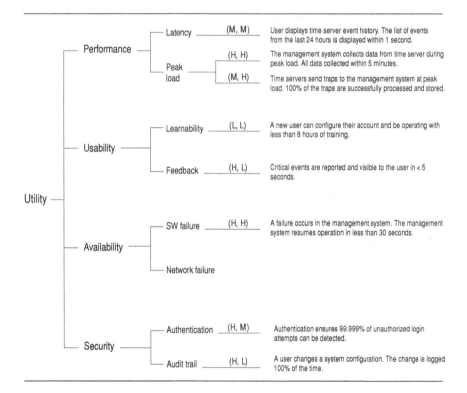

It works as follows. First write the word "Utility" on a sheet of paper. Then write the various quality attributes that constitute utility for your system. For example, you might know, based on the business goals for the system, that the most important qualities for the system are that the system be fast, secure, and easy to modify. In turn, you would write these words underneath "Utility". Next, because we don't really know what any of those terms actually means, we describe the aspect of the quality attribute that we are most concerned with. For example, while "performance" is vague, "latency of database transactions" is a bit less vague. Likewise, while "modifiability" is vague, "ease of adding new codecs" is a bit less vague.

The leaves of the tree are expressed as scenarios, which provide concrete examples of the quality attribute considerations that you just enumerated. For example, for "latency of database transactions", you might create a scenario such as "1000 users simultaneously update their own customer records under normal conditions with an average latency of 1 second". For "ease of adding new codecs", you might create a scenario such as "Customer requests that a new custom codec be added to the system. Codec is added with no side effects in 2 person-weeks of effort".

Finally, the scenarios that you have created must be prioritized. We do this prioritization by using the technique of ranking across two dimensions, resulting in a priority matrix such as the following (where the numbers in the cells are from a set of system scenarios).

| Business Importance/ Technical Risk | L | M | H |
|---|---|---|---|
| L | 5, 6, 17, 20, 22 | 1, 14 | 12, 19 |
| M | 9, 12, 16 | 8, 20 | 3, 13, 15 |
| H | 10, 18, 21 | 4, 7 | 2, 11 |

Our job, as architects, is to focus on the lower-right-hand portion of this table (H, H): those scenarios that are of high business importance and high risk. Once we have satisfactorily addressed those scenarios, we can move to the (M, H) or (H, M) ones, and then move up and to the left until all of the system's scenarios are addressed (or perhaps until we run out of time or budget, as is often the case).

It should be noted that the QAW and the Utility Tree are two different techniques that are aimed at the same goal—eliciting and prioritizing the most important quality attribute requirements, which will be some of your most critical architectural drivers. There is no reason, however, to choose between these techniques. Both are useful and valuable and, in our experience, they have complementary strengths: The QAW tends to focus more on the requirements of external stakeholders, whereas the Utility Tree tends to excel at eliciting the requirements of internal stakeholders. Making all of these stakeholders happy will go a long way toward ensuring the success of your architecture.

### 2.4.3  Primary Functionality

Functionality is the ability of the system to do the work for which it was intended. As opposed to quality attributes, the way the system is structured does not normally influence functionality. You can have all of the functionality of a given system coded in a single enormous module, or you can have it neatly distributed across many smaller, highly cohesive modules. Externally the system will look and work the same way if you consider only functionality. What matters, though, is what happens when you want to make changes to such system. In the former case, changes will be difficult and costly; in the latter case, they should be much easier and cheaper to perform. In terms of architectural design, allocation of functionality to elements, rather than the functionality per se, is what matters. A good architecture is one in which the most common changes are localized in a single or a few elements, and hence easy to make.

When designing an architecture, you need to consider at least the primary functionality. Primary functionality is usually defined as functionality that is critical to achieve the business goals that motivate the development of the system. Other criteria for primary functionality might be that it implies a high level of technical difficulty or that it requires the interaction of many architectural elements. As a rule of thumb, approximately 10 percent of your use cases or user stories are likely to be primary.

There are two important reasons why you need to consider primary functionality when designing an architecture:

1. You need to think how functionality will be allocated to elements (usually modules) to promote modifiability or reusability, and also to plan work assignments.
2. Some quality attribute scenarios are directly connected to the primary functionality in the system. For example, in a movie streaming application, one of the primary use cases is, of course, to watch a movie. This use case is associated with a performance quality attribute scenario such as "Once the user presses play, the movie should begin streaming in no more than 5 seconds". In this case, the quality attribute scenario is directly associated with the primary use case, so making decisions to support this scenario also requires making decisions about how its associated functionality will be supported. This is not the case for all quality attributes. For example, an availability scenario can involve recovery from a system failure, and this failure may occur when any of the system's use cases are being executed.

Decisions regarding the allocation of functionality that are made during architectural design establish a precedent for how the rest of the functionality should be allocated to modules as development progresses. This is usually not the work of the architect; instead, this activity is typically performed as part of the element interaction design process described in Section 2.2.2.

Finally, bad decisions that are made regarding the allocation of functionality result in the accumulation of technical debt. (Of course, these decisions may reveal themselves to be bad only in hindsight.) This debt can be paid through the use of refactoring, although this impacts the project's rate of progress, or velocity (see the sidebar "Refactoring").

---

### Refactoring

If you refactor a software architecture (or part of one), what you are doing is maintaining the same functionality but changing some quality attribute that you care about. Architects often choose to refactor because a portion of the system is difficult to understand, debug, and maintain. Alternatively, they may refactor because part of the system is slow, or prone to failure, or insecure.

The goal of the refactoring in each case is not to change the functionality, but rather to change the quality attribute response. (Of course, additions to functionality are sometimes lumped together with a refactoring exercise, but that is not the core *intent* of the refactoring.) Clearly, if we can maintain the same functionality but change the architecture to achieve different quality attribute responses, these requirement types are orthogonal to each other—that is, they can vary independently.

---

### 2.4.4  Architectural Concerns

Architectural concerns encompass additional aspects that need to be considered as part of architectural design but that are not expressed as traditional requirements. There are several different types of concerns:

- *General concerns.* These are "broad" issues that one deals with in creating the architecture, such as establishing an overall system structure, the allocation of functionality to modules, the allocation of modules to teams, organization of the code base, startup and shutdown, and supporting delivery, deployment, and updates.
- *Specific concerns.* These are more detailed system-internal issues such as exception management, dependency management, configuration, logging, authentication, authorization, caching, and so forth that are common across large numbers of applications. Some specific concerns are addressed in reference architectures (see Section 2.5.1), but others will be unique to your system. Specific concerns also result from previous design decisions. For example, you may need to address session management if you previously decided to use a reference architecture for the development of web applications.

- *Internal requirements*. These requirements are usually not specified explicitly in traditional requirement documents, as customers usually seldom express them. Internal requirements may address aspects that facilitate development, deployment, operation, or maintenance of the system. They are sometimes called "derived requirements".
- *Issues*. These result from analysis activities, such as a design review (see Section 8.6), so they may not be present initially. For instance, an architectural evaluation may uncover a risk that requires some changes to be performed in the current design.

Some of the decisions surrounding architectural concerns might be trivial or obvious. For example, your deployment structure might be a single processor for an embedded system, or a single cell phone for an app. Your reference architecture might be constrained by company policy. Your authentication and authorization policies might be dictated by your enterprise architecture and realized in a shared framework. In other cases, however, the decisions required to satisfy particular concerns may be less obvious—for example, in exception management or input validation or structuring the code base.

From their past experience, wise architects are usually aware of the concerns that are associated with a particular type of system and the need to make design decisions to address them. Inexperienced architects are usually less aware of such concerns; because these concerns tend to be tacit rather than explicit, they may not consider them as part of the design process, which often results in problems later on.

Architectural concerns frequently result in the introduction of new quality attribute scenarios. The concern of "supporting logging", for example, is too vague and needs to be made more specific. Like the quality attribute scenarios that are provided by the customer, these scenarios need to be prioritized. For these scenarios, however, the customer is the development team, operations, or other members of the organization. During design, the architect must consider both the quality attribute scenarios that are provided by the customer and those scenarios that are derived from architectural concerns.

One of the goals of our revision of the ADD method was to elevate the importance of architectural concerns as explicit inputs to the architecture design process, as will be highlighted in our examples and case studies in Chapters 4, 5, and 6.

## 2.4.5 Constraints

You need to catalog the constraints on development as part of the architectural design process. These constraints may take the form of mandated technologies, other systems with which your system needs to interoperate or integrate, laws and standards that must be complied with, the abilities and availability of your developers, deadlines that are non-negotiable, backward compatibility with older versions of systems, and so on. An example of a technical constraint is the use of open source technologies, whereas a nontechnical constraint is that the system must obey the Sarbanes-Oxley Act or that it must be delivered by December 15.

A constraint is a decision over which you have little or no control as an architect. Your job is, as we mentioned in Chapter 1, to *satisfice*: to design the best system that you can, despite the constraints you face. Sometimes you might be able to argue for loosening a constraint, but in most cases you have no choice but to design around the constraints.

## 2.5  Design Concepts: The Building Blocks for Creating Structures

Design is not random, but rather is planned, intentional, rational, and directed. The process of design may seem daunting at first. When facing the "blank page" at the beginning of any design activity, the space of possibilities might seem impossibly huge and complex. However, there is some help here. The software architecture community has created and evolved, over the course of decades, a body of generally accepted design principles that can guide us to create high-quality designs with predictable outcomes.

For example, some well-documented design principles are oriented toward the achievement of specific quality attributes:

- To help achieve high modifiability, aim for good modularity, which means high cohesion and low coupling.
- To help achieve high availability, avoid having any single point of failure.
- To help achieve scalability, avoid having any hard-coded limits for critical resources.
- To help achieve security, limit the points of access to critical resources.
- To help achieve testability, externalize state.
- . . . and so forth.

In each case, these principles have been evolved over decades of dealing with those quality attributes in practice. In addition, we have evolved reusable realizations of these abstract approaches in design and, eventually, in code. We call these reusable realizations *design concepts*, and they are the building blocks from which the structures that make up the architecture are created. Different types of design concepts exist, and here we discuss some of the most commonly used, including reference architectures, deployment patterns, architectural patterns, tactics, and externally developed components (such as frameworks). While the first four are conceptual in nature, the last one is concrete.

### 2.5.1  Reference Architectures

*Reference architectures* are blueprints that provide an overall logical structure for particular types of applications. A reference architecture is a reference model mapped onto one or more architectural patterns. It has been proven in business and technical contexts, and typically comes with a set of supporting artifacts that eases its use.

An example of a reference architecture for the development of web applications is shown in Figure 2.3 on the next page. This reference architecture establishes the main layers for this type of application—presentation, business, and data—as well as the types of elements that occur within the layers and the responsibilities of these elements, such as UI components, business components, data access components, service agents, and so on. Also, this reference architecture introduces cross-cutting concerns, such as security and communication, that need to be addressed. As this example shows, when you select a reference architecture for your application, you also adopt a set of issues that you need to address during design. You may not have an explicit requirement related to communications or security, but the fact that these elements are part of the reference architecture require you to make design decisions about them.

Reference architectures may be confused with architectural styles, but these two concepts are different. Architectural styles (such as "Pipe and Filter" and "Client Server") define types of components and connectors in a specified topology that are useful for structuring an application either logically or physically. Such styles are technology and domain agnostic. Reference architectures, in contrast, provide a structure for applications in specific domains, and they may embody different styles. Also, while architectural styles tend to be popular in academia, reference architectures seem to be preferred by practitioners—which is also why we favor them in our list of design concepts.

While there are many reference architectures, we are not aware of any catalog that contains an extensive list of them.

### 2.5.2  Architectural Design Patterns

*Design patterns* are conceptual solutions to recurring design problems that exist in a defined context. While design patterns originally focused on decisions at the object scale, including instantiation, structuring, and behavior, today there are catalogs with patterns that address decisions at varying levels of granularity. In addition, there are specific patterns to address quality attributes such as security or integration.

While some people argue for the differentiation between what they consider to be architectural patterns and the more fine-grained design patterns, we believe there is no principled difference that can be solely attributed to scale. We consider a pattern to be architectural when its use directly and substantially influences the satisfaction of some of the architectural drivers (see Section 2.2).

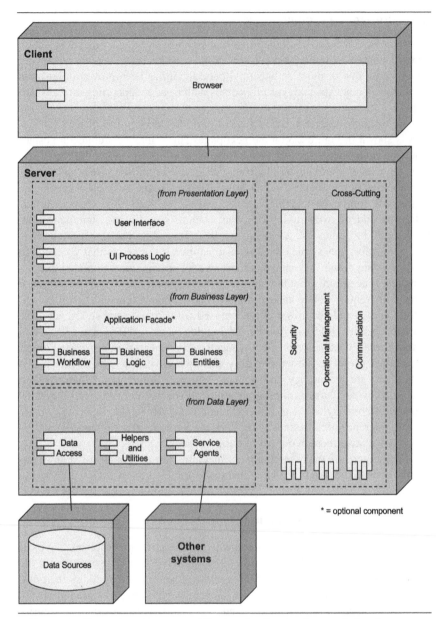

**FIGURE 2.3** Example reference architecture for the development of web applications from the *Microsoft Application Architecture Guide* (Key: UML)

Figure 2.4 shows an example architectural pattern that is useful for structuring the system, the Layers pattern. When you choose a pattern such as this one, you must decide how many layers you will need for your system. Figure 2.5 shows a pattern to support concurrency, which is useful to increase performance. This pattern, too, needs to be instantiated—that is, it needs to be adapted to the specific problem and design context. Instantiation is discussed in Chapter 3.

Although reference architectures may be considered as a type of pattern, we prefer to consider them separately because of the important role they play in structuring an application and because they are more directly connected to technology stacks. Also, a reference architecture typically incorporates other patterns and often constrains these patterns. For example, the reference architecture for web applications shown in Figure 2.3 incorporates the Layers pattern but also establishes how many layers need to be used. This reference architecture also incorporates other patterns such as an Application Facade and Data Access Components.

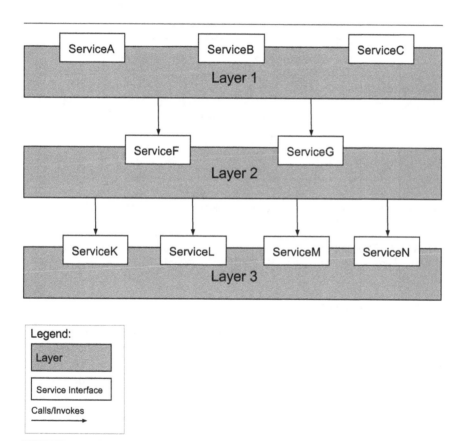

**FIGURE 2.4**  The Layers pattern for structuring an application from *Pattern-Oriented Software Architecture*

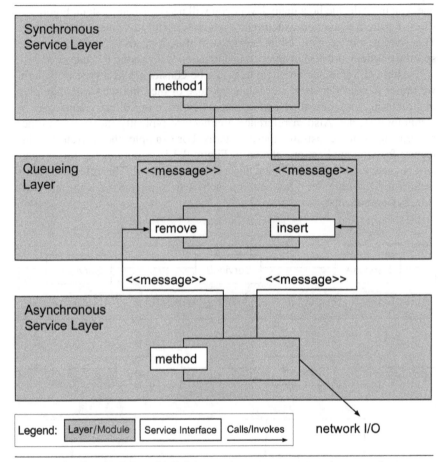

**FIGURE 2.5**  The Half-Sync/Half-Async pattern to support concurrency from *Pattern-Oriented Software Architecture* (Source: Softserve)

### 2.5.3  Deployment Patterns

Another type of pattern that we prefer to consider separately is *deployment patterns*. These patterns provide models on how to physically structure the system to deploy it. Some deployment patterns, such as the one shown in Figure 2.6, are useful to establish an initial physical structure of the system in terms of tiers (physical nodes). More specialized deployment patterns, such as the Load-Balanced Cluster in Figure 2.7, are used to satisfy quality attributes such as availability, performance, and security.

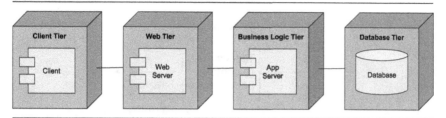

**FIGURE 2.6** Four-tier deployment pattern from the *Microsoft Application Architecture Guide* (Key: UML)

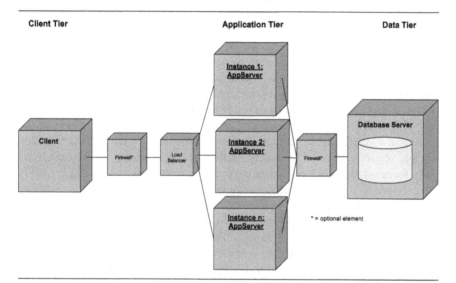

**FIGURE 2.7** Load-Balanced Cluster deployment pattern for performance from the *Microsoft Application Architecture Guide* (Key: UML)

In general, an initial structure for the system is obtained by mapping the logical elements that are obtained from reference architectures (and other patterns) into the physical elements defined by deployment patterns.

## 2.5.4 Tactics

Architects can use collections of fundamental design techniques to achieve a response for particular quality attributes. We call these architectural design primitives *tactics*. Tactics, like design patterns, are techniques that architects have been using for years. We do not invent tactics, but simply capture what architects actually have done in practice, over the decades, to manage quality attribute response goals.

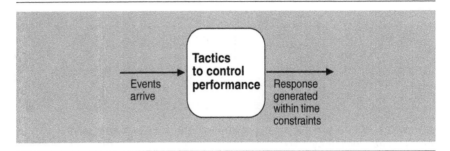

**FIGURE 2.8**   Tactics mediate events and responses.

Tactics are design decisions that influence the control of a quality attribute response. For example, if you want to design a system to have low latency or high throughput, you could make a set of design decisions that would mediate the arrival of events (requests for service), resulting in responses that are produced within some time constraints, as shown in Figure 2.8.

Tactics are both simpler and more primitive than patterns. They focus on the control of a single quality attribute response (although they may, of course, trade off this response with other quality attribute goals). Patterns, in contrast, typically focus on resolving and balancing multiple forces—that is, multiple quality attribute goals. By way of analogy, we can say that a tactic is an atom, whereas a pattern is a molecule.

Tactics provide a top-down way of thinking about design. A tactics categorization begins with a set of design objectives related to the achievement of a quality attribute, and presents the architect with a set of options from which to choose. These options then need to be further instantiated through some combination of patterns, frameworks, and code.

For example, in Figure 2.9, the design objectives for performance are "Control Resource Demand" and "Manage Resources". An architect who wants to create a system with "good" performance needs to choose one or more of these options. That is, the architect needs to decide if controlling resource demand is feasible, and if managing resources is feasible. In some systems, the events arriving at the system can be managed, prioritized, or limited in some way. If this is not possible, then the architect can manage resources only as part of an attempt to generate responses within acceptable time constraints. Within the "Manage Resources" category, an architect might choose to increase resources, introduce concurrency, maintain multiple copies of computations, maintain multiple copies of data, and so forth. These tactics then need to be instantiated. As an example, an architect might choose the Half-Sync/Half-Async pattern (see Figure 2.5) as a way of introducing (and managing) concurrency, or the Load-Balanced Cluster deployment pattern (see Figure 2.7) to maintain multiple copies of computations. As we will see in Chapter 3, the choice, combination, and tailoring of tactics and

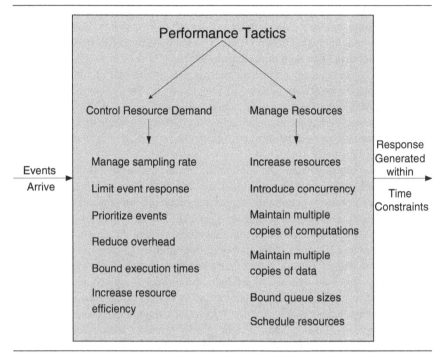

**FIGURE 2.9**  Performance tactics from *Software Architecture in Practice*

patterns are some of the key steps of the ADD process. There are existing tactics categorizations for the quality attributes of availability, interoperability, modifiability, performance, security, testability, and usability.

### 2.5.5  Externally Developed Components

Patterns and tactics are abstract in nature. However, when you are designing a software architecture, you need to make these design concepts concrete and closer to the actual implementation. There are two ways to achieve this: You can code the elements obtained from tactics and patterns or you can associate technologies with one or more of these elements in the architecture. This "buy versus build" choice is one of the most important decisions you will make as an architect.

We consider technologies to be *externally developed components*, because they are not created as part of the development project. Several types of externally developed components exist:

- *Technology families.* A technology family represents a group of specific technologies with common functional purposes. It can serve as a placeholder until a specific product or framework is selected. An example is a relational database management system (RDBMS) or an object-oriented to relational mapper (ORM). Figure 2.10 shows different technology families in the Big Data domain (in regular text).

- *Products.* A product (or software package) refers to a self-contained functional piece of software that can be integrated into the system that is being designed and that requires only minor configuration or coding. An example is a relational database management system, such as Oracle or Microsoft SQL Server. Figure 2.10 shows different products in the Big Data domain (in italics).

- *Application frameworks.* An application framework (or just framework) is a reusable software element, constructed out of patterns and tactics, that provides generic functionality addressing recurring domain and quality attribute concerns across a broad range of applications. Frameworks, when carefully chosen and properly implemented, increase the productivity of programmers. They do so by enabling programmers to focus on business logic and end-user value, rather than underlying technologies and their implementations. As opposed to products, framework functions are generally invoked from the application code or are "injected" using some type of aspect-oriented approach. Frameworks usually require extensive configuration, typically through XML files or other approaches such as annotations in Java. A framework example is Hibernate, which is used to perform object-oriented to relational mapping in Java. Several types of frameworks are available: Full-stack frameworks, such as Spring, are usually associated with reference architectures and address general concerns across the different elements of the reference architecture, while non-full-stack frameworks, such as JSF, address specific functional or quality attribute concerns.

- *Platforms.* A platform provides a complete infrastructure upon which to build and execute applications. Examples of platforms include Java, .Net, or and Google Cloud.

The selection of externally developed components, which is a key aspect of the design process, can be a challenging task because of their extensive number. Here are a few criteria you should consider when selecting externally developed components:

- *Problem that it addresses.* Is it something specific, such as a framework for object-oriented to relational mapping or something more generic, such as a platform?

- *Cost.* What is the cost of the license and, if it is free, what is the cost of support and education?

- *Type of license.* Does it have a license that is compatible with the project goals?

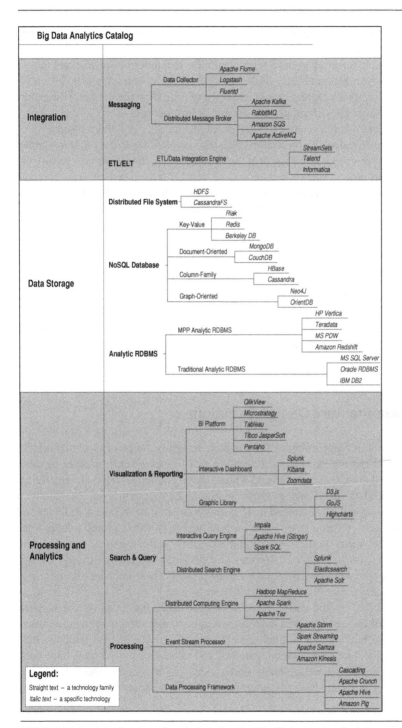

**FIGURE 2.10**   A technology family tree for the Big Data application domain

- *Support.* Is it well supported? Is there extensive documentation about the technology? Is there an extensive user or developer community that you can turn to for advice?
- *Learning curve.* How hard is it to learn this technology? Have others in your organization already mastered it? Are there courses available?
- *Maturity.* Is it a technology that has just appeared on the market, which may be exciting but still relatively unstable or unsupported?
- *Popularity.* Is it a relatively widespread technology? Are there positive testimonials or adoption by mature organizations? Will it be easy to hire people who have deep knowledge of it? Is there an active developer community or user group?
- *Compatibility and ease of integration.* Is it compatible with other technologies used in the project? Can it be integrated easily in the project?
- *Support for critical quality attributes.* Does it limit attributes such as performance? Is it secure and robust?
- *Size.* Will the use of the technology have a negative impact on the size of the application under development?

Unfortunately, the answers to these questions are not always easy to find and the selection of a particular technology may require you do some research or, eventually, to create prototypes that will help you in the selection process. These criteria will have a significant effect on your total cost of ownership.

## 2.6  Architecture Design Decisions

As we said at the beginning of this chapter, design is the process of making decisions. But the act of making a decision is a *process*, not a moment in time. Experienced architects, when faced with a design challenge, typically entertain a set of "candidate" decisions (as shown in Figure 2.1); from this set, they choose a best candidate and instantiate that. They might select this "best" candidate based on experience, constraints, or some form of analysis such as prototyping or simulation. The reality is that an architect will often make a choice and "ride the horse until it drops"—that is, commit to a decision and revisit it only if it appears to be compromising the success of the project. These decisions have serious consequences!

Recall that, in the early stages of design, decisions focus on the biggest, most critical choices that will have substantial downstream consequences: reference architectures, major technologies (such as frameworks), and patterns. Reference architectures, deployment patterns, and other kinds of patterns have been widely discussed—there are many books, websites, and conferences devoted to the creation and validation of patterns and pattern languages. Nevertheless, the output of these activities is always a set of documented patterns. Interpreting the patterns from a pattern catalog is a critical part of the selection activity for an architect. Each candidate pattern must be chosen and its instantiation must be analyzed. For example, if you chose the Layers pattern from Figure 2.4, you would still have many decisions to make: how many layers there will be, how strict the layering will be, which specific services will be placed into each layer, what the interfaces between these functions will be, and so forth. If you chose the Load-Balanced Cluster deployment pattern from Figure 2.7, you would have to decide how many servers will be balanced, how many load balancers you will use, where these servers and load balancers will physically reside, which kinds of networks will connect these servers, which form of encryption you will use on those network connections, which form of health monitoring the load balancers will employ, and so forth. These decisions are important and will affect the success of the instantiated pattern, so they need to be analyzed. In addition, the quality of the *implementation* of these decisions will affect the success of the pattern. As we like to quip, the architecture giveth and the implementation taketh away.

Furthermore, the many catalogs and web pages that present design concepts use different conventions and notations. The focus of our book is on the design method and how it can be used with these external sources. For this reason we just take examples from outside sources and show them here as they were originally presented. This book is not intended to be another design patterns catalog— we want to alert you to the presence of these catalogs and show how they can be an incredibly useful resource for an architect, but they must be interpreted and used with care! In fact, one of your many jobs as an architect is to understand and interpret these catalogs, with their different notations and conventions. This is the reality that you will have to deal with.

Finally, once a design decision has been made, you should think about how you will *document* it. You could, of course, do no documentation. This is, in fact, what is most common in practice. Architectural concepts are often vague and conveyed informally, in "tribal knowledge": personal communications, emails, naming conventions, and so forth. Alternatively, you could create and maintain full, formal documentation, as is done for some projects with demanding quality attribute requirements, such as safety-critical or high-security systems. If you are designing flight-control software, you will probably end up at this end of the spectrum. In between these endpoints is a broad set of possibilities, and in this space we see less formal (and less costly) forms of architecture documentation, such as sketches (as we will discuss in Section 3.7).

The decision of what, when, and how to document should be risk based. You should ask yourself: What is the risk of *not* documenting this decision? Could it be misinterpreted and undermined by future developers? Could it contribute to near-term or long-term problems in the system? For example, if the rationale for layering is not carefully documented, the layering will inevitably break down, losing coherence and tending toward increased coupling. Over time, this trend will increase the system's technical debt, making it harder to find and fix bugs or add new features. To take another example, if the rationale for allocation of a critical resource is not documented, that resource might become an unintended contention area, resulting in bottlenecks and failures.

## 2.7   Summary

In this chapter, we introduced the idea of design as a set of decisions to satisfy requirements and constraints. We also introduced the notion of "architectural" design and showed that it does not differ from design in general, other than that it addresses the satisfaction of *architectural drivers*: the purpose, primary functionality, quality attribute requirements, architectural concerns, and constraints. What makes a decision "architectural"? A decision is architectural if it has nonlocal consequences *and* those consequences matter to the achievement of an architectural driver.

We also discussed why architectural design is so important: because it is the embodiment of early, far-reaching, hard-to-change decisions. These decisions will help you meet your architectural drivers, will determine much of your project's work-breakdown structure, and will affect the tools, skills, and technologies needed to realize the system. Thus architectural design decisions should be scrutinized well, as their consequences are profound. In addition, architecture is a key enabler of agility.

Architectural design is guided by certain principles. For example, to achieve good modularity, high coupling, and low cohesion, the wise architect will probably include some form of layering in the architecture being designed. Similarly, to achieve high availability, an architect will likely choose a pattern involving some form of redundancy and failover, such as active–passive redundancy, where an active server sends real-time updates to a passive server, so that the passive server can replace the active server in case it fails, with no loss of state.

Design concepts, such as reference architectures, deployment patterns, architectural patterns, tactics, and externally developed components, are the building blocks of design, and they form the foundation for architectural design as it is performed using ADD. As you will see in our step-by-step explanation of ADD in Chapter 3, some of the most important design decisions that an architect makes are how design concepts are selected, how they are instantiated, and how they are combined. Also, in Appendix A, we present a design concepts catalog that includes several instances of the design concepts presented here.

From these foundations, an architecture can be confidently and predictably constructed.

## 2.8 Further Reading

A more in-depth treatment of scenarios and architectural drivers can be found in
L. Bass, P. Clements, and R. Kazman, *Software Architecture in Practice,* 3rd ed.,
Addison-Wesley, 2012. Also found in this book is an extensive discussion of ar-
chitectural tactics, which are useful in guiding an architecture to achieve quality
attribute goals. Likewise, this book contains an extensive discussion of QAW and
Utility Trees.

The Mission Thread Workshop is discussed in R. Kazman, M. Gagliardi,
and W. Wood, "Scaling Up Software Architecture Analysis", *Journal of Systems and Software*, 85, 1511–1519, 2012; and in M. Gagliardi, W. Wood, and
T. Morrow, *Introduction to the Mission Thread Workshop*, Software Engineering
Institute Technical Report CMU/SEI-2013-TR-003, 2013.

An overview of discovery prototyping, JRP, JAD, and accelerated systems
analysis can be found in any competent book on systems analysis and design,
such as J. Whitten and L. Bentley, *Systems Analysis and Design Methods,* 7th
ed., McGraw-Hill, 2007. The combination of architectural approaches with Agile
methods will be discussed in Chapter 9.

A catalog of reference architectures and deployment patterns appears in the
book by the Microsoft Patterns and Practices Team: *Microsoft® Application Architecture Guide,* 2nd ed., Microsoft Press, 2009. This book also provides an extensive list of architectural concerns associated with the reference architectures
that are documented.

An extensive collection of architectural design patterns for the construction
of distributed systems can be found in F. Buschmann, K. Henney, and D. Schmidt,
*Pattern-Oriented Software Architecture Volume 4: A Pattern Language for Dis-
tributed Computing*, Wiley, 2007. Other books in the POSA (Patterns Of Software Architecture) series provide additional pattern catalogs. Many other pattern
catalogs specializing in particular application domains and technologies exist. A
few examples are listed here:

- E. Gamma, R. Helm, R. Johnson, and J. Vlissides. *Design Patterns: Ele-
  ments of Reusable Object-Oriented Software*. Addison-Wesley, 1995.
- M. Fowler. *Patterns of Enterprise Application Architecture*. Addi-
  son-Wesley, 2003.
- E. Fernandez-Buglioni. *Security Patterns in Practice: Designing Secure
  Architectures Using Software Patterns*. Wiley, 2013.
- G. Hohpe and B. Woolf. *Enterprise Integration Patterns: Designing, Build-
  ing, and Deploying Messaging Solutions*. Addison-Wesley, 2004.

The evaluation and selection of software packages is discussed in A. Jadhav
and R. Sonar, "Evaluating and Selecting Software Packages: A Review", *Journal
of Information and Software Technology,* 51, 555–563, 2009.

The "bible" for software architecture documentation is P. Clements, F. Bachmann, L. Bass, D. Garlan, J. Ivers, R. Little, P. Merson, R. Nord, and J. Stafford, *Documenting Software Architectures: Views and Beyond*, 2nd ed., Addison-Wesley, 2011.

The technology family tree for the Big Data application domain is based on the Smart Decisions Game by H. Cervantes, S. Haziyev, O. Hrytsay, and R. Kazman, which can be found at http://smartdecisionsgame.com.

# 3

# The Architecture Design Process

In this chapter we provide a detailed discussion of ADD, the design method that is the focus of this book. We begin with an overview of the method and of each one of its steps. This overview is followed by more detailed discussions of different aspects that need to be considered when performing these steps. We suggest different roadmaps that provide guidance on when different types of design concepts can be used depending on which type of system is being designed. We also discuss the identification and selection of design concepts, the production of structures from these design concepts, the definition of interfaces, the production of preliminary documentation, and, finally, a technique to track design progress.

## 3.1 The Need for a Principled Method

In Chapter 2, we discussed the various concepts associated with design. The question is, how do you actually perform design? Performing design to *ensure* that the drivers are satisfied requires a principled method. By "principled", we refer to a method that takes into account all of the relevant aspects that are needed to produce an adequate design. Such a method provides guidance that is necessary to guarantee that your drivers are satisfied. To achieve this goal in a cost-effective, repeatable way, you need a method that guides you in combining and incorporating reusable design concepts.

Performing design adequately is important because architecture design decisions have significant consequences at different points in a project's lifetime. For example, during a pre-sales phase, an appropriate design will allow for a better estimation of cost, scope, and schedule. During development, an appropriate design will be helpful to avoid later rework and facilitate development and deployment. Finally, a clear understanding of what architectural design involves is necessary to better manage aspects of technical debt.

## 3.2 Attribute-Driven Design 3.0

Architecture design is performed in a series of *rounds* across the development of a software project. Each design round may take place within a project increment such as a sprint. Within these rounds, a series of *design iterations* is performed. Perhaps the most important characteristic of the ADD method is that it provides detailed, step-by-step guidance on the tasks that have to be performed inside the design iterations (see Chapter 7 for a comparison with other design methods). When ADD appeared, it was the first method to focus specifically on quality attributes and their achievement through the selection of different types of structures and their representation through views. Another important contribution of ADD was that it recognized that analysis and documentation are an integral part of the design process. Although ADD was and is a major contribution in the field of software architecture, we believe that its adoption within the practitioner community has been limited by a number of inherent weaknesses, as discussed in Section 1.4.

ADD has been used successfully for more than 15 years. The world of software has changed dramatically since ADD's introduction, however, and even more since version 2.0 was published in 2006. For this reason, and to address the weaknesses of version 2.0, we have decided to create ADD 3.0. Henceforth, we will simply refer to this method as ADD. Figure 3.1 shows the steps and artifacts associated with ADD and in the following subsections we provide an overview of the activities in each of its steps.

### 3.2.1 Step 1: Review Inputs

Before starting a design round, you need make sure that the inputs to the design process are available and correct. First, you need to ensure that you are clear about the *purpose* for the design activities that will ensue. The purpose may be, for example, to produce a design for early estimation, to refine an existing design to build a new increment of the system, or to design and generate a prototype to mitigate certain technical risks (see Section 2.4.1 for a discussion of the design

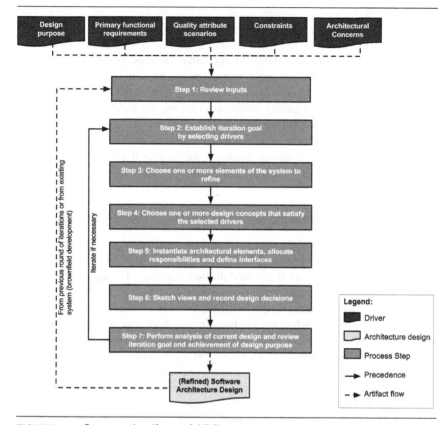

**FIGURE 3.1**    Steps and artifacts of ADD version 3.0

purpose). Also, you need to make sure that the other drivers needed for the design activity are available. These include primary functional requirements, quality attribute scenarios, architectural constraints, and concerns. Finally, if this is not the first design round, or if this is not greenfield development, an additional input that you need to consider is the existing architecture design.

At this point, we assume that primary functionality and quality attribute scenarios have been prioritized, ideally by your most important project stakeholders. (If not, there are techniques that you can employ to elicit and prioritize them, as discussed in Sections 2.4.2 and 2.4.3.) You, as the architect, must now "own" these drivers. You need to check, for example, whether any important stakeholders were overlooked in the original requirements elicitation process, or whether any business conditions have changed since the prioritization was performed. These drivers really do "drive" design, so getting them right and getting their priority right is crucial. We cannot stress this point strongly enough. Software architecture design, like most activities in software engineering, is a "garbage in, garbage out" process. The results of ADD cannot be good if the inputs are poorly formed.

As a rule of thumb, you should be able to start designing if, besides the design purpose, constraints, and initial architectural concerns, you have established the primary use cases and the most important quality attribute scenarios. This, of course, does not mean you will make decisions only about these drivers: You still need to address other quality attribute scenarios, use cases and architectural concerns, but these can be treated later on.

The drivers become part of an architectural design backlog that you should use to perform the different design iterations. We discuss this idea in more depth in Section 3.8.1.

### 3.2.2   Step 2: Establish the Iteration Goal by Selecting Drivers

A design round represents the architecture design activities performed within a development cycle if an iterative development model is used, or the whole set of architecture design activities if a waterfall model is used. Through one or more rounds, you produce an architecture that suits the established design purpose.

A design round is generally performed in a series of design iterations, where each iteration focuses on achieving a particular goal. Such a goal typically involves designing to satisfy a subset of the drivers. For example, an iteration goal could be to create structures from elements that will support a particular performance scenario, or that will enable a use case to be achieved. For this reason, when performing design, you need to establish a goal before you start a particular design iteration.

As we will discuss in Section 3.3, depending on the type of system whose architecture is being designed, there may be a "best"—or at least strongly suggested—ordering of the iteration goals that need to be addressed. For example, for a greenfield system in a mature domain, your initial goal is typically to identify an overall structure for the system by choosing a reference architecture.

### 3.2.3   Step 3: Choose One or More Elements of the System to Refine

Satisfying drivers requires you to produce one or more architectural structures. These structures are composed of interrelated elements, and those elements are generally obtained by refining other elements that you previously identified in an earlier iteration. Refinement can mean decomposition into finer-grained elements (top-down approach), combination of elements into coarser-grained elements (bottom-up approach), or improvement of previously identified elements. For greenfield development, you can start by establishing the system context and then selecting the only available element—that is, the system itself—for refinement by decomposition. For existing systems or for later design iterations in greenfield systems, you normally choose to refine elements that were identified in prior iterations.

The elements that you will select are the ones that are involved in the satisfaction of specific drivers. For this reason, when design is performed for an existing system, you need to have a good understanding of the elements that are part of the as-built architecture of the system. This may involve some "detective work", reverse engineering, or discussions with developers.

We have presented steps 2 and 3 in the order they appear in the method. That is to say, step 2 precedes step 3. However, in some cases you may need to reverse this order. For example, when designing a greenfield system or when fleshing out certain types of reference architectures (as we will show in Chapter 5), you will, at least in the early stages of design, focus on elements of the system and start the iteration by selecting a particular element and then consider the drivers that you want to address.

### 3.2.4 Step 4: Choose One or More Design Concepts That Satisfy the Selected Drivers

Choosing the design concepts is probably the most difficult decision you will face in the design process, because it requires you to identify alternatives among design concepts that can be used to achieve your iteration goal, and to make a selection from these alternatives. As we saw in Section 2.5, different types of design concepts exist, and, for each type, there may be many options. This can result in a considerable number of alternatives that need to be analyzed to make a choice. In Section 3.4, we discuss the identification and selection of design concepts in more detail.

### 3.2.5 Step 5: Instantiate Architectural Elements, Allocate Responsibilities, and Define Interfaces

Once you have selected one or more design concepts, you must make another design decision, which involves *instantiating* elements out of the design concepts that you selected. For example, if you selected the Layers pattern as a design concept, you must decide how many layers will be used, since the pattern itself does not prescribe a specific number. In this example, the layers are the elements that are instantiated. In certain cases, instantiation can mean configuration. For example, you may have dedicated an iteration to selecting technologies and associating them with the elements in your design. In further iterations, you might refine these elements by making finer-grained decisions about how they should be configured to support a particular driver, such as a quality attribute.

After instantiating the elements, you need to allocate responsibilities to each of them. For example, in a typical web-based enterprise system, at least three layers are usually present: the presentation layer, the business layer, and the data layer. The responsibilities of these layers differ: The responsibilities of the presentation layer include managing all of the user interactions, whereas the responsibilities of the data layer include managing the persistence of data.

Instantiating elements is just one of the tasks you need to perform to create structures that satisfy a driver or a concern. The elements that have been instantiated also need to be connected, to allow them to collaborate with one another. This requires the existence of *relationships* between the elements and the exchange of information through some kind of interface. The interface is a contractual specification of how information should flow between the elements. Section 3.5 provides more details on how the different types of design concepts are instantiated and how structures are created, and Section 3.6 discusses how interfaces can be defined.

### 3.2.6   Step 6: Sketch Views and Record Design Decisions

At this point, you have finished performing the design activities for the iteration. Nevertheless, you may not have taken any actions to ensure that the views—the representations of the structures you created—are preserved. For instance, if you performed the previous step in a conference room, you probably ended up with a series of diagrams on a whiteboard. This information is essential, and you need to capture it so that you can later analyze and communicate it to other stakeholders.

The views that you have created are almost certainly incomplete, so these diagrams may need to be revisited and refined in a subsequent iteration. This is typically done to accommodate elements resulting from other design decisions that you will make to support additional drivers. This factor explains why we speak of "sketching" the views in ADD—that is, creating a preliminary type of documentation. The more formal, more fully fleshed-out documentation of these views—should you choose to produce them—occurs only after a number of design iterations have been finished (as part of the architectural documentation activity discussed in Section 1.2.2).

In addition to storing the sketches of the views, you should record the significant decisions that are made in the design iteration, and the reasons that led to these decisions (i.e., the rationale), to facilitate later analysis and understanding of the decisions. For example, decisions about important tradeoffs might be recorded at this time. During a design iteration, decisions are primarily made in steps 4 and 5. Section 3.7 provides further information on how to create preliminary documentation *during* design, including creating sketches, recording design decisions and their rationale.

### 3.2.7   Step 7: Perform Analysis of Current Design and Review Iteration Goal and Achievement of Design Purpose

By the time you reach step 7, you should have created a partial design that addresses the goal established for the iteration. Making sure that this is actually the case is a good idea, so as to avoid unhappy stakeholders and later rework. You can perform the analysis yourself by reviewing the sketches of the views and design decisions that you recorded, but an even better idea is to have someone else help you review this design. We do this for the same reason that organizations frequently have a separate testing/quality assurance group: Another person will not share your assumptions, and will have a different experience base and a different perspective. Pulling in someone with a different point of view can help you find "bugs", in both code and architecture. We discuss analysis in more depth in Chapter 8.

Once the design performed in the iteration has been analyzed, you should review the state of your architecture in terms of the established design purpose. This means considering if, at this point, you have performed enough design iterations to satisfy the drivers that are associated with the design round as well as considering whether the design purpose has been achieved or if additional design rounds are needed in future project increments. Section 3.8 describes simple techniques that allow you to keep track of design progress.

### 3.2.8  Iterate If Necessary

Ideally, you should perform additional iterations and repeat steps 2 to 7 for every driver that was considered as part of the input. More often than not, such iterations are not possible because of time or resource constraints that force you to stop the design activities and move on to the next activities in the development process—typically implementation.

What are the criteria for evaluating if more design iterations are necessary? We let *risk* be our guide. You should at least have addressed the drivers with the highest priorities. Ideally, you should have assured that critical drivers are satisfied or, at least, that the design is "good enough" to satisfy them. Finally, when performing iterative development, you can choose to perform one design round in every project iteration. The first rounds should focus on addressing the drivers, while subsequent rounds focus on making design decisions for other requirements that were not selected as drivers but that need to be addressed nonetheless.

## 3.3  Following a Design Roadmap According to System Type

When writing, you might have experienced the much-dreaded "fear of the blank page". Similarly, when you start designing an architecture, you may face a situation in which you ask yourself, "How do I begin designing?" To answer this question, you need to consider which type of system you are designing.

Design of software systems falls into three broad categories: (1) the design of a *greenfield* system for a mature (i.e., well-known) domain; (2) the design of a greenfield system for a domain that is novel (i.e., a domain that has a less established infrastructure and knowledge base); and (3) the design for making changes to an existing system (*brownfield*). Each one of these categories involves a different roadmap in terms of the sequence of goals that you should perform across the design iterations.

### 3.3.1   Design of Greenfield Systems for Mature Domains

The design of a greenfield system for a mature domain occurs when you are designing an architecture for a system that is built from "scratch" and when this type of system is well known and understood—that is, when there is an established infrastructure of tools and technologies, and an associated knowledge base. Examples of mature domains include the following:

- Traditional desktop applications
- Interactive applications that run on a mobile device
- Enterprise applications accessed from a web browser, which store information in a relational database, and which provide support for partially or fully automating business processes

Since these types of applications are relatively common, some general architectural concerns associated with their design are well known, well supported, and well documented. If you are designing a new system that falls into this category, we recommend the following roadmap (shown in Figure 3.2).

The goal of your **initial** design iteration(s) should be to address the general architectural concern of establishing an initial overall system structure. Is this to be a three-tier client-server application, a peer-to-peer application, a mobile app connecting to a Big Data back-end, and so on? Each of these options will lead you to different architectural solutions, and these solutions will help you to achieve your drivers. To achieve this iteration goal, you will select some design concepts. Specifically, you will typically choose one or more reference architectures and deployment patterns (see Sections 2.5.1 and 2.5.3). You may also select some externally developed components, such as frameworks. The types of frameworks that are typically chosen in early iterations are either "full-stack" frameworks that are associated with the selected reference architectures, or more specific frameworks that are associated with elements established by the reference architecture (see Section 2.5.5). In this first iteration, you should review all of your drivers to select the design concepts, but you will probably pay more attention to the constraints and to quality attributes that are not associated with specific functionalities and that favor particular reference architectures or require particular deployment configurations. Consider an example: If you select a reference architecture for Big Data systems, you have presumably chosen a quality

| Iteration | Goal | Design concepts |
|---|---|---|
| 1 | Establishing an initial overall system structure | 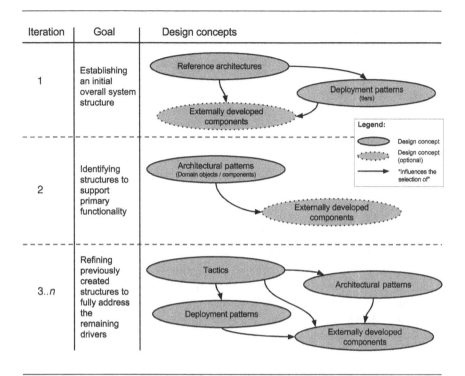 |
| 2 | Identifying structures to support primary functionality | |
| 3..*n* | Refining previously created structures to fully address the remaining drivers | |

**FIGURE 3.2**   Design concept selection roadmap for greenfield systems

attribute such as low latency with high data volumes as your most important driver. Of course, you will make many subsequent decisions to flesh out this early choice, but this driver has already exerted a great influence on your design such as the selection of a particular reference architecture.

The goal of your **next** design iteration(s) should be to identify structures that support the primary functionality. As noted in Section 2.4.3, allocation of functionality (i.e., use cases or user stories) to elements is an important part of architectural design because it has critical downstream implications for modifiability and allocation of work to teams. Furthermore, once functionality has been allocated, the elements that support it can be refined in later iterations to support the quality attributes associated with these functionalities. For example, a performance scenario may be associated with a particular use case. Achieving the performance goal may require making design decisions across all of the elements that participate in the achievement of this use case. To allocate functionality, you usually refine the elements that are associated with the reference architecture by decomposing them. A particular use case may require the identification of multiple elements. For example, if you have selected a web application reference architecture, supporting a use case will probably require you to identify modules across the different layers associated with this reference architecture. Finally, at this point you should also be thinking about allocating functionality—associated with modules—to (teams of) developers.

The goal of your **subsequent** design iterations should be to refine the structures you have previously created to fully address the remaining drivers. Addressing these drivers, and especially quality attributes, will likely require you to use the three major categories of design concepts—tactics, patterns, and externally developed components such as frameworks—as well as commonly accepted design best practices such as modularity, low coupling, and high cohesion. For example, to (partially) satisfy a performance requirement for the search use case in a web application, you might select the "maintain multiple copies of data" tactic and implement this tactic by configuring a cache in a framework that is used inside an element responsible for persisting data.

This roadmap is appropriate for the initial project iterations, but it is also extremely useful for early project estimation activities (see the discussion about the architecture design process during pre-sales in Section 9.1.1). Why have we created such a roadmap? First, because the process of starting an architectural design is always complex. Second, because many of the steps in this roadmap are frequently overlooked or done in an intuitive and ad hoc way, rather than in a well-considered, reflective way. Third, because different types of design concepts exist, and it is not always clear at which point in the design they should be used. This roadmap encapsulates best practices that we have observed in the most competent architecture organizations. Simply put, the use of a roadmap results in better architectures, particularly for less mature architects.

### 3.3.2   Design of Greenfield Systems for Novel Domains

In the case of novel domains, it is more challenging to establish a precise roadmap, because reference architectures may not exist and there may be few, if any, externally developed components that you can use. You are, more than likely, working from first principles and creating your own home-grown solutions. Even in this case, however, general-purpose design concepts such as tactics and patterns can guide you, aided by strategic prototyping. In essence, your iteration goals will mostly be to continuously refine previously created structures to fully address the drivers.

Many times, your design goal will focus on the creation of prototypes so that you can explore possible solutions to the challenge that you are facing. In particular, you may need to focus on quality attributes and design challenges oriented toward issues such as performance, scalability, or security. We discuss the creation of prototypes in Section 3.4.2.

Of course, the notion of "novel" is fluid. Mobile application development was a novel domain 10 or 15 years ago, but now it is a well-established field.

### 3.3.3  Design for an Existing System (Brownfield)

Architecture design for an existing system may occur for different purposes. The most obvious is maintenance—that is, when you need to satisfy new requirements or correct issues, and doing so requires changes to the architecture of an existing system. You may also be making architectural changes to an existing system for the purpose of *refactoring*. When refactoring, you change the architecture of an existing system, without altering its functions, to reduce technical debt, to introduce technology updates, or to fix quality attribute problems (e.g., the system is too slow, or insecure, or frequently crashes).

To be able to choose elements to decompose as part of the design process (step 3 of ADD), you need to first identify which elements are present in the architecture of the existing system. In this sense, before starting the design iterations, your first goal should be to make sure that you have a clear understanding of the existing architecture of the system.

Once you understand the elements, properties, and relationships that constitute the architecture of the system, and the characteristics of the existing code base, you can perform design similar to what is done for greenfield systems after the initial design iteration. Your design iteration goals here will be to identify and refine structures to satisfy architectural drivers, including new functionality and quality attributes, and to address specific architectural concerns. These design iterations will typically not involve establishing a new overall system structure unless you are dealing with a major refactoring.

It might seem that the preceding discussion of the different contexts of design is rather abstract and perhaps even confusing. In the next three chapters we will be presenting examples of design of a system in a mature domain (Chapter 4), design for a system in a relatively novel domain (Chapter 5), and design to modify an existing system (Chapter 6). These extended examples will make the previously described concepts clearer and more concrete.

---

## 3.4  Identifying and Selecting Design Concepts

Freeman Dyson, the English physicist, once said the following: "A good scientist is a person with original ideas. A good engineer is a person who makes a design that works with as few original ideas as possible". This quotation is particularly relevant in the context of software architecture design: Most of the time you don't need to, and shouldn't, reinvent the wheel. Rather, your major design activities are to identify and select design concepts to address the challenges and drivers that you encounter across the design iterations. Design is still an original and creative endeavor, but the creativity resides in the appropriate identification of these existing solutions and then on combining and adapting them to the problem at hand.

### 3.4.1   Identification of Design Concepts

The identification of design concepts can appear to be daunting, because of the vast number of design concepts that exist. There are likely dozens of design patterns and externally developed components that you could use to address any particular issue. To make things worse, these design concepts are scattered across many different sources: in the popular press, in research literature, in books, and on the Internet. Moreover, in many cases, there is no canonical definition of a concept. Different sites, for example, will define the Broker pattern in different, largely informal, ways. Finally, once you have identified the alternatives that might potentially help you achieve the design goals of the iteration, you need to select among them.

To identify which design concepts you need at a particular point, you should consider what we previously discussed regarding the design roadmap. Different points in the design process usually require different types of design concepts. For example, when you are designing a greenfield system in a mature domain, the types of design concepts that will help you initially structure the system are reference architectures and deployment patterns. As you progress in the design process, you will use all of the categories of design concepts: tactics, architecture and design patterns, and externally developed components. Keep in mind that to address a specific design problem, you can and often will use and combine different types of design concepts. For example, when addressing a security driver, you may employ a security pattern, a security tactic, a security framework, or some combination of these.

Once you have more clarity regarding the types of design concepts that you wish to use, you still need to identify alternatives—that is, design candidates. There are several ways to do so, although you will probably use a combination of these techniques rather than a single one:

- *Leverage existing best practices.* You can identify alternatives for your required design concepts by making use of catalogs that are available in printed or online form. Some design concepts, such as patterns, are extensively documented; others, such as externally developed components, are documented in a less thorough way. The benefits of this approach are that you can identify many alternatives, and that you can leverage the considerable knowledge and experience of others. The downsides are that searching for and studying the information can require a considerable amount of time, the quality of the documented knowledge is often unknown, and the assumptions and biases of the authors are unknown.
- *Leverage your own knowledge and experience.* If the system you are designing is similar to other systems you have designed in the past, you will probably want to begin with some of the design concepts that you have used before. The benefit of this approach is that the identification of alternatives is performed rapidly and confidently. The downside is that you may end up using the same ideas repeatedly, even if they are not the most

appropriate for all the design problems that you are facing, and if they have been superseded by newer, better approaches. As the saying goes, "If you give a small child a hammer, all the world looks like a nail".

- *Leverage the knowledge and experience of others.* As an architect, you have background and knowledge that you have gained through the years. This foundation varies from person to person, especially if the types of design problems they have addressed in the past differ. You can leverage this information by performing the identification and selection of design concepts with some of your peers through brainstorming.

### 3.4.2 Selection of Design Concepts

Once you have identified a list of alternative design concepts, you need to select which one is the most appropriate to solve the design problem at hand. You can achieve this in a relatively simple way, by creating a table that lists the pros and cons associated with each alternative and selecting one of the alternatives based on those criteria and your drivers. The table can also include other criteria, such as the cost associated with the use of the alternative. Table 3.1 shows an example of such a table used to support the selection of different reference architectures.

You may also need to perform a more in-depth analysis to select the alternative. Methods such as CBAM (cost benefit analysis method) or SWOT (strengths, weaknesses, opportunities, threats) can help you to perform this analysis (see the sidebar "The Cost Benefit Analysis Method").

**TABLE 3.1**  Example of a Table to Support the Selection of Alternatives

| Name of Alternative | Pros | Cons | Cost |
|---|---|---|---|
| Web application | Can be accessed from a variety of platforms using a standard web browser<br>Fast page loading<br>Simple deployment | Does not support "rich" interaction | Low |
| Rich Internet application | Supports "rich" user interaction<br>Simple deployment and updating | Longer page loading times<br>Requires a runtime environment to be installed on the client browser | Medium |
| Mobile application | Supports "rich" user interaction | Less portability<br>Screen limitations | High |

## The Cost Benefit Analysis Method

The CBAM is a method that guides the selection of design alternatives using a quantitative approach. This method considers that architectural strategies (i.e., combinations of design concepts) affect quality attribute responses, and that the level of each response in turn provides system stakeholders with some benefit called *utility*. Each architectural strategy provides a different level of utility, but also has a cost and takes time to implement. The idea behind the CBAM is that by studying levels of utility and costs of implementation, particular architectural strategies can be selected based on their associated return on investment (ROI). The CBAM was conceived to be performed after an ATAM (architecture tradeoff analysis method), but it is possible to use the CBAM during design—that is, prior to the moment where the architectural evaluation is performed.

The CBAM takes as its input a collection of prioritized traditional quality attribute scenarios, which are then analyzed and refined with additional information. The addition is to consider several levels of response for each scenario:

- The worst-case scenario, which represents the minimum threshold at which a system must perform (utility = 0)
- The best-case scenario, which represents the level after which stakeholders foresee no further utility (utility = 100)
- The current scenario, which represents the level at which the system is already performing (the utility of the current scenario is estimated by stakeholders)
- The desired scenario, which represents the level of response that the stakeholders are hoping to achieve (the utility of the desired scenario is estimated by stakeholders)

Using these data points, we can draw a utility–response curve, as shown in the figure. After the utility–response curve is mapped for each of the different scenarios, a number of contemplated design alternatives may be considered, and their expected response values can be estimated. For example, if we are concerned about mean time to failure, we might consider three different architectural strategies (i.e., redundancy options)—for example, no redundancy, cold spare, and hot spare. For each of these strategies, we could estimate their expected responses (i.e., their expected mean times to failure). In the graph shown here, the "e" represents one such option, placed on the curve based on its expected response measure.

Using these response estimates, the utility values of each architectural strategy can now be determined via interpolation, which provides its expected benefit. The costs of each architectural strategy are also elicited—one would expect hot spare to be the most costly, followed by cold spare and no redundancy.

Given all of this information, architectural strategies can now be selected based on their expected value for cost.

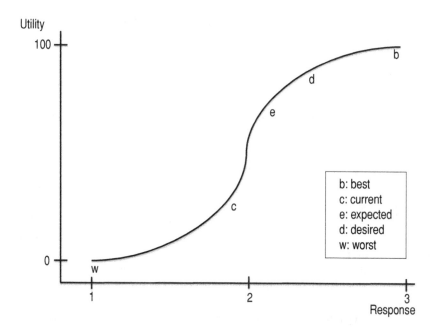

Although the CBAM may seem relatively complex and time-consuming at first, you need to consider that some design decisions can have enormous economic consequences—in terms of their costs, their benefits, and their effects on project schedule. You must decide if you are willing to take the chance of making these decisions solely using a gut-feeling approach versus this more rational and systematic approach.

---

In case the previous analysis techniques do not guide you to make an appropriate selection, you may need to create throwaway prototypes and collect measurements from them. The creation of early throwaway prototypes is a useful technique to help in the selection of externally developed components. This type of prototype is usually created in a "quick and dirty" fashion without too much consideration for maintainability or reuse. For these reasons, it is important to keep in mind that throwaway prototypes should not be used as a basis for further development.

Although the creation of prototypes can be costly compared to analysis (the ratio of costs is between 10 and 5 to 1, according to our sources), certain scenarios strongly motivate the creation of prototypes. Aspects that you should consider when deciding whether you will create a prototype include the following:

- Does the project incorporate emerging technologies?
- Is the technology new in the company?

- Are there certain drivers, particularly quality attributes, whose satisfaction using the selected technology presents risks (i.e., it is not understood if they can be satisfied)?
- Is there a lack of trusted information, internal or external, that provides some degree of certainty that the selected technology will be useful to satisfy the project drivers?
- Are there configuration options associated with the technology that need to be tested or understood?
- Is it unclear whether the selected technology can be integrated with other technologies that are used in the project?

If most of your answers to these questions are "yes", then you should strongly consider the creation of a throwaway prototype.

When identifying and selecting design concepts, you need to keep in mind the *constraints* that are part of the architectural drivers, because some constraints will restrict you from selecting particular alternatives. For example, a constraint might require that all libraries and frameworks in the system do not use the GPL license; thus, even if you have found a framework that could be useful for your needs, you may need to discard it if it has a GPL license. Also, you need to keep in mind that the decisions regarding the selection of design concepts that you have made in previous iterations may restrict the design concepts that you can select in the future because of incompatibilities. For example, if you selected a web application reference architecture for use in an initial iteration, you cannot select a user interface framework intended for local applications in a subsequent iteration.

Finally, you need to remember that even though ADD provides guidance on how to perform the design process, it cannot ensure that you will make appropriate design decisions. Thorough reasoning and considering different alternatives (not just the first thing that comes to mind) are the best means to improve the odds of finding a good solution. We discuss doing "analysis in the design process" in Chapter 8.

## 3.5 Producing Structures

Design concepts per se won't help you satisfy your drivers unless you produce *structures*; that is, you need to identify and connect elements that are derived from the selected design concepts. This process is the *instantiation* of architectural elements in ADD: creating elements and relationships between them, and associating responsibilities with these elements. It is important to remember that the architecture of a software system is composed of a set of structures, which can be grouped into three major categories:

- *Module structures*: composed of logical and static elements that exist at development time, such as files, modules, and classes
- *Component and connector (C&C) structures*: composed of dynamic elements that exist at runtime, such as processes and threads
- *Allocation structures*: composed of both software elements (from a module or C&C structure) and non-software elements that may exist both at development time and at runtime, such as file systems, hardware, and development teams

When you instantiate a design concept, you may actually produce more than one structure. For example, in a particular iteration you may instantiate the Layers pattern, which will result in a Module structure. As part of instantiating this pattern, you will need to choose the number of layers, their relationships, and the specific responsibilities of each layer. As part of the iteration, you may also study how a scenario is supported by the elements that you have just identified. For example, you could create instances of the logical elements in a C&C structure and model how they exchange messages (see Section 3.6). Finally, you may want to decide who will be responsible for implementing the modules inside each of the layers, which is an allocation decision.

### 3.5.1 Instantiating Elements

The instantiation of architectural elements depends on the type of design concept that you are working with:

- *Reference architectures.* In the case of reference architectures, instantiation typically means that you perform some sort of customization. As part of this work, you will add or remove elements that are part of the structure that is defined by the reference architecture. For example, if you are designing a web application that needs to communicate with an external application to handle payments, you will probably need an integration layer in addition to the traditional presentation, business, and data layers.
- *Architectural and design patterns.* These patterns provide a generic structure composed of elements, their relationships and their responsibilities. As this structure is generic, you will need to adapt it to your specific problem. Instantiation usually involves transforming the generic structure defined by the pattern into a specific one that is adapted to the needs of the problem that you are solving. For example, consider the Pipe and Filters architectural pattern. It establishes the basic elements of computation—filters—and their relationships—pipes—but does not specify how many filters you should use for your problem or what their relationships should be. You will instantiate this pattern by defining how many pipes and filters are needed to solve your problem, by establishing the specific responsibilities of each of the filters, and by defining their topology.

- *Deployment patterns.* Similar to the case with architectural and design patterns, the instantiation of deployment patterns generally involves the identification and specification of physical elements. If, for example, you are using a Load-Balanced Cluster pattern, instantiation may involve identifying the number of replicas to be included in the cluster, the load-balancing algorithm, and the physical location of the replicas.
- *Tactics.* This design concept does not prescribe a particular structure, so you will need to use other design concepts to instantiate a tactic. For example, you may select a security tactic of authenticating actors and instantiate it by creating a custom-coded ad hoc solution, or by using a security pattern, or by using an externally developed component such as a security framework.
- *Externally developed components.* The instantiation of these components may or may not imply the creation of new elements. For example, in the case of object-oriented frameworks, instantiation may require you to create specific classes that inherit from the base classes defined in the framework. This will result in new elements. Other approaches, which do not involve the creation of new elements, might include choosing a specific technology from a technology family that was identified in a previous iteration, associating a particular framework to elements that were identified in a previous iteration, or specifying configuration options for an element associated with a particular technology (such as a number of threads in a thread pool).

### 3.5.2  Associating Responsibilities and Identifying Properties

When you are creating elements by instantiating design concepts, you need to consider the responsibilities that are allocated to these elements. For example, if you instantiate the Layers pattern and decide to use the traditional three-layer structure, you might decide that one of the layers will be responsible for managing the interactions with the users (typically known as the presentation layer). When instantiating elements and allocating responsibilities, you should keep in mind the high cohesion/low coupling design principle: Elements should have high cohesion (internally), defined by a narrow set of responsibilities, and low coupling (externally), defined by a lack of knowledge of the implementation details of other elements.

One additional aspect that you need to consider when instantiating design concepts is the properties of the elements. This may involve aspects such as the configuration options, statefulness, resource management, priority, or even hardware characteristics (if the elements that you created are physical nodes) of the chosen technologies. Identifying these properties supports analysis and the documentation of the design rationale.

### 3.5.3  Establishing Relationships Between the Elements

The creation of structures also requires making decisions with respect to the relationships that exist between the elements and their properties. Once again, consider the Layers pattern. You may decide that two layers are connected, but these layers will eventually be allocated to components that are, in turn, allocated to hardware. In such a case, you need to decide how communication will take place between these layers, as they have been allocated to components: Is the communication synchronous or asynchronous? Does it involve some type of network communication? Which type of protocol is used? How much information is transferred and at what rate? These design decisions can have a significant impact with respect to achieving certain quality attributes such as performance.

## 3.6  Defining Interfaces

*Interfaces* are the externally visible properties of elements that establish a contractual specification that allows elements to collaborate and exchange information. There are two categories of interfaces: external and internal.

### 3.6.1  External Interfaces

External interfaces include interfaces from other systems that are *required* by the system that you are developing and interfaces that are *provided* by your system to other systems. Required interfaces are part of the constraints for your system, as you usually cannot influence their specification. Provided interfaces need to be formally defined, which can be performed in a similar way to defining internal interfaces—that is, by considering interactions between the external systems and your system and seeing them as elements of a bigger structure.

Establishing a system context at the beginning of the design process is useful to identify external interfaces. This context can be represented using a system context diagram, as shown in Figure 3.3. Given that external entities and the system under development interact via interfaces, there should be at least one external interface per external system (each relationship in the figure).

### 3.6.2  Internal Interfaces

Internal interfaces are interfaces between the elements that result from the instantiation of design concepts. To identify the relationships and the interface details, you generally need to understand how the elements exchange information at runtime. You can achieve this with the help of modeling tools such as UML sequence diagrams (Figure 3.4), which allow you to model the information that

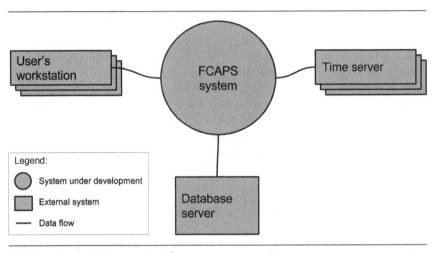

**FIGURE 3.3** A system context diagram

is exchanged between elements during execution to support use cases or quality attribute scenarios. This type of analysis is also useful for identifying relationships between elements: If two elements need to exchange information directly, then a relationship between these elements must exist. The information that is exchanged becomes part of the specification of the interface. Interfaces typically consist of a set of operations (such as methods) with specified parameters, return values, and possibly, exceptions and pre and post conditions. Some interfaces, however, may involve other information exchange mechanisms, such as a component that writes information to a file or database and another component that then accesses this information. Interfaces may also establish quality of service agreements. For example, the execution of an operation specified in the interface may be time-constrained to satisfy a performance quality attribute scenario.

The identification of interfaces is usually not performed equally across all design iterations. When you are starting the design of a greenfield system, for example, your first iterations will produce only abstract elements such as layers, with these elements then being refined in later iterations. The interfaces of abstract elements such as layers are typically underspecified. For example, in an early iteration you might simply specify that the UI layer sends "commands" to the business logic layer, with the business logic layer sending "results" back. As you advance in the design process and particularly when you create structures to address specific use cases and quality attribute scenarios, you will need to refine the interfaces of the specific elements that participate in the interaction.

In some special cases, identification of interfaces is greatly simplified. For example, in the Big Data case study we present in Chapter 5, interfaces are already defined by the technologies that are selected. The specification of interfaces then becomes a relatively trivial task, as the chosen technologies are designed to

(*continues on p. 64*)

The following is an initial sequence diagram for Use Case UC-2 (Detect Fault)[1] from the FCAPS case study in Chapter 4. This diagram shows the interactions between an actor and the five components that participate in UC-2. In creating this diagram, we identify the information that is exchanged, the methods that are invoked, and the values that are passed and returned.

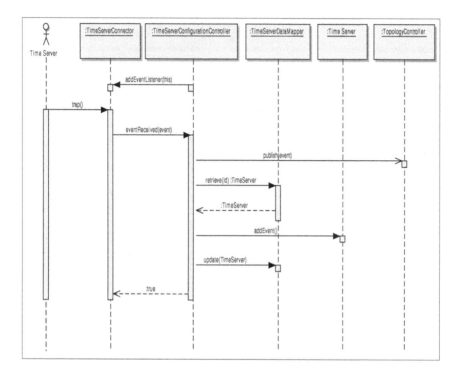

Key: UML

From this interaction, initial methods for the interfaces of the interacting elements can be identified:

**Name: TimeServerConnector**

| Method name | Description |
| --- | --- |
| `boolean addEventListener(:EventListener)` | This method allows components from the business logic to register themselves as listeners to events that are received from the `TimeServers`. |

**FIGURE 3.4** A sequence diagram used to identify interfaces

1. More detail about this example is presented in Chapter 4.

(*continued from p. 62*)

interoperate and hence have already "baked in" many interface assumptions and decisions.

Finally, you need to consider that not all of the internal interfaces of the system element will be identified as part of the design process (see the sidebar "Identifying Interfaces in Element Interaction Design").

---

### Identifying Interfaces in Element Interaction Design

Although defining interfaces is an essential part of the architecture design process, it is important to recognize that not all of the internal interfaces are identified during architectural design. As part of the architecture design process, you typically consider the primary use cases as part of the architectural drivers, and you identify elements (usually modules) that support this primary functionality along with the other drivers. This process will, however, not uncover all of the elements and interfaces for the system that are required to support the entire set of use cases. This lack of specificity is intended: Architecture is about abstraction, so necessarily some information is less important, particularly in the earliest stages of design.

Identifying the modules that support the nonprimary use cases is often necessary for estimation or work-assignment purposes. Identifying their interfaces is also necessary to support the individual development and integration of the modules and to perform unit testing. This identification of modules may be done early in the project life cycle, but it must not be confused with a big design up front (BDUF) approach. This, at most, is a BDUF that, in certain contexts such as early estimation or iteration planning, is hard to avoid.

As an architect, you may identify the set of modules that supports the complete set of use cases for the system or for a particular release of the system, but the identification of the interfaces associated with the modules that support the nonprimary use cases is typically not your responsibility, as it would require a significant amount of your time and does not usually have a major architectural impact. This task, which we call element interaction design (see Section 2.2.2), is usually performed after architectural design ends but before the development of (most of) the modules begins. Although this task should be performed by other members in the development team, you play a critical role in it, since these interfaces must adhere to the architectural design that you established. You, as the architect, must communicate the architecture to the engineers who are responsible for identifying the interfaces and ensure that they understand the rationale for the existing design decisions.

A good way to achieve this communication is to use the *active reviews for intermediate design (ARID)* method. In this method, the architecture design (or part of it) is presented to a group of reviewers—in this case, the engineers who will make use of this design. After the design presentation, a set of scenarios is selected by the participants. The selected scenarios are used for the core of the exercise, where the reviewers use the elements present in the architecture to satisfy them. In standard ARID, the reviewers are asked to write code or pseudo-code for the purpose of identifying interfaces. Alternatively, the architect can present the architecture, select a nonprimary functional scenario and ask the participants to identify the interfaces of the components that support the scenario using sequence diagrams or a similar method.

Aside from the fact that the architectural design is reviewed in this exercise, there are additional benefits to this approach. Specifically, in a single meeting, the architecture design or part of it is presented to the entire team, and agreements can be reached with respect to how the interfaces should be defined (e.g., the level of detail or aspects such as parameter passing, data types, or exception management).

## 3.7   Creating Preliminary Documentation During Design

A software architecture is typically documented as a set of *views*, which represent the different structures that compose the architecture. The formal documentation of these views is not part of the design process. Structures, however, are produced as part of design. Capturing them, even in an informal manner (i.e., as sketches), along with the design decisions that led you to create these structures, is a task that should be performed as part of normal design activities.

### 3.7.1   Recording Sketches of the Views

When you produce structures by instantiating the design concepts that you have selected to address a particular design problem, you will typically not produce these structures in your mind, but rather will create some *sketches* of them. In the simplest case, you will produce these sketches on a whiteboard, a flip-chart, or even a piece of paper. Otherwise, you may use a modeling tool in which you will draw the structures. The sketches that you produce are the initial documentation for your architecture that you should capture and may flesh out later, if necessary. When you create sketches, you don't need to always use a more formal language such as UML. If you use some informal notation, you should at least be careful in maintaining consistency in the use of symbols. Eventually, you will need to add a legend to your diagrams to provide clarity and avoid ambiguity.

You should develop discipline in writing down the responsibilities that you allocate to the elements as you create the structures. The reasons for this are simple: As you identify an element, you are determining some responsibilities for that element in your mind. Writing it down *at that moment* ensures that you won't have to remember it later. Also, it is easier to write down the responsibilities associated with your elements gradually, rather than compiling all of them at a later time.

Creating this preliminary documentation as you design requires some discipline. But the benefits are worth the effort—you will be able to produce the more detailed architecture documentation relatively easily and quickly at a later point. One simple way that you can document responsibilities if you are using a whiteboard, a flip-chart, or a PowerPoint slide is to take a photo of the sketch that you have produced and paste it in a document, along with a table that summarizes the responsibilities of every element depicted in the diagram (Figure 3.5 provides an example). If you are using a computer-aided software engineering (CASE) tool, you can select an element to create and use the text area that usually appears in the properties sheet of the element to document its responsibilities, and then generate the documentation automatically.

---

This diagram presents a sketch of a module view depicting the overall system structure from the case study in Chapter 5.

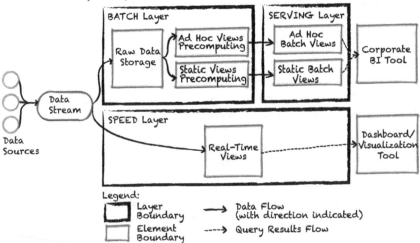

The diagram is complemented with a table that describes the element's responsibilities:

| Element | Responsibility |
|---|---|
| Data stream | This element collects data from all data sources in real time and dispatches it to both the batch layer and the speed layer for processing. |
| Batch layer | This layer is responsible for storing raw data and precomputing the batch views to be stored in the serving layer. |
| ... | ... |

**FIGURE 3.5** Sample preliminary documentation

Of course, it is not necessary to document *everything*. The three purposes of documentation are analysis, construction, and education. At the moment you are designing, you should choose a documentation purpose and then document to fulfill that purpose, based on your risk mitigation concerns. For example, if you have a critical quality attribute scenario that your architecture design needs to satisfy, and if you will need to prove this requirement is met in an analysis, then you must take care to document the information that is relevant for the analysis to be satisfactory. Alternatively, if you anticipate having to train new team members, then you should make a sketch of a C&C view of the system, showing how it operates and how the elements interact at runtime, and perhaps construct a crude module view of the system, showing at least the major layers or subsystems.

Finally, it is a good idea to remember, as you are documenting, that your design may eventually be analyzed. Consequently, you need to think about which information should be documented to support this analysis (see the sidebar "Scenario-Based Documentation").

---

## Scenario-Based Documentation

An analysis of an architecture design is based on your most important use cases and quality attribute scenarios. Simply put, a scenario is selected and you must explain to reviewers how the architecture supports the scenario, and justify your decisions. To start preparing for the analysis *while* you design, it is useful to produce and document structures that contain the elements that are involved in the satisfaction of a scenario. This should come naturally given that the design process is guided by scenarios, but keeping this point firmly in mind is always helpful.

During the design process, you should at least try to capture the following elements in a single document:

- The primary presentation: the diagram that represents the structure that you produced
- The element responsibilities table: it will help you record the responsibilities of the elements that are present in the structure
- The relevant design decisions, and their rationales (see Section 3.7.2)

You might also capture two other pieces of information:

- A runtime representation of the element's interaction—for example, a sequence diagram
- The initial interface specifications (which can also be captured in a separate document)

As you can see, all of this information needs to be produced as part of the design process. One way or another, you need to decide which elements are present in the system and how they interact. The only question is whether you bother to write this information down, or whether its sole representation is in the code.

If you follow the approach that we advocate here, at the end of the design you will have a set of preliminary views documented, in which each of the views is associated with a particular scenario, and you will have this documentation at little cost. This preliminary documentation can be used "as is" to analyze the design, and particularly through scenario-based evaluations.

### 3.7.2   Recording Design Decisions

In each design iteration, you make important design decisions to achieve your iteration goal. As we saw previously, these design decisions include the following:

- Selecting a design concept from several alternatives
- Creating structures by instantiating the selected design concept
- Establishing relationships between elements and defining interfaces
- Allocating resources (e.g., people, hardware, computation)
- Others

When you study a diagram that represents an architecture, you see the end product of a thought process, but it may not be easy to understand the decisions that were made to achieve this result. Recording design decisions *beyond* the representation of the chosen elements, relationships, and properties is fundamental to help in understanding how you arrived at the result: the design rationale.

When your iteration goal involves satisfying a specific quality attribute scenario, some of the decisions that you make will play significant roles in your ability to achieve the scenario response measure. These are, therefore, the decisions that you should take the greatest care in recording. You should record these decisions because they are essential to facilitate analysis of the design you created; then to facilitate implementation; and, still later, to aid in understanding of the architecture (e.g., during maintenance). Also *every* design decision is "good enough" but seldom optimal, so you need to justify the decisions made, and possibly revisit the remaining risks later.

You might think that recording design decisions is a tedious task. In reality, depending on the criticality of the system being developed, you can adjust the amount of information that is recorded. For example, to record a minimum of information, you can use a simple table such as the one shown in Table 3.2. If you decide to record more than this minimum, the following information can prove useful:

- What evidence was produced to justify decisions?
- Who did what?
- Why were shortcuts taken?

**TABLE 3.2**   Example of a Table to Document Design Decisions

| Driver | Design Decisions and Location | Rationale and Assumptions |
|---|---|---|
| QA-1 | **Introduce concurrency** (tactic) in the `TimeServerConnector` and `FaultDetectionService` | Concurrency should be introduced to be able to receive and process several events (traps) simultaneously. |
| QA-2 | Use of a **messaging** pattern through the introduction of a message queue in the communications layer | Although the use of a message queue may seem to go against the performance imposed by the scenario, a message queue was chosen because some implementations have high performance and, furthermore, this will be helpful to support QA-3. |
| ... | ... | ... |

- Why were tradeoffs made?
- What assumptions did you make?

And, in the same way that we suggest you record responsibilities as you identify elements, you should record the design decisions as you make them. The reason for this is simple: If you leave it until later, you may not remember why you did things.

## 3.8   Tracking Design Progress

Even though ADD provides clear guidelines to perform design systematically, it does not provide a mechanism to track design progress. When you are performing design, however, there are several questions that you want to answer:

- How much design do we need to do?
- How much design has been done so far?
- Are we finished?

Agile practices such as the use of backlogs and Kanban boards can help you track the design progress and answer these questions. These techniques are not limited to Agile methods, of course. Any development project using any methodology should track progress.

### 3.8.1   Use of an Architectural Backlog

The concept of an architecture (or design) backlog has been proposed by several authors (see Section 7.1). This is similar to what is found in Agile development methods such as Scrum. The basic idea is that you need to create a list of the pending actions that still need to be performed as part of the architecture design process.

Initially, you should populate the design backlog with your drivers, but other activities that support the design of the architecture can also be included. For example:

- Creation of a prototype to test a particular technology or to address a specific quality attribute risk
- Exploration and understanding of existing assets (possibly requiring reverse engineering)
- Issues uncovered in a review of the design
- Review of a partial design that was performed on a previous iteration

For example, when using Scrum, the sprint backlog and the design backlog are not independent: Some features in the sprint backlog may require architecture design to be performed, so they will generate items that go into the architectural design backlog. These two backlogs can be managed separately, however. The design backlog may even be managed internally, as it contains several items that are typically not discussed or prioritized by the customer (or product owner).

Also, additional architectural concerns may arise as decisions are made. For example, if you choose a reference architecture, you will probably need to add specific architectural concerns, or quality attribute scenarios derived from them, to the architectural design backlog. An example of such a concern is the management of sessions for a web application reference architecture.

### 3.8.2   Use of a Design Kanban Board

As design is performed in rounds and as a series of iterations within these rounds, you need to have a way of tracking the design's degree of advancement. You must also decide whether you need to continue making more design decisions (i.e., performing additional iterations). One tool that can be used to facilitate this task is a Kanban board, such as the one shown in Figure 3.6

At the beginning of a design round, the inputs to the design process become entries in the backlog. Initially, that activity occurs in step 1 of ADD; the different entries in your backlog for this design round should be added to the "Not Yet Addressed" column of the board (except if you have some entries that were not concluded in previous design rounds that you wish to address here). When you begin a design iteration, in step 2 of ADD, the backlog entries that correspond to the drivers that you plan to address as part of the design iteration goal should be moved to the "Partially Addressed" column. Finally, once you finish an iteration and the analysis of your design decisions reveals that a particular driver has been addressed (step 7 of ADD), the entry should be moved to the "Completely Addressed" column of the board. It is important to establish clear criteria that will allow a driver to be moved to the "Completely Addressed" column (think of this as the "Definition of Addressed" criteria, similar to the "Definition of Done"

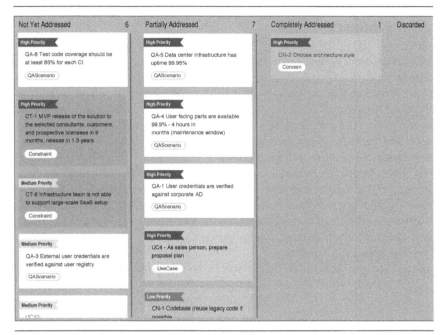

| Not Yet Addressed | 6 | Partially Addressed | 7 | Completely Addressed | 1 | Discarded |
|---|---|---|---|---|---|---|

**High Priority**
QA-8 Test code coverage should be at least 85% for each CI
( QAScenario )

**High Priority**
CT-1 MVP release of the solution to the selected consultants, customers, and prospective licensees in 9 months, release in 1.5 years
( Constraint )

**Medium Priority**
CT-6 Infrastructure team is not able to support large-scale SaaS setup
( Constraint )

**Medium Priority**
QA-3 External user credentials are verified against user registry
( QAScenario )

**Medium Priority**
UC10.

**High Priority**
QA-5 Data center infrastructure has uptime 99.95%
( QAScenario )

**High Priority**
QA-4 User facing parts are available 99.9% - 4 hours in months (maintenance window)
( QAScenario )

**High Priority**
QA-1 User credentials are verified against corporate AD
( QAScenario )

**High Priority**
UC4 - As sales person, prepare proposal plan
( UseCase )

**Low Priority**
CN-1 Codebase (reuse legacy code if possible

**High Priority**
CN-2 Choose architecture style
( Concern )

**FIGURE 3.6**  A Kanban board used to track design progress

criteria used in Scrum). A criterion may be, for example, that the driver has been analyzed or that it has been implemented in a prototype. Also, drivers that are selected for a particular iteration may not be completely addressed in that particular iteration, in which case they should remain in the "Partially Addressed" column and, in preparation for subsequent iterations, you should consider how they can be allocated to the elements that exist at this point.

It can be useful to select a technique that will allow you to differentiate the entries in the board according to their priority. For example, you might use different colors of Post-it notes depending on the priority.

With such a board, it is easy to visually track the advancement of design, as you can quickly see how many of the (most important) drivers are being or have been addressed in the design round. This technique also helps you decide whether you need to perform additional iterations as, ideally, the design round is terminated when a majority of your drivers (or at least the ones with the highest priority) are located under the "Completely Addressed" column.

## 3.9  Summary

In this chapter, we presented a detailed walk-through of the Attribute-Driven Design method, version 3.0. We also discussed several important aspects that need
to be considered in the various steps of the design process. These aspects include the use of a backlog, the various possible design roadmaps (for greenfield,
brownfield, and novel contexts), the identification and selection of design concepts and their use in producing structures, the definition of interfaces, and the
production of preliminary documentation.

Even though the overall architecture development life cycle includes documenting and analyzing architecture as activities that are separate from design, we
have argued that a clean separation of these activities is artificial and harmful. We
stress that preliminary documentation and analysis activities need to be regularly
performed as integral parts of the design process.

In Chapters 4, 5, and 6, we will instantiate ADD 3.0 in several extended examples, showing how the method works in the real world, in both greenfield and
brownfield contexts.

## 3.10  Further Reading

Some of the concepts of ADD 3.0 were first introduced in an IEEE Software
article: H. Cervantes, P. Velasco, and R. Kazman, "A Principled Way of Using Frameworks in Architectural Design", *IEEE Software*, 46–53, March/April
2013. Version 2.0 of ADD was first documented in the SEI Technical Report:
R. Wojcik, F. Bachmann, L. Bass, P. Clements, P. Merson, R. Nord, and B. Wood,
"Attribute-Driven Design (ADD), Version 2.0", SEI/CMU Technical Report
CMU/SEI-2006-TR-023, 2006. An extended example of using ADD 2.0 was
documented in W. Wood, "A Practical Example of Applying Attribute-Driven Design (ADD), Version 2.0", SEI/CMU Technical Report: CMU/SEI-2007-TR-005.

Several alternative methods exist to support the design of software architectures. These are discussed in more detail and referenced in Chapter 7.

The concept of an architecture backlog is discussed in C. Hofmeister,
P. Kruchten, R. Nord, H. Obbink, A. Ran, and P. America, "A General Model of
Software Architecture Design Derived from Five Industrial Approaches", *Journal
of Systems and Software,* 80:106–126, 2007.

The ARID method is discussed in P. Clements, R. Kazman, and M. Klein,
*Evaluating Software Architectures: Methods and Case Studies,* Addison-Wesley,
2002.

The CBAM method is presented in L. Bass, P. Clements, and R. Kazman,
*Software Architecture in Practice,* 3rd ed., Addison-Wesley, 2013.

The ways in which an architecture can be documented are covered extensively in P. Clements et al. *Documenting Software Architectures: Views and Beyond*, 2nd ed., Addison-Wesley, 2011. More Agile approaches to documenting are discussed in books such as S. Brown, *Software Architecture for Developers*. Lean Publishing, 2015.

The importance and challenges of capturing design rationale are discussed in A. Tang, M. Ali Babar, I. Gorton, and J. Han, "A Survey of Architecture Design Rationale", *Journal of Systems and Software*, 79(12):1792–1804, 2007. A minimalistic technique for capturing rationale is discussed in U. Zdun, R. Capilla, H. Tran, and O. Zimmermann, "Sustainable Architectural Design Decisions", *IEEE Software*, 30(6):46–53, 2013.

# 4

# Case Study: FCAPS System

We now present a case study of using ADD 3.0 for a greenfield system in a mature domain. This case study details an initial design round composed of three iterations and is based on a real-world example. We first present the business context, and then we summarize the requirements for the system. This is followed by a step-by-step summary of the activities that are performed during the ADD iterations.

## 4.1  Business Case

In 2006, a large telecommunications company wanted to expand its Internet Protocol (IP) network to support "carrier-class services", and more specifically high-quality voice over IP (VOIP) systems. One important aspect to achieve this goal was synchronization of the VOIP servers and other equipment. Poor synchronization results in low quality of service (QoS), degraded performance, and unhappy customers. To achieve the required level of synchronization, the company wanted to deploy a network of time servers that support the Network Time Protocol (NTP). Time servers are formed into groups that typically correspond to geographical regions. Within these regions, time servers are organized hierarchically in levels or *strata*, where time servers placed in the upper level of the hierarchy (stratum 1) are equipped with hardware (e.g., Cesium Oscillator, GPS signal) that provides precise time. Time servers that are lower in the hierarchy use NTP to request time from servers in the upper levels or from their peers.

Many pieces of equipment depend on the time provided by time servers in the network, so one priority for the company was to correct any problems that occur on the time servers. Such problems may require dispatching a technician to perform physical maintenance on the time servers, such as rebooting. Another priority for the company was to collect data from the time servers to monitor the performance of the synchronization framework.

In the initial deployment plans, the company wanted to field 100 time servers of a particular model. Besides NTP, time servers support the Simple Network Management Protocol (SNMP), which provides three basic operations:

- `set()` operations: change configuration variables (e.g., connected peers)
- `get()` operations: retrieve configuration variables or performance data
- `trap()` operations: notifications of exceptional events such as the loss or restoration of the GPS signal or changes in the time reference

To achieve the company's goals, a management system for the time servers needed to be developed. This system needed to conform to the FCAPS model, which is a standard model for network management. The letters in the acronym stand for:

- *Fault management.* The goal of fault management is to recognize, isolate, correct, and log faults that occur in the network. In this case, these faults correspond to traps generated by time servers or other problems such as loss of communication between the management system and the time servers.
- *Configuration management.* This includes gathering and storing configurations from network devices, thereby simplifying the configuration of devices and tracking changes that are made to device configurations. In this system, besides changing individual configuration variables, it is necessary to be able to deploy a specific configuration to several time servers.
- *Accounting.* The goal here is to gather device information. In this context, this includes tracking device hardware and firmware versions, hardware equipment, and other components of the system.
- *Performance management.* This category focuses on determining the efficiency of the current network. By collecting and analyzing performance data, the network health can be monitored. In this case, delay, offset, and jitter measures are collected from the time servers.
- *Security management.* This is the process of controlling access to assets in the network. In this case, there are two important types of users: technicians and administrators. Technicians can visualize trap information and configurations but cannot make changes; administrators are technicians who can visualize the same information but can also make changes to configurations, including adding and removing time servers from the network.

Once the initial network was deployed, the company planned to extend it by adding time servers from newer models that might potentially support management protocols other than SNMP.

The remainder of this chapter describes a design for this system, created using ADD 3.0.

## 4.2  System Requirements

Requirement elicitation activities had been previously performed, and the following is a summary of the most relevant requirements collected.

### 4.2.1  Use Case Model

The use case model in Figure 4.1 presents the most relevant use cases that support the FCAPS model in the system. Other use cases are not shown.

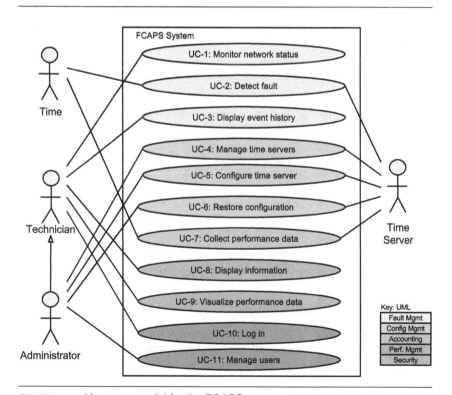

**FIGURE 4.1**  Use case model for the FCAPS system

Each of these use cases is described in the following table:

| Use Case | Description |
|---|---|
| UC-1: Monitor network status | A user monitors the time servers in a hierarchical representation of the whole network. Problematic devices are highlighted, along with the logical regions where they are grouped. The user can expand and collapse the network representation. This representation is updated continuously as faults are detected or repaired. |
| UC-2: Detect fault | Periodically the management system contacts the time servers to see if they are "alive". If a time server does not respond, or if a trap that signals a problem or a return to a normal state of operation is received, the event is stored and the network representation observed by the users is updated accordingly. |
| UC-3: Display event history | Stored events associated with a particular time server or group of time servers are displayed. These can be filtered by various criteria such as type or severity. |
| UC-4: Manage time servers | The administrator adds a time server to, or removes a time server from, the network. |
| UC-5: Configure time server | An administrator changes configuration parameters associated with a particular time server. The parameters are sent to the device and are also stored locally. |
| UC-6: Restore configuration | A locally stored configuration is sent to one or more time servers. |
| UC-7: Collect performance data | Network performance data (delay, offset, and jitter) is collected periodically from the time servers. |
| UC-8: Display information | The user displays stored information about the time server—configuration values and other parameters such as the server name. |
| UC-9: Visualize performance data | The user displays network performance measures (delay, offset, jitter) in a graphical way to view and analyze network performance. |
| UC-10: Log in | A user logs into the system through a login/password screen. Upon successful login, the user is presented with different options according to their role. |
| U-11: Manage users | The administrator adds or removes a user or modifies user permissions. |

## 4.2.2   Quality Attribute Scenarios

In addition to these use cases, a number of quality attribute scenarios were elicited and documented. The six most relevant ones are presented in the following table. For each scenario, we also identify the use case that it is associated with.

| ID | Quality Attribute | Scenario | Associated Use Case |
|---|---|---|---|
| QA-1 | Performance | Several time servers send traps to the management system at peak load; 100% of the traps are successfully processed and stored. | UC-2 |
| QA-2 | Modifiability | A new time server management protocol is introduced to the system as part of an update. The protocol is added successfully without any changes to the core components of the system. | UC-5 |
| QA-3 | Availability | A failure occurs in the management system during normal operation. The management system resumes operation in less than 30 seconds. | All |
| QA-4 | Performance | The management system collects performance data from a time server during peak load. The management system collects all performance data within 5 minutes, while processing all user requests, to ensure no loss of data due to CON-5. | UC-7 |
| QA-5 | Performance, usability | A user displays the event history of a particular time server during normal operation. The list of events from the last 24 hours is displayed within 1 second. | UC-3 |
| QA-6 | Security | A user performs a change in the system during normal operation. It is possible to know who performed the operation and when it was performed 100% of the time. | All |

### 4.2.3  Constraints

Finally, a set of constraints on the system and its implementation were collected. These are presented in the following table.

| ID | Constraint |
|---|---|
| CON-1 | A minimum of 50 simultaneous users must be supported. |
| CON-2 | The system must be accessed through a web browser (Chrome V3.0+, Firefox V4+, IE8+) in different platforms: Windows, OSX, and Linux. |
| CON-3 | An existing relational database server must be used. This server cannot be used for other purposes than hosting the database. |
| CON-4 | The network connection to user workstations can have low bandwidth but is generally reliable. |
| CON-5 | Performance data needs to be collected in intervals of no more than 5 minutes, as higher intervals result in time servers discarding data. |
| CON-6 | Events from the last 30 days must be stored. |

### 4.2.4   Architectural Concerns

Given that this is greenfield development, only a few general architectural concerns are identified initially, as shown in the following table.

| ID | Concern |
| --- | --- |
| CRN-1 | Establishing an overall initial system structure. |
| CRN-2 | Leverage the team's knowledge about Java technologies, including Spring, JSF, Swing, Hibernate, Java Web Start and JMS frameworks, and the Java language. |
| CRN-3 | Allocate work to members of the development team. |

Given these sets of inputs, we are now ready to proceed to describe the design process, as described in Section 3.2. In this chapter, we present only the final results of the requirements collection process. The job of collecting these requirements is nontrivial, but is beyond the scope of this chapter.

## 4.3   The Design Process

We now ready to make the leap from the world of requirements and business concerns to the world of design. This is perhaps the most important job for an architect—translating requirements into design decisions. Of course, many other decisions and duties are important, but this is the core of what it means to be an architect: making design decisions with far-reaching consequences.

### 4.3.1   ADD Step 1: Review Inputs

The first step of the ADD method involves reviewing the inputs and identifying which requirements will be considered as drivers (i.e., which will be included in the design backlog). The inputs are summarized in the following table.

| Category | Details |
| --- | --- |
| Design purpose | This is a greenfield system from a mature domain. The purpose is to produce a sufficiently detailed design to support the construction of the system. |
| Primary functional requirements | From the use cases presented in Section 4.2.1, the primary ones were determined to be: |
| | UC-1: Because it directly supports the core business |
| | UC-2: Because it directly supports the core business |
| | UC-7: Because of the technical issues associated with it (see QA-4) |

| Quality attribute scenarios | The scenarios were described in Section 4.2.2. They have now been prioritized (as discussed in Section 2.4.2) as follows: |
|---|---|

| Scenario ID | Importance to the Customer | Difficulty of Implementation According to the Architect |
|---|---|---|
| QA-1 | High | High |
| QA-2 | High | Medium |
| QA-3 | High | High |
| QA-4 | High | High |
| QA-5 | Medium | Medium |
| QA-6 | Medium | Low |

| | From this list, only QA-1, QA-2, QA-3, and QA-4 are selected as drivers. |
|---|---|
| Constraints | All of the constraints discussed in Section 4.2.3 are included as drivers. |
| Architectural concerns | All of the architectural concerns discussed in Section 4.2.4 are included as drivers. |

## 4.3.2 Iteration 1: Establishing an Overall System Structure

This section presents the results of the activities that are performed in each of the steps of ADD in the first iteration of the design process.

### 4.3.2.1 Step 2: Establish Iteration Goal by Selecting Drivers

This is the first iteration in the design of a greenfield system, so the iteration goal is to achieve the architectural concern CNR-1 of *establishing an overall system structure* (see Section 3.3.1).

Although this iteration is driven by a general architectural concern, the architect must keep in mind *all* of the drivers that may influence the general structure of the system. In particular, the architect must be mindful of the following:

- QA-1: Performance
- QA-2: Modifiability
- QA-3: Availability
- QA-4: Performance
- CON-2: System must be accessed through a web browser in different platforms—Windows, OSX, and Linux
- CON-3: A relational database server must be used
- CON-4: Network connection to users workstations can have low bandwidth and be unreliable
- CRN-2: Leverage team's knowledge about Java technologies

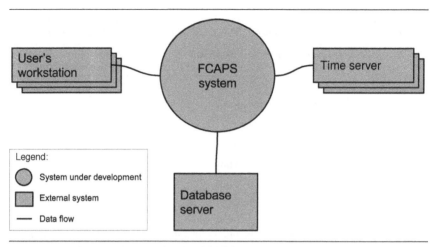

**FIGURE 4.2** Context diagram for the FCAPS system

**4.3.2.2** Step 3: Choose One or More Elements of the System to Refine
This is a greenfield development effort, so in this case the element to refine is the entire FCAPS system, which is shown in Figure 4.2. In this case, refinement is performed through decomposition.

**4.3.2.3** Step 4: Choose One or More Design Concepts That Satisfy the Selected Drivers
In this initial iteration, given the goal of structuring the entire system, design concepts are selected according to the roadmap presented in Section 3.3.1. The following table summarizes the selection of design decisions. Note that all of the design concepts used in this case study are also described in Appendix A.

| Design Decisions and Location | Rationale |
|---|---|
| Logically structure the client part of the system using the **Rich Client Application** reference architecture | The Rich Client Application (RCA) reference architecture (see Section A.1.2) supports the development of applications that are installed in the users' PC. These applications support rich user interface capabilities that are needed for displaying the network topology and performance graphs (UC-1). These capabilities are also helpful in achieving QA-5, even if this design decision is not a driver. Although these types of applications do not run in a web browser (CON-2), they can be installed from a web browser using a technology such as Java Web Start. |

| Design Decisions and Location | Rationale | |
|---|---|---|
| | **Discarded alternatives:** | |
| | **Alternative** | **Reason for Discarding** |
| | Rich Internet applications (RIA) | This reference architecture (see Section A.1.3) is oriented toward the development of applications with a rich user interface that runs inside a web browser. Although this type of application supports a rich user interface and can be upgraded easily, this option was discarded because it was believed that plugins for executing RIA were less broadly available than the Java Virtual Machine. |
| | Web applications | This reference architecture (see Section A.1.1) is oriented toward the development of applications that are accessed from a web browser. Although this reference architecture facilitates deployment and updating, it was discarded because it is difficult to provide a rich user interface experience. |
| | Mobile applications | This reference architecture (see Section A.1.4) is oriented toward the development of applications that are deployed in handheld devices. This alternative was discarded because this type of device was not considered for accessing the system. |
| Logically structure the server part of the system using the **Service Application** reference architecture | Service applications (see Section A.1.5) do not provide a user interface but rather expose services that are consumed by other applications. No other alternatives were considered and discarded, as the architect was familiar with this reference architecture and considered it fully adequate to meet the requirements. | |
| Physically structure the application using the **three-tier deployment pattern** | Since the system must be accessed from a web browser (CON-2) and an existing database server must also be used (CON-3), a three-tier deployment is appropriate (see Section A.2.2). At this point, it is clear that some type of replication will be needed on both the web/app tier and the database tier to support QA-3, but this will be addressed later (in iteration 3). Discarded alternatives include other $n$-tier patterns with $n\,!= 3$. The two-tier alternative is discarded because an existing legacy database server needs to be incorporated into the system and this cannot be used for any other purpose, according to CON-3. All $n > 3$ alternatives are discarded because at this point no other servers are necessary for the solution. | |

*(continues)*

| Design Decisions and Location | Rationale |
|---|---|
| Build the user interface of the client application using the Swing Java framework and other Java technologies | The standard framework for building Java Rich Clients ensures portability (CON-2) and it is what the developers were already familiar with (CRN-3). Discarded alternatives: The Eclipse SWT (Standard Widget Toolkit) framework was considered, but the developers were not as familiar with it. |
| Deploy the application using the Java Web Start technology | Access to the application is obtained via a web browser, which launches the installer (CON-2). This technology also facilitates updating because client code is reloaded only when a new version is available. As updates are not expected to occur frequently, this is beneficial for low-bandwidth situations (CON-4). The alternative would be the use of applets, but they need to be reloaded every time the web page is loaded, which increases the bandwidth requirements. |

#### 4.3.2.4 Step 5: Instantiate Architectural Elements, Allocate Responsibilities, and Define Interfaces

The instantiation design decisions considered and made are summarized in the following table:

| Design Decision and Location | Rationale |
|---|---|
| Remove local data sources in the rich client application | It is believed that there is no need to store data locally, as the network connection is generally reliable. Also, communication with the server is handled in the data layer. Internal communication between components in the client is managed through local method calls and does not need particular support. |
| Create a module dedicated to accessing the time servers in the data layer of the Service Application reference architecture | The service agents component from the reference architecture is adapted to abstract the access to the time servers. This will further facilitate the achievement of QA-2 and will play a critical role in the achievement of UC-2 and UC-7. |

The results of these instantiation decisions are recorded in the next step. In this initial iteration, it is typically too early to precisely define functionality and interfaces. In the next iteration, which is dedicated to defining functionality in more detail, interfaces will begin to be defined.

#### 4.3.2.5 Step 6: Sketch Views and Record Design Decisions

The diagram in Figure 4.3 shows the sketch of a module view of the two reference architectures that were selected for the client and server applications. These have now been adapted according to the design decisions we have made.

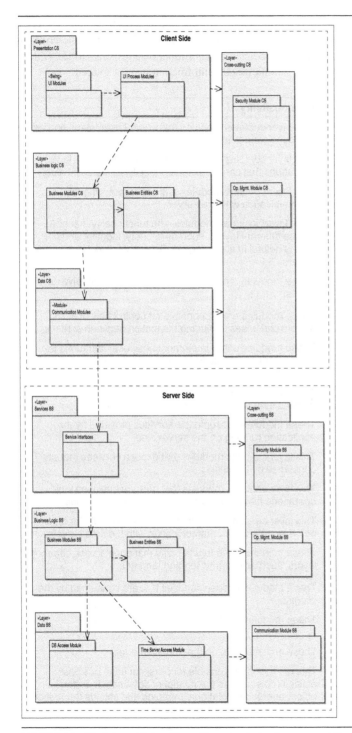

**FIGURE 4.3** Modules obtained from the selected reference architectures (Key: UML)

This sketch was created using a CASE tool. In the tool, each element is selected and a short description of its responsibilities is captured. Note that the descriptions at this point are quite crude, just indicating major functional responsibilities, with no details. The following table summarizes the information that is captured:

| Element | Responsibility |
|---|---|
| Presentation client side (CS) | This layer contains modules that control user interaction and use case control flow. |
| Business logic CS | This layer contains modules that perform business logic operations that can be executed locally on the client side. |
| Data CS | This layer contains modules that are responsible for communication with the server. |
| Cross-cutting CS | This "layer" includes modules with functionality that goes across different layers, such as security, logging, and I/O. This is helpful in achieving QA-6, even if it is not one of the drivers. |
| UI modules | These modules render the user interface and receive user inputs. |
| UI process modules | These modules are responsible for control flow of all the system use cases (including navigation between screens). |
| Business modules CS | These modules either implement business operations that can be performed locally or expose business functionality from the server side. |
| Business entities CS | These entities make up the domain model. They may be less detailed than those on the server side. |
| Communication modules CS | These modules consume the services provided by the application running on the server side. |
| Services server side (SS) | This layer contains modules that expose services that are consumed by the clients. |
| Business Logic SS | This layer contains modules that perform business logic operations that require processing on the server side. |
| Data SS | This layer contains modules that are responsible for data persistence and for communication with the time servers. |
| Cross-cutting SS | These modules have functionality that goes across different layers, such as security, logging, and I/O. |
| Service interfaces SS | These modules expose services that are consumed by the clients. |
| Business modules SS | These modules implement business operations. |
| Business entities SS | These entities make up the domain model. |
| DB access module | This module is responsible for persistence of business entities (objects) into the relational database. It performs object-oriented to relational mapping and shields the rest of the application from persistence details. |

| Element | Responsibility |
|---------|----------------|
| Time server access module | This module is responsible for communication with the time servers. It isolates and abstracts operations with the time servers to support communication with different types of time servers (see QA-2). |

The deployment diagram in Figure 4.4 sketches an allocation view that illustrates where the components associated with the modules in the previous diagram will be deployed.

The responsibilities of the elements are summarized here:

| Element | Responsibility |
|---------|----------------|
| User workstation | The user's PC, which hosts the client side logic of the application |
| Application server | The server that hosts server side logic of the application and also serves web pages |
| Database server | The server that hosts the legacy relational database |
| Time server | The set of (external) time servers |

Also, information about relationships between some elements in the diagram that is worth recording is summarized in the following table:

| Relationship | Description |
|--------------|-------------|
| Between web/app server and database server | Communication with the database will be done using the JDBC protocol. |
| Between web/app server and time server | The SNMP protocol is used (at least initially). |

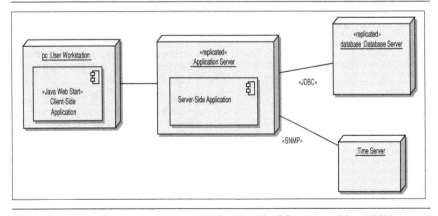

**FIGURE 4.4** Initial deployment diagram for the FCAPS system (Key: UML)

**4.3.2.6** Step 7: Perform Analysis of Current Design and Review Iteration Goal and Achievement of Design Purpose

The following table summarizes the design progress using the Kanban board technique discussed in Section 3.8.2.

| Not Addressed | Partially Addressed | Completely Addressed | Design Decisions Made During the Iteration |
|---|---|---|---|
| | UC-1 | | Selected reference architecture establishes the modules that will support this functionality. |
| | UC-2 | | Selected reference architecture establishes the modules that will support this functionality. |
| | UC-7 | | Selected reference architecture establishes the modules that will support this functionality. |
| QA-1 | | | No relevant decisions made, as it is necessary to identify the elements that participate in the use case that is associated with the scenario. |
| | QA-2 | | Introduction of a time server access module in the data layer on the server application that encapsulates communication with the time servers. The details of this component and its interfaces have not been defined yet. |
| | QA-3 | | Identification of the elements derived from the deployment pattern that will need to be replicated. |
| QA-4 | | | No relevant decisions made, as it is necessary to identify the elements that participate in the use case that is associated with the scenario. |
| | CON-1 | | Structuring the system using 3 tiers will allow multiple clients to connect to the application server. Decisions regarding concurrent access have not been made yet. |
| | | CON-2 | Use of Java Web Start technology allows access through a web browser to download the Rich Client. Since the Rich Client is being programmed in Java, this supports execution under Windows, OSX, and Linux. |

| Not Addressed | Partially Addressed | Completely Addressed | Design Decisions Made During the Iteration |
|---|---|---|---|
| | | CON-3 | Physically structure the application using the 3-tier deployment pattern, and isolate the database by providing database access components in the data layer of the application server. |
| | CON-4 | | Use of Java Web Start technology requires the client to be downloaded only the first time, and then when upgrades occur. This is helpful to support limited-bandwidth connections. More decisions need to be made regarding the communication between the presentation and the business logic layers. |
| CON-5 | | | No relevant decisions made. |
| CON-6 | | | No relevant decisions made. |
| | | CRN-1 | Selection of reference architectures and deployment pattern. |
| | CRN-2 | | Technologies that have been considered up to this point take into account the knowledge of the developers. Other technologies still need to be selected (e.g., communication with the time servers). |
| CRN-3 | | | No relevant decisions made. |

### 4.3.3  Iteration 2: Identifying Structures to Support Primary Functionality

This section presents the results of the activities that are performed in each of the steps of ADD in the *second* iteration of the design process for the FCAPS system. In this iteration, we move from the generic and coarse-grained descriptions of functionality used in iteration 1 to more detailed decisions that will drive implementation and hence the formation of development teams.

This movement from the generic to the specific is intentional, and built into the ADD method. We cannot design everything up front, so we need to be disciplined about which decisions we make, and when, to ensure that the design is done in a systematic way, addressing the biggest risks first and moving from there to ever finer details. Our goal for the first iteration was to establish an overall system structure. Now that this goal has been met, our new goal for this second iteration is to reason about the units of implementation, which affect team formation, interfaces, and the means by which development tasks may be distributed, outsourced, and implemented in sprints.

### 4.3.3.1 Step 2: Establish Iteration Goal by Selecting Drivers

The goal of this iteration is to address the general architectural concern of *identifying structures to support primary functionality*. Identifying these elements is useful not only for understanding how functionality is supported, but also for addressing CRN-3—that is, the allocation of work to members of the development team.

In this second iteration, besides CRN-3, the architect considers the system's primary use cases:

- UC-1
- UC-2
- UC-7

### 4.3.3.2 Step 3: Choose One or More Elements of the System to Refine

The elements that will be refined in this iteration are the modules located in the different layers defined by the two reference architectures from the previous iteration. In general, the support of functionality in this system requires the collaboration of components associated with modules that are located in the different layers.

### 4.3.3.3 Step 4: Choose One or More Design Concepts That Satisfy the Selected Drivers

In this iteration, several design concepts—in this case, architectural design patterns—are selected from the book *Pattern Oriented Software Architecture, Volume 4*. The following table summarizes the design decisions. The words in **bold** in the following table refer to architectural patterns from this book, and can be found in Appendix A.

| Design Decisions and Location | Rationale and Assumptions |
|---|---|
| Create a **Domain Model** for the application | Before starting a functional decomposition, it is necessary to create an initial domain model for the system, identifying the major entities in the domain, along with their relationships. |
| | There are no good alternatives. A domain model must eventually be created, or it will emerge in a suboptimal fashion, leading to an ad hoc architecture that is hard to understand and maintain. |
| Identify **Domain Objects** that map to functional requirements | Each distinct functional element of the application needs to be encapsulated in a self-contained building block—a domain object. |
| | One possible alternative is to not consider domain objects and instead directly decompose layers into modules, but this increases the risk of not considering a requirement. |

| Design Decisions and Location | Rationale and Assumptions |
|---|---|
| Decompose **Domain Objects** into general and specialized **Components** | Domain objects represent complete sets of functionality, but this functionality is supported by finer-grained elements located within the layers. The "components" in this pattern are what we have referred to as modules. |
| | Specialization of modules is associated with the layers where they are located (e.g., UI modules). |
| | There are no good alternatives to decomposing the layers into modules to support functionality. |
| Use Spring framework and Hibernate | Spring is a widely used framework to support enterprise application development. Hibernate is an object to relational mapping (ORM) framework that integrates well with Spring. |
| | An alternative that was considered for application development is JEE. Spring was eventually selected because it was considered more "lightweight" and the development team was already familiar with it, resulting in greater and earlier productivity. |
| | Other ORM frameworks were not considered, as the development team already was familiar with, and happy with the performance of, Hibernate. |

**4.3.3.4**  Step 5: Instantiate Architectural Elements, Allocate Responsibilities, and Define Interfaces

The instantiation design decisions made in this iteration are summarized in the following table:

| Design Decisions and Location | Rationale |
|---|---|
| Create only an initial domain model | The entities that participate in the primary use cases need to be identified and modeled but only an initial domain model is created, to accelerate this phase of design. |
| Map the system use cases to domain objects | An initial identification of domain objects can be made by analyzing the system's use cases. To address CRN-3, domain objects are identified for all of the use cases in Section 4.2.1. |
| Decompose the domain objects across the layers to identify layer-specific modules with an explicit interface | This technique ensures that modules that support all of the functionalities are identified. |
| | The architect will perform this task just for the primary use cases. This allows another team member to identify the rest of the modules, thereby allocating work among team members. |
| | Having established the set of modules, the architect realizes the need to test these modules, so a new architectural concern is identified here: |
| | CRN-4: A majority of modules shall be unit tested. |
| | Only "a majority of modules" are covered by this concern because the modules that implement user interface functionality are difficult to test independently. |

*(continues)*

| Design Decisions and Location | Rationale |
| --- | --- |
| Connect components associated with modules using Spring | This framework uses an inversion of control approach that allows different aspects to be supported and the modules to be unit-tested (CRN-4). |
| Associate frameworks with a module in the data layer | ORM mapping is encapsulated in the modules that are contained in the data layer. The Hibernate framework previously selected is associated with these modules. |

While the structures and interfaces are identified in this step of the method, they are captured in the next step.

### 4.3.3.5   Step 6: Sketch Views and Record Design Decisions
As a result of the decisions made in step 5, several diagrams are created.

- Figure 4.5 shows an initial domain model for the system.
- Figure 4.6 shows the domain objects that are instantiated for the use case model in Section 4.2.1.
- Figure 4.7 shows a sketch of a module view with modules that are derived from the business objects and associated with the primary use cases. Note that explicit interfaces are not shown but their existence is assumed.

The responsibilities for the elements identified in Figure 4.7 are summarized in the table that begins on page 95.

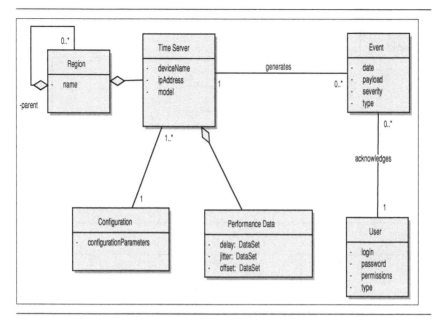

**FIGURE 4.5** Initial domain model (Key: UML)

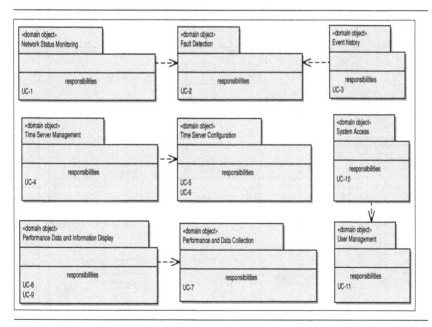

**FIGURE 4.6** Domain objects associated with the use case model (Key: UML)

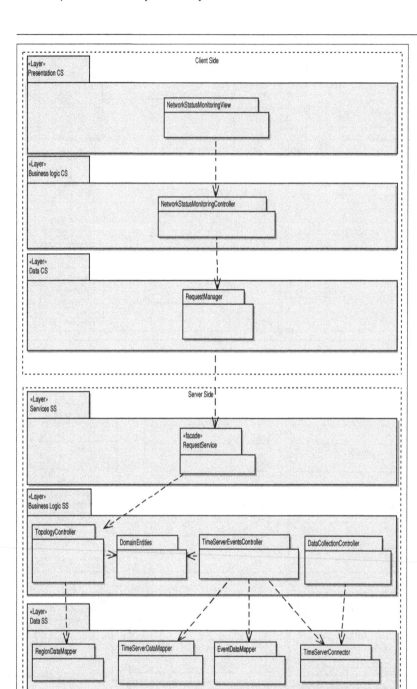

**FIGURE 4.7** Modules that support the primary use cases (Key: UML)

| Element | Responsibility |
|---------|----------------|
| NetworkStatusMonitoringView | Displays the network representation and updates it when events are received. This component embodies both UI components and UI process components from the reference architecture. |
| NetworkStatusMonitoringController | Responsible for providing the necessary information to the presentation layer for displaying the network representation. |
| RequestManager | Responsible for communication with the server-side logic. |
| RequestService | Provides a facade that receives requests from the clients. |
| TopologyController | Contains business logic related to the topological information. |
| DomainEntities | Contains the entities from the domain model (server side). |
| TimeServerEventsController | Contains business logic related to the management of events. |
| DataCollectionController | Contains logic to perform data collection and storage. |
| RegionDataMapper | Responsible for persistence operations (CRUD) related to the regions. |
| TimeServerDataMapper | Responsible for persistence operations (CRUD) related to the time servers. |
| EventDataMapper | Responsible for persistence operations (CRUD) related to the events. |
| TimeServerConnector | Responsible for communication with the time servers. It isolates and abstracts operations with the time servers to support communication with different types of time servers (see QA-2). |

The following sequence diagrams for UC-1 and UC-2 were created in the previous step of the method to define interfaces (as discussed in Section 3.6). A similar diagram was also created for UC-7 but is not shown here due to space limitations.

### UC-1: Monitor Network Status

Figure 4.8 shows an initial sequence diagram for UC-1 (monitor network status). It shows how the user representation of the topology is displayed on startup (after the user has successfully logged into the system). Upon launch, the topology is requested from the `TopologyController` on the server. This element retrieves the root region through the `RegionDataMapper` and returns it to the client. The client can then populate the view by traversing the relationships within the `Region` class.

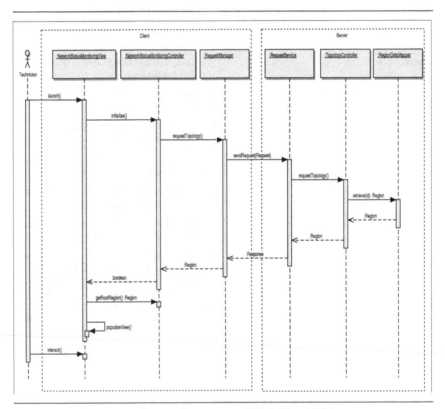

**FIGURE 4.8** Sequence diagram for use case UC-1 (Key: UML)

From the interactions identified in the sequence diagram, initial methods for the interfaces of the interacting elements can be identified:

| Method Name | Description |
|---|---|
| **Element:** `NetworkStatusMonitoringContoller` | |
| `boolean initialize()` | Opens up the network representation so that users can interact with it. |
| `Region getRootRegion()` | Returns a reference to the root region and the neighbors of this object (excluding traps). |
| **Element:** `RequestManager` | |
| `Region requestTopology()` | Requests the topology. This method returns a reference to the root region from which it is possible to navigate through the complete topology. |
| **Element:** `RequestService` | |
| `Response sendRequest(Request req)` | This method receives a request. Only this method is exposed in the service interface. This simplifies the addition of other functionality in the future without having to modify the existing service interface. |
| **Element:** `TopologyController` | |
| `Region requestTopology()` | Requests the topology. This method returns a reference to the root region from which it is possible to navigate through the complete topology. |
| **Element:** `RegionDataMapper` | |
| `Region retrieve(int id)` | Returns a `Region` from its `id`. |

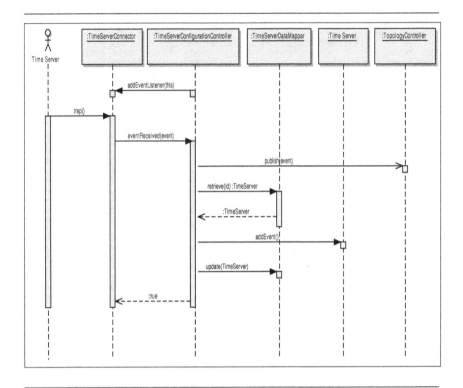

**FIGURE 4.9** Sequence diagram for use case UC-2 (Key: UML)

### UC-2: Detect Fault

Figure 4.9 shows an initial sequence diagram for UC-2 (detect fault) shows only the components on the server side. The interaction starts with a TimeServer sending a trap, which is received by the TimeServerConnector. The trap is transformed into an Event and sent to the TimeServerConfigurationController. The Event is sent asynchronously to the TopologyController for publication to the clients and is then persisted.

From this interaction, initial methods for the interfaces of the interacting elements can be identified:

| Method Name | Description |
|---|---|
| **Element:** `TimeServerConnector` | |
| `boolean addEventListener (EventListener el)` | This method allows components from the business logic to register themselves as listeners to events that are received from the time servers. |
| **Element:** `TimeServerConfigurationController` | |
| `boolean eventReceived(Event evt)` | This callback method is invoked when an event is received. |
| **Element:** `TopologyController` | |
| `publish(Event evt)` | This method notifies the clients that a new event has occurred. |
| **Element:** `TimeServerDataMapper` | |
| `TimeServer retrieve(int id)` | Retrieves a `TimeServer` identified by its `id`. |
| `boolean update(TimeServer ts)` | Persists changes in a `TimeServer`. |

**4.3.3.6**  Step 7: Perform Analysis of Current Design and Review Iteration
Goal and Achievement of Design Purpose
The decisions made in this iteration provided an initial understanding of how functionality is supported in the system. The modules associated with the primary use cases were identified by the architect, and the modules associated with the rest of the functionality were identified by another team member. From the complete list of modules, a work assignment table was created (not shown here) to address CRN-3.

Also, as part of module identification, a new architectural concern was identified and added to the Kanban board. Drivers that were completely addressed in the previous iteration are removed from the table.

| Not Addressed | Partially Addressed | Completely Addressed | Design Decisions Made During the Iteration |
|---|---|---|---|
| | | UC-1 | Modules across the layers and preliminary interfaces to support this use case have been identified. |
| | | UC-2 | Modules across the layers and preliminary interfaces to support this use case have been identified. |
| | | UC-7 | Modules across the layers and preliminary interfaces to support this use case have been identified. |
| | QA-1 | | The elements that support the associated use case (UC-2) have been identified. |
| | QA-2 | | The elements that support the associated use case (UC-5) have been identified. |
| | QA-3 | | No relevant decisions made. |
| | QA-4 | | The elements that support the associated use case (UC-7) have been identified. |
| | CON-1 | | No relevant decisions made. |
| | CON-4 | | No relevant decisions made. |
| | CON-5 | | Modules responsible for collecting data have been identified. |
| | CON-6 | | Modules responsible for collecting data storage been identified. |
| | CRN-2 | | Additional technologies were identified and selected considering the team's knowledge. |
| | | CRN-3 | Modules associated with all of the use cases have been identified and a work assignment matrix has been created (not shown). |
| | CRN-4 | | The architectural concern of unit-testing modules, which was introduced in this new iteration, is partially solved through the use of an inversion of control approach to connect the components associated with the modules. |

### 4.3.4   Iteration 3: Addressing Quality Attribute Scenario Driver (QA-3)

This section presents the results of the activities that are performed in each of the steps of ADD in the third iteration of the design process. Building on the fundamental structural decisions made in iterations 1 and 2, we can now start to reason about the fulfillment of some of the more important quality attributes. This iteration focuses on just one of these quality attribute scenarios.

#### 4.3.4.1   Step 2: Establish Iteration Goal by Selecting Drivers

For this iteration, the architect focuses on the QA-3 quality attribute scenario: A failure occurs in the management system during operation. The management system resumes operation in less than 30 seconds.

#### 4.3.4.2   Step 3: Choose One or More Elements of the System to Refine

For this availability scenario, the elements that will be refined are the physical nodes that were identified during the first iteration:

- Application server
- Database server

#### 4.3.4.3   Step 4: Choose One or More Design Concepts That Satisfy the Selected Drivers

The design concepts used in this iteration are the following:

| Design Decisions and Location | Rationale and Assumptions |
| --- | --- |
| Introduce the **active redundancy** tactic by replicating the application server and other critical components such as the database | By replicating the critical elements, the system can withstand the failure of one of the replicated elements without affecting functionality. |
| Introduce an element from the **message queue** technology family | Traps received from the time servers are placed in the message queue and then retrieved by the application. Use of a queue will guarantee that traps are processed and delivered in order (QA-1). |

#### 4.3.4.4   Step 5: Instantiate Architectural Elements, Allocate Responsibilities, and Define Interfaces

The instantiation design decisions are summarized in the following table:

| Design Decisions and Location | Rationale |
|---|---|
| Deploy message queue on a separate node | Deploying the message queue on a separate node will guarantee that no traps are lost in case of application failure. This node is replicated using the tactic of active redundancy, but only one copy receives and treats events coming from the network devices. |
| Use active redundancy and load balancing in the application server | Because two replicas of the application server are active at any time, it makes sense to distribute and balance the load among the replicas. This tactic can be achieved through the use of the Load-Balanced Cluster pattern (see Section A.2.3).<br><br>This introduces a new architectural concern, CRN-5: Manage state in replicas. |
| Implement load balancing and redundancy using technology support | Many technological options for load balancing and redundancy can be implemented without having to develop an ad hoc solution that would be less mature and harder to support. |

The results of these instantiation decisions are recorded in the next step.

### 4.3.4.5 Step 6: Sketch Views and Record Design Decisions
Figure 4.10 shows a refined deployment diagram that includes the introduction of redundancy in the system.

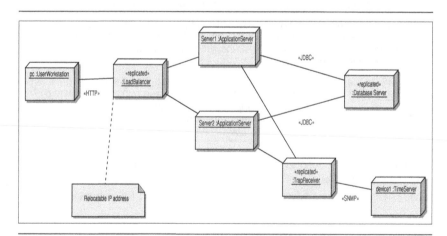

**FIGURE 4.10** Refined deployment diagram (Key: UML)

The following table describes responsibilities for elements that have not been listed previously (in iteration 1):

| Element | Responsibility |
| --- | --- |
| LoadBalancer | Dispatches (and balances the load of) requests coming from clients to the application servers. The load balancer also presents a unique IP address to the clients. |
| TrapReceiver | Receives traps from network devices, converts them into events, and puts these events into a persistent message queue. |

The UML sequence diagram shown in figure 4.11 illustrates how the TrapReceiver that was introduced in this iteration exchanges messages with other elements shown in the deployment diagram to support UC-2 (detect fault), which is associated with both QA-3 (availability) and QA-1 (performance).

As the purpose of this diagram is to illustrate the communication that occurs between the physical nodes, the names of the methods are only preliminary; they will be refined in further iterations.

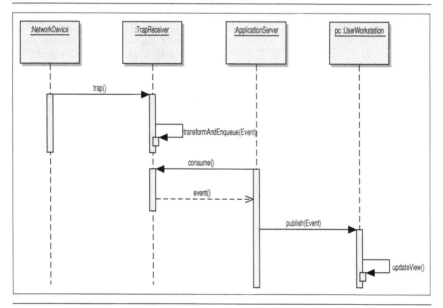

**FIGURE 4.11** Sequence diagram illustrating the messages exchanged between the physical nodes to support UC-2 (Key: UML)

**4.3.4.6** Step 7: Perform Analysis of Current Design and Review Iteration Goal and Achievement of Design Purpose

In this iteration, important design decisions have been made to address QA-3, which also impacted QA-1. The following table summarizes the status of the different drivers and the decisions that were made during the iteration. Drivers that were completely addressed in the previous iteration have been removed from the table.

| Not Addressed | Partially Addressed | Completely Addressed | Design Decisions Made During the Iteration |
|---|---|---|---|
| | QA-1 | | The introduction of a separate replicated trap receiver node can help ensure 100% of the traps are processed, even in the case of a failure of the application server. Furthermore, because trap reception is performed in a separate node, this approach reduces application server processing load, thereby helping performance. |
| | | | Because specific technologies have not been chosen, this driver is marked as "partially addressed". |
| | QA-2 | | No relevant decisions made. |
| | QA-3 | | By making the application server redundant, we reduce the probability of failure of the system. Furthermore, if the load balancer fails, a passive replica is activated within the required time period. |
| | | | Because specific technologies have not been chosen (message queue), this driver is marked as "partially addressed". |
| | QA-4 | | No relevant decisions made. |
| | CON-1 | | Replication of the application server and the use of a load balancer will help in supporting multiple user requests. |
| | CON-4 | | No relevant decisions made. |
| | CON-5 | | No relevant decisions made. |
| | CON-6 | | No relevant decisions made. |
| | CRN-2 | | No relevant decisions made. |
| | CRN-4 | | No relevant decisions made. |
| CRN-5 | | | This new architectural concern is introduced in this iteration: manage state in replicas. At this point, no relevant decisions have been made. |

## 4.4 Summary

In this chapter, we presented an example of using ADD to design a greenfield system in a mature domain. We illustrated three iterations with different foci: addressing a general concern, addressing functionality, and addressing one key quality attribute scenario.

The example followed the roadmap discussed in Section 3.3.1. It is interesting to observe that in the first iteration, two different reference architectures were used to structure the system. Also, the selection of externally developed components—in this case, frameworks—was carried out across the different iterations. Finally, the example illustrates how new architectural concerns appear as the design progresses.

This example demonstrates how architectural concerns, primary use cases, and quality attribute scenarios can be addressed as part of architectural design. In a real system, more iterations would be necessary to create a complete architecture design by addressing other scenarios with high priority.

In this example, we assumed that the architect is using a CASE tool during design, so diagrams were produced using UML. This is certainly not mandatory, as we will see in the case study presented in Chapter 5. Also, note that it is relatively simple to generate preliminary view sketches by using the information that is generated as part of the design process.

## 4.5 Further Reading

Appendix A provides descriptions and bibliographical references of all the design concepts used in this case study.

# 5

# Case Study: Big Data System

With Serge Haziyev and Olha Hrytsay

We now present an extended design example of using ADD 3.0 in a greenfield system for a challenging domain—that of Big Data. As of the time of writing, this domain was still relatively new and rapidly evolving. As such, the architects could not solely rely on past experience to guide them. They instead complemented the design process with periodic analyses and strategic prototyping, as we will now describe.

## 5.1 Business Case

This case study involves an Internet company that provides popular content and online services to millions of web users. Besides providing information externally, the company collects and analyzes massive logs of data that are generated from its infrastructure (e.g., application and server logs, system metrics). Such an approach of dealing with computer-generated log messages is also called *log management* (http://en.wikipedia.org/wiki/Log_management_and_intelligence).

Because of very fast infrastructure growth, the company's IT department realizes that the existing in-house systems can no longer process the required log data volume and velocity. Moreover, requests for a new system are coming from other company stakeholders, including product managers and data scientists, who would like to leverage the various kinds of data that can be collected from multiple data sources, not just logs.

The *marketecture* diagram (informal depiction of the system's structure) shown in Figure 5.1 represents the desired solution from a functional perspective for three major groups of users.

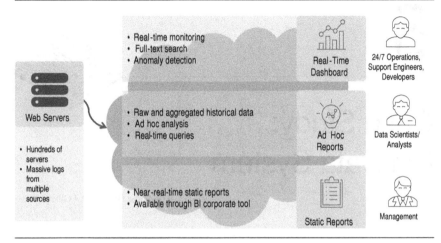

**FIGURE 5.1**   Marketecture diagram for the Big Data system

## 5.2   System Requirements

Requirement elicitation activities have been previously performed. The most important requirements collected are summarized here. They comprise a set of primary use cases, a set of quality attribute scenarios, a set of constraints, and a set of architectural concerns.

### 5.2.1   Use Case Model

The primary use cases for the system are described in the following table.

| Use Case | Description |
| --- | --- |
| UC-1: Monitor online services | On-duty operations staff can monitor the current state of services and IT infrastructure (such as web server load, user activities, and errors) through a real-time operational dashboard, which enables them to quickly react to issues. |
| UC-2: Troubleshoot online service issues | Operations, support engineers, and developers can do troubleshooting and root-cause analysis on the latest collected logs by searching log patterns and filtering log messages. |
| UC-3: Provide management reports | Corporate users, such as IT and product managers, can see historical information through predefined (static) reports in a corporate BI (business intelligence) tool, such as those showing system load over time, product usage, service level agreement (SLA) violations, and quality of releases. |

| Use Case | Description |
|---|---|
| UC-4: Support data analytics | Data scientists and analysts can do ad hoc data analysis through SQL-like queries to find specific data patterns and correlations to improve infrastructure capacity planning and customer satisfaction. |
| UC-5: Anomaly detection | The operations team should be notified 24/7 about any unusual behavior of the system. To support this notification plan, the system shall implement real-time anomaly detection and alerting (future requirement). |
| UC-6: Provide security reports | Security analysts should be provided with the ability to investigate potential security and compliance issues by exploring audit log entries that include destination and source addresses, a time stamp, and user login information (future requirement). |

## 5.2.2 Quality Attribute Scenarios

The most relevant quality attribute (raw) scenarios are presented in the following table. For each scenario, we also identify the use case that it is associated with.

| ID | Quality Attribute | Scenario | Associated Use Case |
|---|---|---|---|
| QA-1 | Performance | The system shall collect up to 15,000 events/ second from approximately 300 web servers. | UC-1, 2, 5 |
| QA-2 | Performance | The system shall automatically refresh the real-time monitoring dashboard for on-duty operations staff with < 1 min latency. | UC-1 |
| QA-3 | Performance | The system shall provide real-time search queries for emergency troubleshooting with < 10 seconds query execution time, for the last 2 weeks of data. | UC-2 |
| QA-4 | Performance | The system shall provide near-real-time static reports with per-minute aggregation for business users with < 15 min latency, < 5 seconds report load. | UC-3, 6 |
| QA-5 | Performance | The system shall provide ad hoc (i.e., non-predefined) SQL-like human-time queries for raw and aggregated historical data, with < 2 minutes query execution time. Results should be available for query in < 1 hour. | UC-4 |
| QA-6 | Scalability | The system shall store raw data for the last 2 weeks available for emergency troubleshooting (via full-text search through logs). | UC-2 |
| QA-7 | Scalability | The system shall store raw data for the last 60 days (approximately 1 TB of raw data per day, approximately 60 TB in total). | UC-4 |

(*continues*)

| ID | Quality Attribute | Scenario | Associated Use Case |
|---|---|---|---|
| QA-8 | Scalability | The system shall store per-minute aggregated data for 1 year (approximately 40 TB) and per-hour aggregated data for 10 years (approximately 50 TB). | UC-3, 4, 6 |
| QA-9 | Extensibility | The system shall support adding new data sources by just updating a configuration, with no interruption of ongoing data collection. | UC-1, 2, 5 |
| QA-10 | Availability | The system shall continue operating with no downtime if any single node or component fails. | All use cases |
| QA-11 | Deployability | The system deployment procedure shall be fully automated and support a number of environments: development, test, and production. | All use cases |

### 5.2.3 Constraints

The constraints associated with the system are presented in the following table.

| ID | Constraint |
|---|---|
| CON-1 | The system shall be composed primarily of open source technologies (for cost reasons). For those components where the value/cost of using proprietary technology is much higher, proprietary technology may be used. |
| CON-2 | The system shall use the corporate BI tool with a SQL interface for static reports (e.g., MicroStrategy, QlikView, Tableau). |
| CON-3 | The system shall support two specific deployment environments: private cloud (with VMware vSphere Hypervisor) and public cloud (Amazon Web Services). Architecture and technology decisions should be made to keep deployment vendor as agnostic as possible. |

### 5.2.4 Architectural Concerns

The initial architectural concerns that are considered are shown in the following table.

| ID | Concern |
|---|---|
| CRN-1 | Establishing an initial overall structure as this is a greenfield system. |
| CRN-2 | Leverage the team's knowledge of the Apache Big Data ecosystem. |

## 5.3 The Design Process

Now that we have enumerated the requirements, we are ready to begin the first iteration of ADD. This is a system from a relatively novel domain that is being created from scratch. Hence we follow the roadmap of design for greenfield systems in mature domains (as discussed in Section 3.3.1), albeit with some modifications to address the uncertainties inherent in the Big Data domain, such as the rapid emergence and evolution of technologies.

### 5.3.1 ADD Step 1: Review Inputs

The first step of the method involves reviewing the inputs. They are summarized in the following table.

| Category | Details |
|---|---|
| Design purpose | This is a greenfield system in a relatively novel domain. The organization will perform development following an Agile process with short iterations so that developers can quickly receive real-world feedback and continue modifying the system. At the same time, an architectural design is needed to make conscious decisions to satisfy architectural drivers and avoid unnecessary rework. |
| Primary functional requirements | From the use cases presented in Section 5.2.1, the following ones are designated as *primary*:<br>• UC-1<br>• UC-2<br>• UC-3<br>• UC-4 |
| Quality attribute scenarios | The following table illustrates the priority of the primary quality attribute scenarios, as ranked by the customer and architect (as discussed in Section 3.3.2). Note that quality attributes scenarios with lower priorities exist but are not shown here. |

| Scenario ID | Importance to Customer | Difficulty of Implementation According to Architect |
|---|---|---|
| QA-1 | High | High |
| QA-2 | High | Medium |
| QA-3 | Medium | Medium |
| QA-4 | High | High |
| QA-5 | Medium | High |
| QA-6 | Medium | Medium |
| QA-7 | Medium | Medium |
| QA-8 | High | Medium |
| QA-9 | High | Medium |
| QA-10 | High | Medium |
| QA-11 | Medium | High |

*(continues)*

| Category | Details |
|---|---|
| Constraints | See Section 5.2.3. |
| Architectural concerns | All of the architectural concerns presented in Section 5.2.4 are included as drivers. |

## 5.3.2   Iteration 1: Reference Architecture and Overall System Structure

This section presents the results of the activities that are performed in each of the steps of the ADD method in the first iteration of the design process.

### 5.3.2.1   Step 2: Establish Iteration Goal by Selecting Drivers

This is the first iteration in the design of a greenfield system, so the iteration goal is to establish an initial overall structure for the system (CRN-1). Even though this first iteration is driven by a general architectural concern, the architect must keep in mind all of the drivers and, in particular, constraints and quality attributes:

- CON-1: Leverage open source technologies whenever applicable
- CON-2: Use corporate BI tool with SQL interface for static reports
- CON-3: Two deployment environments: private and public clouds
- QA-1, 2, 3, 4, 5: Performance
- QA-6, 7, 8: Scalability
- QA-9: Extensibility
- QA-10: Availability
- QA-11: Deployability

### 5.3.2.2   Step 3: Choose One or More Elements of the System to Refine

Again, as this is greenfield development, and we are in the initial iteration, the element to refine is the entire system.

### 5.3.2.3   Step 4: Choose One or More Design Concepts That Satisfy the Selected Drivers

In this iteration, design concepts are selected from a group of data analytics reference architectures (a list of such reference architectures can be found in the design concepts catalog of the Smart Decisions Game; see the Further Reading section for more information).

| Design Decisions and Location | Rationale |
| --- | --- |
| Build the application as an instance of the Lambda (reference) architecture | The Lambda architecture, shown in Figure 5.2, is a reference architecture that splits the processing of a data stream into two streams: the "speed layer", which supports access to real-time data (UC-1, UC-2, UC-5), and a layer that groups the "batch" and "serving" layers, which supports access to historical data (UC-3, UC-4, UC-6). (The creators of the Lambda architecture refer to these as "layers", but this is different from prior—and more standard—usages of this term, which typically refer to a grouping of modules. Here the layers are groups of runtime components.) While the batch layer is based on immutable nonrelational techniques, the speed layer is based on streaming techniques to support strict real-time processing requirements. |
| | Immutability in this case means that the data is not updated or deleted when it is collected; that is, it can be only appended. As all data is collected, no data can be lost and a machine or human error can be tolerated. For example, if a software engineer made an occasional mistake in processing or viewing logic, once that problem is resolved, the collected data can be used to replay and recompute the views from scratch. |
| | For the reader's convenience we describe the basic concepts of the Lambda architecture by walking through five steps: |
| | 1. All data received from multiple data sources is dispatched through the data stream element to both the batch layer and the speed layer for processing. |
| | 2. The batch layer acts as a landing zone that corresponds to the master dataset element (as an immutable, append-only set of raw data), and also precomputes information that will be used by the batch views. |
| | 3. The serving layer contains precalculated and aggregated views optimized for querying with low latency, which is often required by reporting solutions. |
| | 4. The speed layer processes and provides access to recent data through real-time views that are not available in the serving layer due to the high latency of batch processing. |
| | 5. All data in the system is available for querying, whether it is historical or recent, representing the key Lambda architecture principle: *query = function (batch data + real-time data).* |
| | The parallel streams provide "complexity isolation", meaning that design decisions, development, and execution of each stream can be done independently, which has been shown to increase fault tolerance, scalability, and modifiability (see Table 5.1). |
| | Figure 5.3 depicts the architectural tradeoffs between these alternatives, and demonstrates the differences between the reference architectures in terms of four quality dimensions: scalability, support for ad hoc analysis, unstructured data processing capabilities, and real-time analysis capabilities: |
| | As Figure 5.3 shows, the Lambda architecture provides the best tradeoff between scalability and ad hoc analysis. |

*(continues)*

| Design Decisions and Location | Rationale |
|---|---|
| Use fault tolerance and no single point of failure principle for all elements in the system | Fault tolerance has become a standard for most Big Data technologies and the Lambda architecture already implies a number of design decisions to build a robust and fault-tolerant system, as noted above. |
| | However, we will need to make sure, in all subsequent design and deployment decisions, that all candidate technologies will support the QA-10 requirement by providing fault-tolerant configurations and adhering to the "no single point of failure" principle. |

**TABLE 5.1** Alternatives and Reasons for Discarding

| Alternative | Reason for Discarding |
|---|---|
| Traditional relational | This reference architecture is based on traditional relational model principles and SQL-based DBMSs, which are considered highly efficient for complex ad hoc read queries. |
| | This is, however, the least appropriate alternative because of scalability and real-time processing limitations. |
| Extended relational | Although this reference architecture is completely based on relational model principles and SQL-based DBMSs, it intensively uses massive parallel processing (MPP) and in-memory techniques to improve scalability and extensibility. |
| | It is less appropriate because of its high cost and real-time processing limitations. |
| Pure nonrelational | This reference architecture does not rely on relational model principles. It is often built on techniques such as NoSQL and MapReduce, and is effective for processing semistructured and unstructured data. |
| | This alternative is closer to the goal in terms of cost economy and scalability, but ad hoc analysis is limited. |
| Data refinery | A non-relational component performs an extract–transform–load (ETL) process to refine semistructured/unstructured data and load it, cleansed, into a data warehouse (a relational database) for further analysis. |
| | It is less appropriate for this solution mostly because of its high cost and significant deficiencies in terms of real-time processing capabilities. |

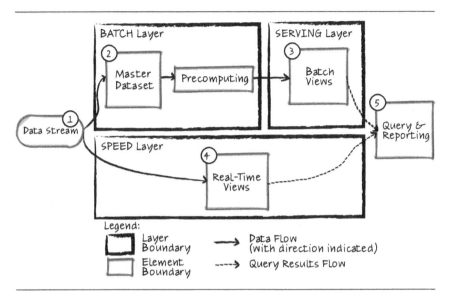

**FIGURE 5.2**  Lambda Architecture

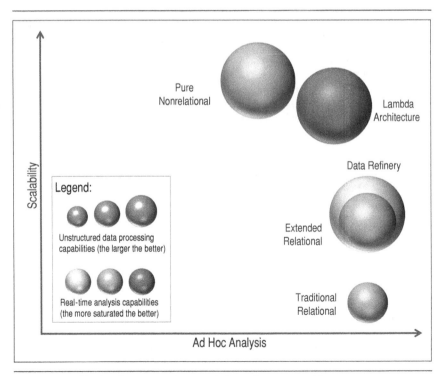

**FIGURE 5.3**  Tradeoffs among data analytics reference architectures

**5.3.2.4**   Step 5: Instantiate Architectural Elements, Allocate Responsibilities, and Define Interfaces

The instantiation design decisions considered and made are summarized in the following table.

| Design Decision and Location | Rationale |
|---|---|
| Split the Query and Reporting element into two subelements associated with the drivers | The Query and Reporting element in the Lambda architecture is divided into the following two sub-elements. They are associated with drivers as follows:<br><br>• Corporate BI tool (UC-3, UC-4, QA-4, QA-5, CON-2)<br>• Dashboard/visualization tool (UC-1, UC-2, QA-2, QA-3)<br><br>This division is driven by knowledge of the domain and the availability of tools. The guiding rationale is to have flexibility in selecting appropriate technologies—there could not be one single "universal" tool to satisfy all of these use cases, constraints, and quality attributes. Thus, we choose to separate concerns, which should give us more design options. Another difference from the "standard" Lambda architecture is that we may not need to merge the results of queries: According to our use cases, they can be executed independently for batch and real-time views. |
| Split the Precomputing and Batch Views elements into subelements associated with Ad Hoc and Static Views | These elements are decomposed into two subelements each:<br><br>• Ad Hoc Views Precomputing and Ad Hoc Batch Views (UC-4, QA-5)<br>• Static Views Precomputing and Static Batch Views (UC-3, QA-4, CON-2)<br><br>The reason for this subdivision is the same as with the previous case: It gives us more flexibility to select the optimal patterns and technologies. If we discover, in subsequent design iterations, that there is one approach to address these two concerns simultaneously, it will be simple to merge these elements. |
| Change semantics and name of the Master Dataset to Raw Data Storage | This is more than just a name change; it is also a change in semantics. According to QA-7, the system shall store raw data for least 60 days. Thus older data can be archived and stored using other storage technologies (or even deleted). The Master Dataset has more responsibilities: It includes raw data storage as well as archived data. To simplify this case, the study of archived data will not be addressed. |

In this initial iteration it is typically too early to precisely define functionality and interfaces.

**5.3.2.5**   Step 6: Sketch Views and Record Design Decisions

Figure 5.4 shows the result of the prior instantiation design decisions. The table that begins on the next page summarizes each element's responsibilities.

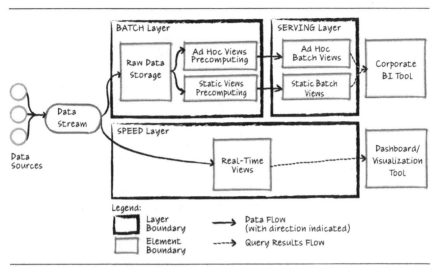

**FIGURE 5.4**  Instantiation of the Lambda architecture

| Element | Responsibility |
|---|---|
| Data Sources | Web servers that generate logs and system metrics (e.g., Apache access and error log, Linux sysstat). |
| Data Stream | This element collects data from all data sources in real-time and dispatches it to both the Batch Layer and the Speed Layer for processing. |
| Batch Layer | This layer is responsible for storing raw data and precomputing the batch views to be stored in the Serving Layer. |
| Serving Layer | This layer exposes the batch views in a data store (with no random writes, but batch updates and random reads), so that they can be queried with low latency. |
| Speed Layer | This layer processes and provides access to recent data, which is not available yet in the serving layer due to the high latency of batch processing, through a set of real-time views. |
| Raw Data Storage | This element is a part of the batch layer and is responsible for storing raw data (immutable, append only) for a specified period of time (QA-7). |
| Ad Hoc Views Precomputing | This element is a part of the Batch Layer and is responsible for precomputing the Ad Hoc Batch Views. The precomputing represents batch operations over raw data that transform it to a state suitable for fast human-time querying. |
| Static Views Precomputing | This element is a part of the Batch Layer and is responsible for precomputing the Static Batch Views. The precomputing represents batch operations over raw data that transform it to a state suitable for fast human-time querying. |

(*continues*)

| Element | Responsibility |
|---|---|
| Ad Hoc Batch Views | This element is a part of the Serving Layer and contains precalculated and aggregated data optimized for ad hoc low-latency queries (QA-5) executed by data scientists/analysts. |
| Static Batch Views | This element is a part of the Serving Layer and contains precalculated and aggregated data optimized for predefined low-latency queries (QA-4) generated by a corporate BI tool. |
| Real-Time Views | This element is a part of the Speed Layer and contains indexed logs optimized for ad hoc, low-latency search queries (QA-3) executed by operations and engineering staff. |
| Corporate BI Tool | This business intelligence tool is licensed to be used across different departments. The tool supports a SQL interface (such as ODBC or JDBC) and can be connected to multiple data sources, including this system (UC-3, UC-4, CON-2). |
| Dashboard/ Visualization Tool | The operations team uses this real-time operational dashboard to monitor online services, search for important messages in logs, and quickly react to potential issues (UC-1, UC-2). |

**5.3.2.6** Step 7: Perform Analysis of Current Design and Review Iteration Goal and Achievement of Design Purpose

The decisions made in this iteration address important early considerations affecting the overall system structure. You do not need to start from a "blank page", because the selected reference architecture already offers a proven initial decomposition and data flow that significantly saves design time and effort. Further design decisions will need to be made to selected candidate technologies and more details provided on how use cases and quality attributes will be supported.

The following table summarizes the design progress using the Kanban board technique discussed in Section 3.8.2.

| Not Addressed | Partially Addressed | Completely Addressed | Design Decisions Made During the Iteration |
|---|---|---|---|
| | UC-1 | | Use Lambda architecture to provide access to real-time data. No detailed decisions of which dashboard technology to use have been made. |
| | UC-2 | | Use Lambda architecture to provide access to real-time data. No detailed decisions of which search technology to use have been made. |
| | UC-3 | | Use Lambda architecture to provide access to historical data. No detailed decisions of which storage and query technologies to use have been made. |

| Not Addressed | Partially Addressed | Completely Addressed | Design Decisions Made During the Iteration |
|---|---|---|---|
| | UC-4 | | Use Lambda architecture to provide access to historical data. No detailed decisions of which storage and query technologies to use have been made. |
| | UC-5 | | This use case has been omitted in this iteration as nonprimary, although the Lambda architecture supports it and we will address it in subsequent iterations. |
| | UC-6 | | This use case has been omitted in this iteration as nonprimary, although from an architectural standpoint it is similar to UC-3. |
| | QA-1 | | Potential data sources for the Data Stream element have been identified. No detailed decisions of which technologies to use for the data stream element have been made. |
| | QA-3 | | The Real-Time Views element has been identified. No detailed decisions of which storage and query technology to use have been made. |
| | QA-4 | | The Static Batch Views element has been identified and its responsibilities have been established. No detailed decisions of which storage technology to use have been made. |
| | QA-5 | | The Ad Hoc Batch Views element has been identified and its responsibilities have been established. No detailed decisions of which storage and query technology to use have been made. |
| | QA-6 | | The Real-Time Views element's responsibilities have been established. No detailed decisions of which storage and query technology to use have been made. |
| | QA-7 | | The Raw Data Storage element has been identified and its responsibilities have been established. No detailed decisions of which storage technology to use have been made. |

*(continues)*

| Not Addressed | Partially Addressed | Completely Addressed | Design Decisions Made During the Iteration |
|---|---|---|---|
| | QA-8 | | The Ad Hoc and Static Batch Views elements have been identified and their responsibilities have been established. No detailed decisions of which storage technologies to use have been made. |
| | QA-10 | | It has been decided that all technologies chosen to implement the system elements support QA-10 by providing fault-tolerance configuration and no single point of failure. |
| | CON-2 | | The Corporate BI Tool element has been identified. No detailed decisions on how this constraint will be met have been made. |
| | CRN-1 | | An overall logical structure of the system has been established but the physical structure still needs to be defined. |
| CRN-2 | | | No relevant decisions made |

### 5.3.3   Iteration 2: Selection of Technologies

This section presents the results of the activities that are performed in each of the steps of ADD in the second iteration of the design process.

Technology choices often influence the system architecture, meaning that we need to select technologies at the earliest stages of architecture design. Choosing technologies starts with the identification and selection of technology families that are further instantiated into specific technologies. Starting with technology families allows us to make specific technologies interchangeable and thus keep the right level of technology agnosticism to avoid vendor lock-in (and as a result, there is less risk and less cost to change a technology to a better one in the future).

In this iteration we will show a technology tree that helps us choose optimal building blocks when designing Big Data greenfield systems.

### **5.3.3.1** Step 2: Establish Iteration Goal by Selecting Drivers

The goal of this iteration is to address CRN-2 (leverage the team's knowledge of the Apache Big Data ecosystem) by selecting technologies to support system requirements defined in Section 5.2, particularly keeping in mind CON-1 (favor open source technologies).

### **5.3.3.2** Step 3: Choose One or More Elements of the System to Refine

The reference architecture selected in the previous iteration (the Lambda architecture) was decomposed into elements that facilitate the selection of technology families and their associated specific technologies. These elements include the Data Stream, Raw Data Storage, Ad Hoc and Static Views Precomputing, Ad Hoc and Static Batch Views, Real-Time Views, and Dashboard/Visualization Tool.

### **5.3.3.3** Step 4: Choose One or More Design Concepts That Satisfy the Selected Drivers

The design concepts used in this iteration are externally developed components. Initially, technology families are selected and associated with the elements to be refined. A technology family represents a group of technologies with common functional purposes (see Section 2.5.5). The family names are indicative of their function, and some specific technologies may belong to several families at the same time, but having such a classification helps us make rational design decisions that eventually pay off in less rework and better readiness for changes. The history of the software industry shows that technology implementations are emerging, evolving, and disappearing much faster than the patterns and principles represented by their families.

Figure 5.5 illustrates family groups, technology families (in regular text), and their associated specific technologies (in italic text) for the Big Data domain. Further details about a number of these technologies can be found in the design concepts catalog of the Smart Decisions Game (see the Further Reading section).

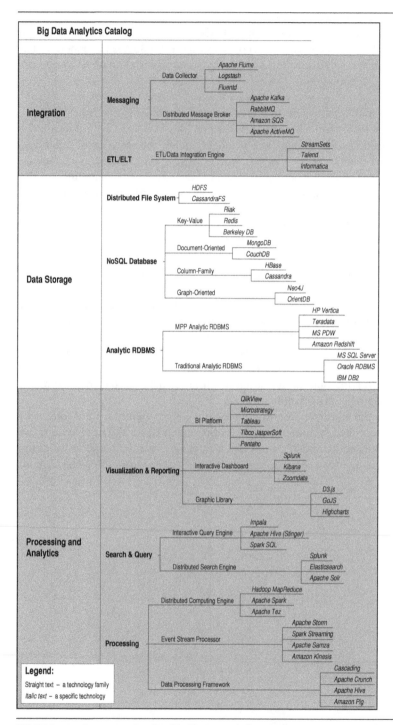

**FIGURE 5.5**   An example of a Big Data analytics design concepts catalog (Source: Softserve)

The BI Platform family group and related technologies are not considered further in this design exercise because the corporate BI tool is external to the target system.

| Design Decisions and Location | Rationale and Assumptions |
|---|---|
| Select the Data Collector family for the Data Stream element | Data Collector is a technology family (and an architectural pattern) that collects, aggregates, and transfers log data for later use. Usually Data Collector implementations offer out-of-the-box plug-ins for integrating with popular event sources and destinations.<br><br>The destinations are the Raw Data Storage and Real-Time Views elements, which will also be addressed in this iteration. |

| Alternative | Reason for Discarding |
|---|---|
| ETL Engine | The main purpose of ETL engines is to perform batch transformations, rather than per-event operations. This means that real-time performance and scalability criteria (QA-1, QA-2) will be extremely difficult to meet (if it is possible to meet them at all). |
| Distributed Message Broker | Although this technology family can be solely used to implement the Data Stream element, it provides less support for extensibility (QA-9) and, therefore, is better suited as a complement to the data collector. This can be achieved, for example, using Flavka—a combination of Apache Flume (Data Collector) and Apache Kafka (Distributed Message Broker). |

| Design Decisions and Location | Rationale and Assumptions |
|---|---|
| Select the Distributed File System family for the Raw Data Storage element | According to the Lambda architecture principles, the Raw Data Storage element must be immutable. Thus new data should not modify existing data, but just be appended to the dataset. Data will be read in batch operations for transforming raw data to Batch Views. For these purposes, we can confidently choose a Distributed File System. |

| Alternative | Reason for Discarding |
|---|---|
| NoSQL Database | Although NoSQL databases (especially column-family and document-oriented) can be used for storing raw data, such as logs, this will cause unnecessary overhead in resource consumption (mostly memory consumption because of caching mechanisms) and maintainability (because of the need of configuring and evolving a schema). |
| Analytic RDBMS | All relational databases including analytic capabilities are based on the relational model, forming tables and rows. This works very well for executing complex queries, but this option is awkward (and expensive) for storing semistructured logs in their raw format. |

*(continues)*

| Design Decisions and Location | Rationale and Assumptions |
|---|---|
| Select Interactive Query Engine family for both the Static and Ad Hoc Batch Views elements | As we stated in the previous iteration, the Batch Views element is refined into two elements, the Static and Ad Hoc Batch Views, to support two use cases: the generation of static reports (UC-3, 6) and the support for ad hoc querying (UC-4). |
| | The main design decision is to use the same technology family for both Static and Ad Hoc Batch Views—namely, the Interactive Query Engine. These engines allow analytic database capabilities over data stored in a Distributed File System (thus this technology family is also selected implicitly). If we select a technology that is fast enough, it can be used for both elements. |
| | The benefit of using a single technology family is that we do not need to have separate storage technologies for reporting and querying data. |

| Alternative | Reason for Discarding |
|---|---|
| NoSQL Database | The Static Batch Views element can be implemented with the Materialized View pattern, by storing data in a form that is ready for querying and displaying in a reporting system (a corporate BI tool). The NoSQL Database family is often used for this purpose because it provides good scalability and, being open source, satisfies QA-8 (approximately 90 TB of aggregated data) and CON-1 (open source license). |
| | However, NoSQL databases are not good options to use as data warehouses for ad hoc queries because they were not designed for analytic purposes. Although they can be used for this purpose, this application will result in significant performance penalties. |
| | This alternative is therefore discarded as it can be used only for the Static Batch Views, but is ineffective for Ad Hoc Batch Views |
| Analytic RDBMS | Ad hoc queries can be any queries that are supported by a SQL-like interface. The query result must be returned within "human" time (QA-5). The described scenario is exactly what a data warehouse is used for. This pattern is usually implemented with Analytic RDBMS technologies following the Kimball or Inmon design approaches. At the same time, it will be quite costly to satisfy the scalability requirement of having approximately 90 TB of aggregated data. The cost per terabyte in MPP analytic databases is significantly higher (up to 30 times) than the same amount of data in a NoSQL database or a distributed file system (such as Hadoop). |

| Design Decisions and Location | Rationale and Assumptions | |
|---|---|---|
| | **Alternative** | **Reason for Discarding** |
| | Analytic RDBMS | This alternative is rejected because even if it can be used for both Static and Ad Hoc Batch Views, the technologies associated with this family are costly compared to (open source) Hadoop-based alternatives. |
| Use Data Processing Framework for the Views Precomputing elements | As we have already selected the Distributed File System family for Raw Data Storage and Batch Views, the next step is to choose a solution for data transformation from the Raw Data Storage to the format used in the Batch Views. The decision is to select Data Processing Framework as this technology family allows data processing pipelines to be created using abstractions that support faster development and better maintainability. | |
| | **Alternative** | **Reason for Discarding** |
| | Distributed Computing Engine | Most Distributed Computing Engine technologies are designed for batch data processing, but require substantial knowledge of low-level primitives (e.g., for writing MapReduce tasks). |
| | Event Stream Processor | This is designed for real-time streaming processing; it is ineffective for batch operations. |
| Select Distributed Search Engine for the Real-Time Views element | The Real-Time Views element is responsible for full-text search over recent logs and for feeding an operational dashboard with real-time monitoring data (UC-1, UC-2). Distributed Search Engine is a technology family that serves just such purposes. | |
| | **Alternative** | **Reason for Discarding** |
| | NoSQL Database | Some NoSQL databases provide keyword search or text search, but these are not as powerful and fast as search engines that also provide text-processing features such as stemming and geolocation. |
| | Analytic RDBMS | Some databases provide full-text search capabilities (e.g., MS SQL Server); however, they are less desirable from extensibility, maintenance, and cost standpoints. |
| | Distributed File System and Interactive Query Engine | This approach works well for batch historical data; however, the latency of storing and processing will be too high for real-time data. |

*(continues)*

| Design Decisions and Location | Rationale and Assumptions |
|---|---|
| Automate deployment of the system with Puppet scripts | Puppet scripts can be used for both Private Cloud (e.g., VMware) and Public Cloud (e.g., AWS) deployments. This supports the satisfaction of CON-3. Puppet allows automating the deployment process as well as managing the configuration of a system. There is a library of predefined scripts written by the Puppet community to automate the deployment of many popular open source technologies. |

**5.3.3.4** Step 5: Instantiate Architectural Elements, Allocate Responsibilities, and Define Interfaces

In this iteration, instantiation is performed by associating specific technologies with the technology families that were previously selected. The instantiation design decisions considered and made are summarized in the following table:

| Design Decision and Location | Rationale | |
|---|---|---|
| Use Apache Flume from the Data Collector family for the Data Stream element | As a primary candidate technology, we will select Apache Flume. It provides the required configurability to support QA-9 (adding new data sources by just updating a configuration at run-time). | |
| | **Alternative** | **Reason for Discarding** |
| | Logstash or Fluentd | Although Logstash and Fluentd are quite popular technologies (perhaps as popular as Flume) and will satisfy the requirements, we have to make a choice and select only one. An extra argument for choosing Flume is its support by three major Hadoop distribution vendors. |
| Use HDFS from the Distributed File System family for the Raw Data Storage element | For this technology, we can confidently choose HDFS, which was designed to support exactly this type of usage scenario for large data sets (QA-7, storing approximately 60 TB of raw data). There are also a number of Hadoop file formats in which to store data in HDFS, such as text file, SequenceFile, RCFile, ORCFile, Avro, and Parquet. The selection of a file format will be addressed in the third iteration. | |
| | **Alternative** | **Reason for Discarding** |
| | CassandraFS | This technology is dependent on a NoSQL Database (Cassandra), whereas we have chosen Distributed File System alone. |

| Design Decision and Location | Rationale | |
|---|---|---|
| Use Impala from the Interactive Query Engine family for both the Static and Ad Hoc Batch Views elements | We select Impala as a primary candidate technology, as it offers competitive performance (although it is still not as fast as the top Analytic RDBMS platforms) and an ODBC interface for connectivity with a corporate BI tool.<br><br>Keeping possible performance issues in mind, we plan a proof-of-concept in the next iterations to make sure this technology selection satisfies QA-4 (less than 5 seconds report load) and QA-5 (less than 2 minutes ad hoc query execution time). | |
| | **Alternative** | **Reason for Discarding** |
| | Apache Hive (Stinger) | Although Hive improved performance thanks to the Stinger initiative, the speed of queries is still slow compared to other alternatives such as Impala and Spark SQL. |
| | Spark SQL | Spark is a very promising technology for Big Data analytics, but the use case of serving as a SQL adapter for a BI tool might not be optimal for Spark SQL. The downside is the high memory requirements and long query time of noncached data. In contrast, Impala has been designed and optimized for this exact scenario. |
| Use Elasticsearch from the Distributed Search Engine family for the Real-Time Views elements. Use Kibana from the Interactive Dashboard family for the Dashboard/Visualization Tool element. | As a primary candidate technology, we select Elasticsearch, since it also provides a visualization tool: an interactive dashboard called Kibana.<br><br>Although Kibana is a relatively simple dashboard without role-based security (at least, at the moment of designing this solution), it satisfies use cases UC-1, 2 and QA-2 (auto-refresh dashboard with a less than 1 minute period).<br><br>Elasticsearch also provides a domain-specific language (Query DSL) that is supported by Kibana to query, filter, and visualize time series. | |
| | **Alternative** | **Reason for Discarding** |
| | Splunk | Splunk also provides indexing and visualization capabilities (offering more features than Elasticsearch and Kibana); however, CON-1 drives us to prefer an open source solution. |
| Use Hive from the Data Processing Framework for the Views Precomputing elements | We select Hive as a primary technology candidate, although we will need to make sure that QA-4 (less than 15 minutes latency) is satisfied by creating a proof-of-concept prototype in a subsequent iteration.<br><br>Hive provides a SQL-like language, just like Impala (which has been already selected in this iteration); thus it allows us to leverage the skills of data warehouse designers when writing data transformation scripts. | |
| | **Alternative** | **Reason for Discarding** |
| | Cascading or Apache Pig | We disqualified Cascading and Pig so that we can minimize development time by leveraging the SQL skills of an existing development team. |

The data exchanged between the elements will be defined more precisely in subsequent iterations. The format of this data constitutes the "interfaces" between the elements.

### 5.3.3.5   Step 6: Sketch Views and Record Design Decisions

Figure 5.6 illustrates the result of the instantiation decisions. The responsibilities of the elements shown in the diagram were discussed in step 6 of Iteration 1. The following table summarizes the technology families and candidate specific technologies selected for these elements:

| Element | Technology Family | Candidate Technology |
| --- | --- | --- |
| Data Stream | Data Collector | Apache Flume |
| Raw Data Storage | Distributed File System | HDFS |
| Ad Hoc Views Precomputing | Data Processing Framework | Apache Hive |
| Static Views Precomputing | Data Processing Framework | Apache Hive |
| Ad Hoc Batch Views | Interactive Query Engine | Impala |
| Static Batch Views | Interactive Query Engine | Impala |
| Real-Time Views | Distributed Search Engine | Elasticsearch |
| Dashboard/ Visualization Tool | Interactive Dashboard | Kibana |

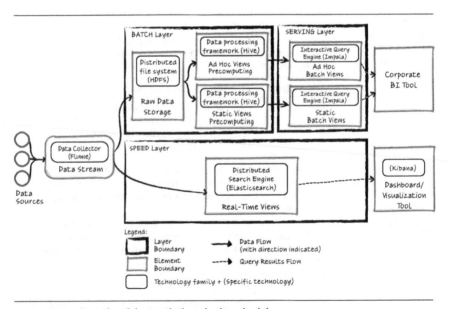

**FIGURE 5.6**   Iteration 2 instantiation design decisions

The next table explains the relationships between elements based on the selected technologies:

| Source Element | Destination Element | Relationship Description |
|---|---|---|
| Data Sources (logs) | Data Stream (Flume) | To be defined in the next iteration |
| Data Stream (Flume) | Raw Data Storage (HDFS) | Network communication (push) through Flume HDFS sink |
| Raw Data Storage (HDFS) | Views Precomputing (Apache Hive) | Local and network communication encapsulated through Hive |
| Views Precomputing (Apache Hive) | Batch Views (Impala) | Local and network communication encapsulated through Hive |
| Batch Views (Impala) | Corporate BI Tool | Network communication (pull) through ODBC API |
| Data Stream (Flume) | Real-Time Views (Elasticsearch) | Network communication (push) through Flume Elasticsearch sink |
| Real-Time Views (Elasticsearch) | Dashboard/ Visualization Tool (Kibana) | Network communication (pull) through Elasticsearch API |

**5.3.3.6** Step 7: Perform Analysis of Current Design and Review Iteration Goal and Achievement If Design Purpose

The following Kanban table summarizes the design progress and the decisions made during the iteration. Note that drivers that were completely addressed in the previous iteration are not shown.

| Not Addressed | Partially Addressed | Completely Addressed | Design Decisions Made During the Iteration |
|---|---|---|---|
| | UC-1 | | Use Distributed Search Engine (Elasticsearch) and Interactive Dashboard (Kibana) to display real-time monitoring information. |
| | | | Pending: Model indexes and create UI mockup. |
| | UC-2 | | Use Distributed Search Engine (Elasticsearch) and Interactive Dashboard (Kibana) for full-text search over recent log data. |
| | | | Pending: Model indexes and create a proof-of-concept. |
| | UC-3 UC-4 | | Use Interactive Query Engine (Impala) for the Batch Views elements. |
| | | | Pending: Model data and typical reports. |

*(continues)*

| Not Addressed | Partially Addressed | Completely Addressed | Design Decisions Made During the Iteration |
|---|---|---|---|
| | UC-6 | | This use case has been omitted in this iteration as nonprimary, although it is similar to UC-3 from an architectural standpoint. |
| | QA-1 | | Use Data Collector (Apache Flume) for the Data Stream element. Pending: Configuration, proof-of-concept, and performance tests. |
| | QA-2 QA-3 | | Use Distributed Search Engine (Elasticsearch) and Interactive Dashboard (Kibana). Pending: Proof-of-concept and performance tests. |
| | QA-4 | | Use Interactive Query Engine (Impala) for the Static Batch Views element. Pending: Model data, proof-of-concept, and performance tests. |
| | QA-5 | | Use Interactive Query Engine (Impala) for the Ad Hoc Batch Views element. Pending: Model data, proof-of-concept, and performance tests. |
| | QA-6 | | Use Distributed Search Engine (Elasticsearch) for the Real-Time Views element. Pending: Do capacity planning. |
| | QA-7 | | Use Distributed File System (HDFS) for the Raw Data Storage element. Pending: Select file format and do capacity planning. |
| | QA-8 | | Use Distributed File System (HDFS) as storage for Batch Views. Pending: Select file format and do capacity planning. |
| | QA-9 | | Use Data Collector (Apache Flume) for the Data Stream element. Pending: Configuration and proof-of-concept. |
| | QA-10 | | Use fault tolerance in all system elements. Pending: Stress test. |
| | | QA-11 | Use Puppet scripts to automate the deployment process for different environments. |

| Not Addressed | Partially Addressed | Completely Addressed | Design Decisions Made During the Iteration |
|---|---|---|---|
| | | CON-1 | All the selected technologies are open source. |
| | | CON-2 | Use Interactive Query Engine (Impala) with ODBC interface. |
| | | CON-3 | All selected technologies can be deployed to both private cloud (VMware) and public cloud (AWS) environments using Puppet scripts. |
| | CRN-1 | | No relevant decisions made. |
| | | CRN-2 | Technologies from the Apache Big Data ecosystem were selected and associated with the different elements in the reference architecture. |

### 5.3.4   Iteration 3: Refinement of the Data Stream Element

This section presents the results of the activities that are performed in each of the steps of ADD for the third iteration of the design process.

Some design decisions made in this iteration require the creation of a proof-of-concept prototype, as they cannot be addressed in a purely conceptual manner. Given that the Big Data field is young and technologies are rapidly evolving, proofs-of-concepts of key elements are necessary to mitigate technology risks (e.g., incompatibility, slow performance, unsatisfactory reliability, limitations of claimed features) and to have the option to switch to an alternative early in the design and development process, thereby saving overall time and budget by avoiding later rework.

#### 5.3.4.1   Step 2: Establish the Iteration Goal by Selecting Drivers
The goal of this iteration is to address several concerns associated with the selection of Apache Flume, as the technology to be used for the Data Collector element. Apache Flume provides a reference structure—a data-flow model—depicted in the informal diagram shown in Figure 5.7.

The elements in Flume's structure include:

- The source: consumes events delivered to it by external data sources such as web servers
- The channel: stores events received by the source
- The sink: removes events from the channel and puts them in an external repository (i.e., destination)

The selection of Apache Flume raises several specific architectural concerns that need to be addressed:

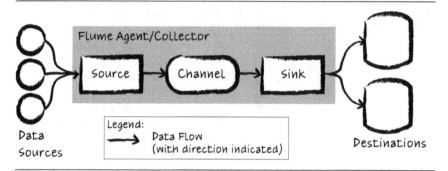

**FIGURE 5.7** Apache Flume data-flow reference structure

- Selecting a mechanism for getting data from the external sources
- Selecting specific input formats in the Source element
- Selecting a file data format in which to store the events
- Selecting a mechanism for the channeling events in the channel
- Establishing a deployment topology for the Data Source elements

Addressing these specific architectural concerns will contribute to the satisfaction of the following quality attributes:

- QA-1 (Performance)
- QA-7 (Scalability)
- QA-9 (Extensibility)
- QA-10 (Availability)

**5.3.4.2   Step 3: Choose One or More Elements of the System to Refine**
In this iteration, the focus is on the elements in Flume's structure.

**5.3.4.3   Step 4: Choose One or More Design Concepts That Satisfy the Selected Drivers**
In this iteration most of the decisions are about instantiation, since they primarily involve configuring the elements that are already established by Flume. The only selection design decision involves choosing tactics to satisfy the availability and performance quality attributes.

| Design Decisions and Location | Rationale and Assumptions |
|---|---|
| Use Flume in agent/ collector configuration. Agents are co-located on the web servers, and the collector runs in the Data Stream element. | A Flume instance can run in two modes: as an agent (directly co-located in the data sources) or as a collector (which combines data streams from multiple agents and writes to destinations).<br><br>From these two modes, Flume can be used in different configurations. The decision is to use Flume in both agent and collector configuration: The agents are co-located with the data sources and the Collector runs in the Data Stream element. |

| Alternative | Reason for Discarding |
|---|---|
| Flume agents are on each web server and write events directly to sinks (no collectors) | Generates heavy traffic from 300-plus simultaneous connections to sinks (HDFS and Elasticsearch). Produces multiple (per web server) files in HDFS, which is suboptimal for this distributed file system (rather than having larger files that aggregate data from multiple web servers). |
| Flume collectors receive events directly from web servers (no agents) and write to sinks | Does not support failover mode. If a collector node fails, the connected web servers will lose a receiver. |

| Design Decisions and Location | Rationale and Assumptions |
|---|---|
| Introduce the tactic of "maintaining multiples copies of computations" by using a load-balanced, failover tiered configuration | Out of the possible topology alternatives, the selected one is a load-balanced and failover tiered topology based on performance (QA-1, 15,000 events/second) and availability (QA-10, no single point of failure) quality attribute scenarios. |

| Alternative | Reason for Discarding |
|---|---|
| Not replicating the collector | This would decrease performance and availability. |

**5.3.4.4** Step 5: Instantiate Architectural Elements, Allocate Responsibilities, and Define Interfaces

The instantiation design decisions made in this iteration are summarized in the following table:

| Design Decisions and Location | Rationale and Assumptions |
|---|---|
| Use access and error logs from the Apache HTTP Server as input formats | The system requirements include the collection and analysis of logs such as web server load, user activities, and errors. In reality, there could be tens (and sometimes hundreds) of data source types. |
| | For the development of the proof-of-concept, a single type of data source system is considered: an Apache HTTP server ("web server"). The data to be collected includes user activities that will be tracked through an access log and system errors through an error log. |
| | The web server access log records all requests processed by the server. A log entry might look like this: |
| | `143.21.52.246 - - [19/Jun/2014:12:15:17 +0000] "GET /test.html HTTP/1.1" 200 341 "-" "Mozilla/5.0 (X11; Linux x86_64; rv:6.0a1) Gecko/20110421 Firefox/6.0a1".` |
| | This example consists of the following data fields: client IP address, client identity, user ID, time stamp, request method, request URL, request protocol, response code, response size, referrer, user agent. |
| | The web server error log sends diagnostic information and records any errors that it encounters when processing user requests. For example: |
| | `[19/Jun/2014:14:23:15 +0000] [error] [client 50.83.180.156] Directory index forbidden by rule: /home/httpd/` |
| | This example consists of the following data fields: time stamp, severity level, client IP address, message. |
| | Further data modeling and technology configuration will be based on these two types of logs and the described fields. |

| | |
|---|---|
| Log files are piped through an IP port in the source element of Flume agent | Apache Flume is configured to pipe log data through an IP port, such as by using syslog. |

| Alternative | Reason for Discarding |
|---|---|
| Read from a log file (e.g., running the UNIX command `tail -F access_log`) | This option looks the simplest but does not guarantee event delivery (events can be lost), which is stated in the Flume user guide. |

| Design Decisions and Location | Rationale and Assumptions |
|---|---|
| Identify event channeling methods for both the agents and the collector; make final decision through prototyping | The ingested events from the Source element are staged in the Channel element. At the moment Flume offers three possible options to configure the channel:<br><br>1. Memory channel: in-memory queue; faster, but if any events are left in the memory queue when a Flume process dies, they cannot be recovered.<br>2. File channel: durable and backed up by the local file system.<br>3. Apache Kafka: an approach in which Kafka serves as a distributed and highly available channel.<br><br>The selection from these options actually is a "classic" tradeoff of performance versus availability (or what is sometimes termed durability). Although we do not have an explicit durability scenario, we understand that with the future system extension (UC-6, security reports), this requirement becomes more critical. This is an example of an architectural concern, in the sense that it does not appear in any requirements document, but the architect has to deal with it nonetheless.<br><br>Given these options and no publicly available information about the performance consequences, this is a good candidate for prototyping and making a decision based on the results. Another rationale for prototyping and performance measurement is the need to calculate the required hardware resources. As a consequence, a new concern is identified and added to the backlog:<br><br>▪ CRN-3: Data modeling and developing proof-of-concept prototypes for key system elements |
| Select Avro as a specific file format for storing raw data in the HDFS sink | One decision that needs to be made when designing a solution based on Hadoop is the selection of an optimal file format. Hadoop supports a variety of formats that provide different functionalities, compression, and performance results depending on stored data and usage scenarios.<br><br>In this case the main scenarios are related to quality attributes such as performance (QA-1, 15,000 events/second), scalability (QA-7, approximately 60 TB of raw data), and extensibility (QA-9, adding new data sources). When we translate these requirements to file format traits, they will be impacted by performance (how fast data can be pushed by the Data Stream), a compression factor (less space to store), and ease of schema evolution (when adding new log formats or changing existing ones).<br><br>We select Avro, as it supports rich data structures, provides good compression levels (with the Snappy compression codec), and is flexible enough to accommodate schema changes (employing a self-describing format where data is stored with its schema). |

*(continues)*

| Design Decisions and Location | Rationale and Assumptions | |
|---|---|---|
| | **Alternative** | **Reason for Discarding** |
| | Text file (plain text, CSV, XML, JSON) | The compression ratio is poor compared with binary file formats (e.g., Avro). Also, text files do not support block compression, which is necessary when storing files larger than the size of an HDFS block. |
| | SequenceFile | Does not support flexible schema evolution. Consists of binary key/value pairs and does not store metadata with the data. |
| | RCFile | This Hadoop columnar file format does not support schema evolution, and writing requires more CPU and memory compared with non-columnar formats. |
| | ORCFile | Optimized RCFile provides better compression and faster querying, but has the same drawbacks as RCFile in terms of schema evolution, at the expense of writing performance. |
| | Parquet | Parquet is a columnar file format that partially supports schema evolution, but still is slower for write operations compared with non-columnar file formats. |

**5.3.4.5** Step 6: Sketch Views and Record Design Decisions

Figure 5.8 illustrates the result of the instantiation decisions.

| Element | Responsibility |
|---|---|
| Flume agent | Consume log events generated by a web server, split text log entries to separate fields, and deliver the parsed event records to a collector. |
| Flume collector | Collect event records from multiple agents in a load-balanced and fault-tolerant manner and deliver them to destinations (HDFS and Elasticsearch) for further persistency and processing. |

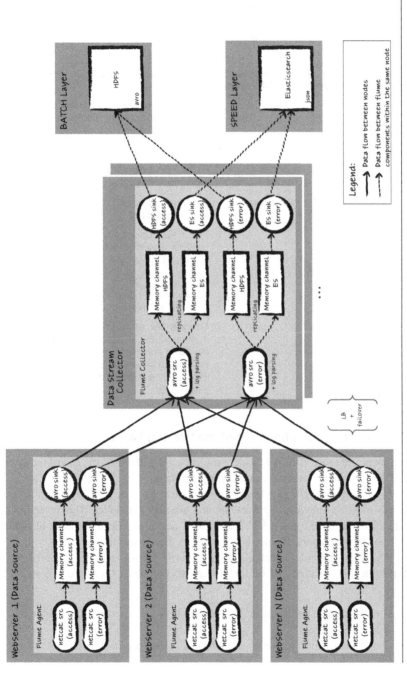

**FIGURE 5.8**  Iteration 3 instantiation design decisions

**5.3.4.6** Step 7: Perform Analysis of Current Design and Review Iteration Goal and Achievement of Design Purpose

The following Kanban table summarizes the design progress and the decisions made during the iteration. Note that drivers that were completely addressed in the previous iteration are not shown.

| Not Addressed | Partially Addressed | Completely Addressed | Design Decisions Made During the Iteration |
|---|---|---|---|
| | UC-1<br>UC-2<br>UC-3<br>UC-4 | | Refinement of the Data Stream element. Decisions about other elements that participate in these use cases still need to be made. |
| | | QA-1 | Flume load-balanced, failover tiered configuration is selected. |
| | | QA-9 | Usage of Flume and Avro format for storing raw data. |
| | QA-10 | | Flume load-balanced, failover tiered configuration is selected.<br><br>Decisions on other elements that participate in this scenario still need to be made. |
| | CRN-1 | | Tiers were identified for the Flume collector and storage. |
| CRN-3 | | | This is a new architectural concern that was introduced in this iteration: data modeling and developing proof-of-concept prototypes for key system elements. At this point, no relevant decisions have been made. |

### 5.3.5 Iteration 4: Refinement of the Serving Layer

We now present the results of the activities that are performed in each of the steps of ADD in the fourth iteration of the design process.

We selected the Serving Layer for refinement (not the Batch Layer) because the risk of not achieving requirements is higher for this layer. This layer is directly involved in use cases UC-3 and UC-4 and a number of quality attribute scenarios in which performance and scalability are critical factors.

As in the previous iteration, design activities involve the creation of prototypes. In this iteration, UI prototypes are also created. There are at least two reasons for this:

- It will facilitate receiving early feedback from users, which can help to update requirements.
- Data visualization scenarios often have an influence on data modeling.

**5.3.5.1**  Step 2: Establish the Iteration Goal by Selecting Drivers
The goal of this iteration is to address the newly identified concern of data modeling and developing proof-of-concept prototypes for key system elements (CRN-3) so as to satisfy the primary use cases and system requirements associated with the analysis and visualization of historic data. These use cases include:

- UC-3
- UC-4

    The quality attribute scenarios associated with these use cases are:

- QA-4 (Performance)
- QA-5 (Performance)
- QA-7 (Scalability)
- QA-8 (Scalability)

**5.3.5.2**  Step 3: Choose One or More Elements of the System to Refine
In this iteration, the elements that are refined are the ones that support historical data, which include the Serving Layer elements: the Ad Hoc and Static Batch Views. Given that both types of elements use the same technology (Impala), the decisions made in this iteration affect both types of elements.

**5.3.5.3**  Step 4: Choose One or More Design Concepts That Satisfy the Selected Drivers
As in the previous iteration, the design activities here involve the configuration of the technologies that were associated with the elements. For this reason, no new design concepts are selected and all of the decisions belong to the instantiation category.

**5.3.5.4**  Step 5: Instantiate Architectural Elements, Allocate Responsibilities, and Define Interfaces
In this iteration, design concepts are instantiated based on the best practices of using the chosen technologies.

| Design Decisions and Location | Rationale and Assumptions |
| --- | --- |
| Select Parquet as a file format for Impala in the Batch Views | The decision-making process for selecting a file format for Batch Views is similar to that in the previous iteration, where we selected a format for raw data storage. The data usage scenario is somewhat different, however. The previous case was about fast writing, effectively storing data, and extending data formats. This case is focused on fast querying (QA-4, less than 5 seconds report load; QA-5, less than 2 minutes ad hoc query execution time), although scalability (QA-8, approximately 90 TB of aggregated data) and extensibility (QA-9, adding new data sources) drivers are still relevant.

Out of all the available alternatives, the Parquet file format looks like the most promising option to satisfy these requirements. |

*(continues)*

| Design Decisions and Location | Rationale and Assumptions |
| --- | --- |
| Select Parquet as a file format for Impala in the Batch Views | In Parquet, a columnar structure represents relational tables on computer clusters and is designed for fast query processing, which is important for ad hoc data exploration and static reports. In addition, Parquet is optimized for Impala, which we selected as a primary technology for the interactive query engine during the second iteration. Finally, it provides a good compression ratio and allows some schema extension, by adding new columns at the end of the structure. |

| Alternative | Reason for Discarding |
| --- | --- |
| Text file (plain text, CSV, XML, JSON) | Slow for reads, especially when querying individual columns. Also does not support block compression, which is necessary when storing files larger than the size of an HDFS block. |
| SequenceFile | Slow for reads, especially when querying individual columns. |
| RCFile | The first columnar file format adopted in Hadoop. Does not support schema evolution. |
| ORCFile | Provides better compression and faster querying than RCFile, but has the same drawbacks as RCFile in terms of schema evolution. Compared with Parquet, the compression ratio is better, but query performance is slower. Another major limitation is that it is not supported by Impala. |
| Avro | Although Avro is considered the best multipurpose storage format for Hadoop, its query performance is noticeably slower compared with columnar formats, such as RCFile, ORCFile, and Parquet. |

| Design Decisions and Location | Rationale and Assumptions |
|---|---|
| Use the star schema as a data model in the Batch Views | In the previous iteration, we selected Impala as a single technology for the Batch Views components, which impacts both static reports (UC-3, 6) and ad hoc querying (UC-4). |

The star schema technique was selected for two reasons:

- Impala was designed for analytical queries, so it naturally provides good support for star schema data modeling.
- Ad hoc querying in combination with BI tools requires data to be well modeled to simplify query complexity and, as a result, allow faster query performance.

In our case, the star schema was designed to have small-dimension (in terms of number of rows) tables to avoid joins between big tables, as this typically consumes large amounts of system resources and affects query execution performance. Small-dimension tables can fit in memory and joins can be performed more effectively.

| Alternative | Reason for Discarding |
|---|---|
| Flat tables | Flat tables are typically represented in the format of wide denormalized tables that contain all measures and dimension attributes.<br><br>Flat tables can cause significant performance issues when querying against large volumes of data. |

#### 5.3.5.5 Step 6: Sketch Views and Record Design Decisions

Figure 5.9 depicts the star schema data model implemented using Impala and Parquet.

The screenshot in Figure 5.10 presents a sample static report implemented with Tableau to demonstrate a possible view through a corporate BI tool. The report was created using test data stored in Parquet and provided by Impala through the ODBC interface.

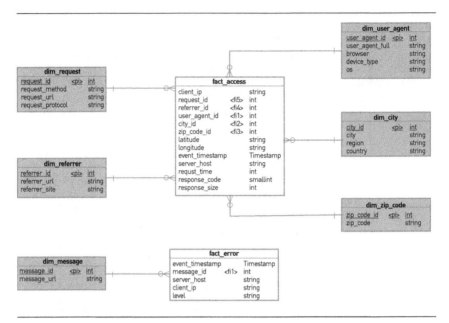

**FIGURE 5.9** Star schema implemented in Impala and Parquet

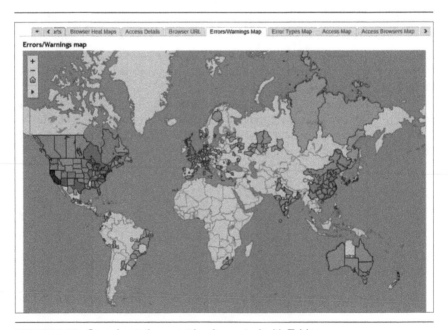

**FIGURE 5.10** Sample static report implemented with Tableau

**5.3.5.6** Step 7: Perform Analysis of Current Design and Review Iteration Goal and Achievement of Design Purpose

The following Kanban table summarizes the design progress and the decisions made during the iteration. Note that drivers that were completely addressed in the previous iteration are not shown.

| Not Addressed | Partially Addressed | Completely Addressed | Design Decisions Made During the Iteration |
|---|---|---|---|
| | UC-3 UC-4 | | Refinement of the Serving Layer, which is used in the use case. Decisions on other elements that participate in these use cases still need to be made. |
| | QA-4 QA-5 QA-8 | | Use Parquet and star schema. Performance tests are still required and thus a new concern is introduced: <br> ▪ CRN-4: Develop performance tests. |
| | CRN-1 | | No relevant decisions made. |
| | CRN-3 | | Data modeling and proof-of-concept prototypes were developed for the elements in the Serving Layer, but the same activity remains to be completed for the elements in the Speed Layer. |

## 5.4 Summary

In this chapter we presented an extended example of using ADD 3.0 in a relatively novel domain, that of Big Data. As this example shows, architectural design can require many detailed decisions to be made to ensure that the quality attributes will be satisfied.

Also, this example shows that a large number of decisions rely on knowledge of many different patterns and technologies. The more novel the domain, the more likely that preexisting information (e.g., design concepts catalog, books of patterns, and reference architectures) will not be available for it. In such a case, you need to rely on your own judgment and experience, or you need to perform experiments and build prototypes. One way or another, such decisions must be made.

This instance of ADD also differed from the example presented in Chapter 4 in that we spent relatively little time and effort on building sequence diagrams as a means of deriving interface specifications. The example presented here relied on a relatively simple data-flow architecture with a modest number of components, so sequence diagrams were not needed to understand the relationships between the components. The "contracts" between the elements were determined by the information exchanged, as exemplified in step 5 of Iteration 3 (Section 5.3.4.4).

## 5.5  Further Reading

The design of a data warehouse has been extensively studied. Two good approaches are documented in R. Kimball and M. Ross, *The Data Warehouse Toolkit,* 3rd ed., Wiley, 2013; and W. Inmon, *Building the Data Warehouse,* 4th ed., Wiley, 2005.

The Lambda architecture was first presented by N. Marz and J. Warren, *Big Data: Principles and Best Practices of Scalable Realtime Data Systems*, Manning, 2015.

A good discussion of how to engineer for scalability can be found in M. Abbott and M. Fisher, *The Art of Scalability: Scalable Web Architecture, Processes, and Organizations for the Modern Enterprise,* Addison-Wesley, 2010.

P. Sadalage and M. Fowler. *NoSQL Distilled: A Brief Guide to the Emerging World of Polyglot Persistence*, Addison-Wesley, 2009.

A discussion of how and when to prototype as part of the architecture design process can be found in H-M Chen, R. Kazman, and S. Haziyev, "Strategic Prototyping for Developing Big Data Systems", *IEEE Software*, March/April 2016.

A design concepts catalog that includes many of the reference architectures and technologies used in this case study is part of the Smart Decisions Game, which can be found at H. Cervantes, S. Haziyev, O. Hrytsay, and R. Kazman, "Smart Decisions Game", http://smartdecisionsgame.com.

# 6

# Case Study: Banking System

Chapters 4 and 5 were both instances of greenfield development. In truth, that kind of development is relatively rare. Most of the time you, as an architect, will be working on evolving an existing system rather than creating one from scratch. In this chapter, we present an example of using ADD 3.0 for a brownfield system in a mature domain (as discussed in Section 3.3.3). We first present the business context and then examine the project's existing architectural documentation. This is followed by a step-by-step summary of the activities that are performed during the ADD iterations to evolve the system. While this is a real system, some of the details have been changed to protect the identities of the actors.

## 6.1  Business Case

In 2010, the government of a Latin American country issued a regulation that required banking institutions to digitally sign bank statements. To comply with the regulation, "ACME Bank" decided to commission the development of a software system, which we will call BankStat, whose main purpose was the generation of digitally signed bank statements.

Figure 6.1 presents a context diagram that illustrates how the BankStat system works. At its core, the system executes a batch process, which retrieves raw bank statement information from a data source (an external database) and then performs a series of validations on this data to generate the bank statements and prepare them for digital signature by an external provider. The statements are sent to the provider, which returns the signed bank statements. These statements are then stored by BankStat for further processing, including sending the statements to customers. This batch process is triggered automatically once a month and, during its execution, approximately 2 million bank statements are processed.

The following quality attributes scenarios are primary for this system:

- *Reliability:* Under normal operating conditions, the batch process is executed in its entirety 100% of the time.
- *Performance:* Under normal operating conditions, when the batch process starts, 2 million bank statements are read, processed, and sent to the signing provider in at most one hour.
- *Availability:* During normal processing, a failure may occur when reading information from the data source or when sending information for digital signature. A notification is then sent to the administrator, who manually restarts the process. When it is restarted, only the information that had not already been processed is treated.

Due to time constraints imposed by the government, only the core batch process for the system was developed and put into production. This initial release, however, did not provide a friendly interface with the system, which is necessary to monitor the state of the bank statement processing, to request the reprocessing of incorrect statements. and to generate reports. In the first release, the process could only be started or stopped manually from a console. For a second release of the system, the ACME Bank requested an extension of the BankStat system to better address these shortcomings.

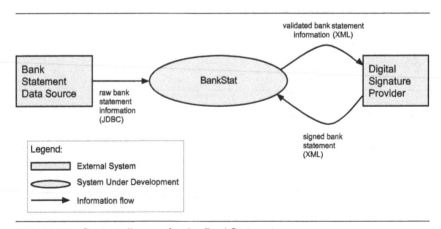

**FIGURE 6.1** Context diagram for the BankStat system

The following subsections present the drivers for this second release of the system.

### 6.1.1 Use Case Model

Figure 6.2 presents the use case model for the second release of BankStat. These use cases are described in more detail here:

| Use Case | Description |
| --- | --- |
| UC-1: Query and reprocess statements | The user manually requests the reprocessing of a number of statements. The user specifies criteria to query and select the statements that must be reprocessed. The user can, for example, select a period of interest or status of the statements that he is interested in (e.g., processed, signed, non-signed). |
| UC-2: Log in | The user logs in to the system. |
| UC-3: Generate report | The user generates reports regarding the process. |
| UC-4: Query users log | The administrator queries user logs to display the activities of a particular user or groups of users. Information can be filtered using criteria such as dates or types of operations. |

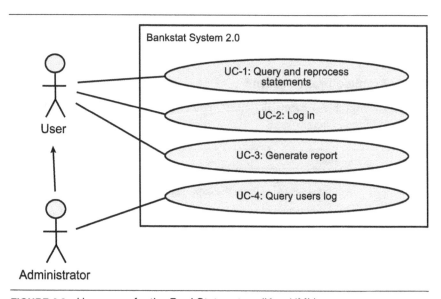

**FIGURE 6.2** Use cases for the BankStat system (Key: UML)

### 6.1.2 Quality Attribute Scenarios

The following table presents the new quality attribute scenario that is considered for this extension of the system.

| ID | Quality Attribute | Scenario | Associated Use Case |
|---|---|---|---|
| QA-1 | Security | A user performs any operation on the system, at any moment, and 100% of the operations performed by the user are recorded by the system in the operations log. | UC-4 |

### 6.1.3 Constraints

The following table presents the constraints that are considered for this extension of the system.

| ID | Constraint |
|---|---|
| CON-1 | The user's accounts and permissions are handled by an existing user directory server that is used by various applications in the bank. |
| CON-2 | Communication with the data source must be realized using JDBC. |
| CON-3 | Communication with the digital signature provider system is performed using web services. These web services receive and return the information in an XML format that adheres to specifications established by the government. |
| CON-4 | The system must be accessed from a web browser, although the access is available only from the bank's intranet. |

### 6.1.4 Architectural Concerns

The following table presents the concerns that are initially considered for this extension of the system.

| ID | Concern |
|---|---|
| CRN-1 | The system shall be programmed using Java and Java-related technologies to leverage the expertise of the development team. |
| CRN-2 | The introduction of new functionality must, as far as possible, avoid modifications to the existing batch processing core. |

## 6.2 Existing Architectural Documentation

This section presents a simplified version of the system's views, which provide relevant information for the changes in the architecture.

### 6.2.1 Module View

The package diagram shown in Figure 6.3 depicts the system layers and the modules that they contain.

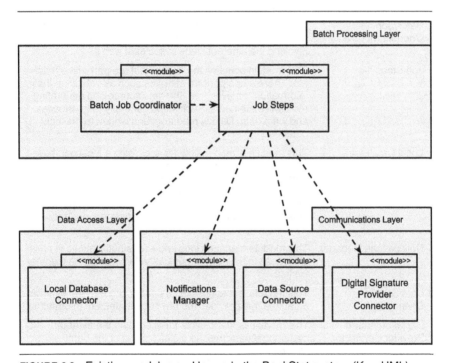

**FIGURE 6.3** Existing modules and layers in the BankStat system (Key: UML)

The responsibilities of the elements depicted in the diagram are described in the following table.

| Element | Responsibility |
| --- | --- |
| Batch Processing Layer | This layer contains modules that perform the batch process. These components are developed using the Spring Batch framework. |
| Data Access Layer | This layer contains modules that store and retrieve data from a local database, which is used by the modules in the Batch Processing Layer. |
| Communications Layer | This layer contains modules that support communication with the external digital signature provider and the bank statement data source. |
| Batch Job Coordinator | This module is responsible for coordinating the execution of the batch process, including launching the process and invoking the different steps associated with it. |
| Job Steps | This module contains the "steps" that are part of the batch job. These steps perform activities such as validating the information retrieved from the data source and generating the bank statements. Such steps generally read, process, and write data. Data is read from and written to the local database. |
| Local Database Connector | This module is responsible for accessing a local database used by the job steps to exchange information while performing the batch process. We refer to this database as "local" to differentiate it from the external data source; this database is used only locally (i.e., internally) by the application, even if it is deployed in a different node (see the next section). |
| Notifications Manager | This module manages logs and sends notifications in case of issues such as a communication failure with the external system. |
| Data Source Connector | This module is responsible for connecting with the external database that provides the raw bank statement information. |
| Digital Signature Provider Connector | This module is responsible for accessing the external system that performs the digital signing of the bank statements. |

## 6.2.2 Allocation View

The deployment diagram shown in Figure 6.4 presents an allocation view consisting of nodes and their relationships.

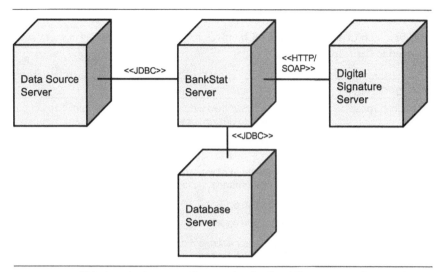

**FIGURE 6.4** Existing deployment diagram for the BankStat system (Key: UML)

The responsibilities of the elements depicted in the diagram are described in the following table.

| Element | Responsibility |
| --- | --- |
| Data Source Server | This server hosts a database that contains the raw data used to produce the bank statements. |
| BankStat Server | This server hosts the main batch process that is responsible for retrieving information from the Data Source Server, validating the information, and sending the information to the Digital Signature Server for signing. |
| Database Server | This server hosts a database that is used locally by the batch process in the BankStat Server to hold the state and information used in the execution of the batch process. |
| Digital Signature Server | This server, which is provided by an external entity, is responsible receiving, digitally signing, and returning the bank statements. The server exposes web services that receive and produce XML information. |

## 6.3 The Design Process

We now describe the design process through the different steps of ADD (as discussed in Section 3.2). As this is not a huge change to the existing system, the architect expects that the design activities will require only a single iteration of ADD.

### 6.3.1 ADD Step 1: Review Inputs

The first step of the ADD method involves reviewing the inputs. They are summarized in the following table.

| Category | Details |
|---|---|
| Design purpose | This is a brownfield system in a mature domain. The purpose is to design for the next system release. |
| Primary functional requirements | The primary use case for this release is UC-1. |
| Quality attribute scenarios | This extension of the system involves only a few quality attribute scenarios, so they are all considered as primary. |
| Constraints | See Section 6.1.3. |
| Architectural concerns | See Section 6.1.4. |
| Existing architecture design | Since this is brownfield development, an additional input is the existing architecture design, which was described in the previous section. |

### 6.3.2 Iteration 1: Supporting the New Drivers

This section presents the results of the activities that are performed in each of the steps of ADD in the single iteration performed in this example.

**6.3.2.1** Step 2: Establish Iteration Goal by Selecting Drivers
Only a limited number of drivers need to be addressed, so the architect has decided that a single iteration is sufficient. The goal of this iteration is to modify the existing design to support all of the new drivers listed in Section 6.1

**6.3.2.2** Step 3: Choose One or More Elements of the System to Refine
The elements to refine include the main modules from BankStat and the node where the system is deployed (BankStat Server). In addition to refining these modules, the physical node where the application is hosted is a candidate for refinement.

**6.3.2.3** Step 4: Choose One or More Design Concepts That Satisfy the Selected Drivers
The following table summarizes the design decisions made with respect to the selection of design concepts.

| Design Decisions and Location | Rationale |
|---|---|
| Use the Web Application Reference architecture | The use cases that are being introduced in the system require interaction through a web browser (CON-4). Since there are no requirements for rich user interaction, the Web Application architecture is selected (see Section A.1.1). <br> Discarded alternatives: <br> • Rich Internet application (see Section A.1.3), as it would require additional development effort and there are no requirements for a rich user interface. |
| Select the Spring Security framework to manage authorization and authentication | Security is a complex topic, and writing ad hoc code to support it is difficult and error prone. The needs for this application include managing authorization and authentication and an activity log. All of these features are available in the Spring Security framework, which can easily be integrated into the existing user directory server (CON-1) and is Java related (CRN-1). <br> Discarded alternatives: <br> • Ad hoc code: Challenging, error-prone, takes significant time to develop. <br> • Other frameworks: The first release of the solution has already been developed using Spring technologies. Hence it makes sense to continue using other technologies from the Spring platform, as they can be easily integrated with the existing frameworks. |
| Use the Shared Database Integration pattern to obtain information about the state of bank statements | The interactive part of the system needs to query the database that is used locally by the batch process to display the state of bank statement processing. The batch and interactive parts of the system can be seen as two different applications (or subsystems) that share data that is contained in the same database. The Shared Database Integration pattern can be used in this context to support the interaction between these systems. This approach does not require changes to be made in the existing parts of the system (CRN-2). <br> Discarded alternatives: <br> • Obtaining the information through an API, which would require modifications in the existing modules and would have a negative impact on performance. |
| Deploy using a three-tier deployment model | Deploying the web part of the application will be done in a separate server. Thus, the deployment of this part of the application can be seen as an instance of the three-tier deployment model (see Section A.2.2). The benefit of this approach is that the server that hosts the batch process will not have to process the interactive requests, so performance will not be hindered. <br> Discarded alternatives: <br> • Hosting the application in the same server where the batch process is hosted. This would save some server costs, but could limit performance of either the batch process or the interactive functions. |

**6.3.2.4** Step 5: Instantiate Architectural Elements, Allocate Responsibilities, and Define Interfaces

The instantiated design decisions considered and made are summarized in the following table.

| Design Decision and Location | Rationale |
| --- | --- |
| Host the web application in a separate server | This choice avoids performance reductions on the batch server and increases security (QA-1). |
| Configure Spring Security to use an external user directory server | This is to address CON-1. |

The results of these instantiation decisions are recorded in the next step.

**6.3.2.5** Step 6: Sketch Views and Record Design Decisions

The deployment diagram shown in Figure 6.5 depicts the new server that will host the application and the external user directory server, along with their connections to the existing nodes.

The responsibilities of the newly introduced elements are described in the following table.

| Element | Responsibility |
| --- | --- |
| Web/App Server | Hosts the interactive part of the application. |
| Auth Server | Existing server that manages users and permissions for multiple applications in the bank (CON-1). |

The package diagram shown in Figure 6.6 illustrates how the reference architecture is instantiated and identifies the modules that are introduced to support the primary use case (UC-1). It also shows how these newly introduced elements are integrated with the existing layers and modules from the previous system release.

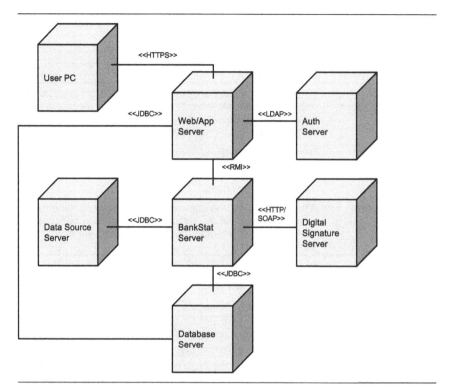

**FIGURE 6.5** Refined deployment diagram (Key: UML)

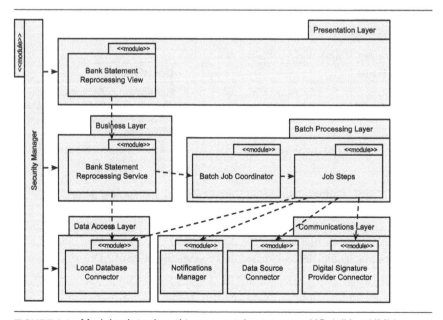

**FIGURE 6.6** Modules introduced to support the use case UC-1 (Key: UML)

The responsibilities of the newly introduced elements are described in the following table.

| Element | Responsibility |
|---|---|
| Bank Statement Reprocessing View | This module displays a view that allows the user to query the state of bank statements that have been processed. It also allows the user to select from these statements the ones that need to be reprocessed. |
| Bank Statement Reprocessing Service | This module manages requests from the view, which include requesting bank statement information, marking bank statements that need to be reprocessed, and triggering the restart of the batch job. |
| Security Manager | This module, which is implemented using Spring Security, handles authentication, authorization, and the activity log (QA-1). It is also integrated with the external user directory server (CON-1). |

The sequence diagram shown in Figure 6.7 illustrates how UC-1 is performed. The user requests the state of bank statements to be displayed. This information is retrieved from the local database by the Local Database Connector. Once displayed, the user selects the statements to reprocess. These bank statements are marked for reprocessing (by changing a flag) and the information is updated on the local database. Finally, the batch job is restarted. Note that the interactions with the system are recorded by Spring Security in the view. In addition, the invocation of the Batch Job Coordinator is asynchronous, which avoids the problem of blocking the user interface.

From the interactions identified in the sequence diagram, initial methods for the interfaces of the interacting elements can be identified.

`BankStatementReprocessingService`

| Method Name | Description |
|---|---|
| `BankStatement [] get BSStatus(criteria)` | Retrieves a collection of bank statements according to diverse criteria, including periods in time or status. |
| `boolean reprocess(BankStatement [])` | Requests the reprocessing of a collection of bank statements. |

**6.3.2.6**  Step 7: Perform Analysis of Current Design and Review Iteration
Goal and Achievement of Design Purpose
The following Kanban table summarizes the status of the various architectural drivers and the decisions that were made during the iteration to address them. As all the drivers were completely addressed, just a single iteration of ADD was required.

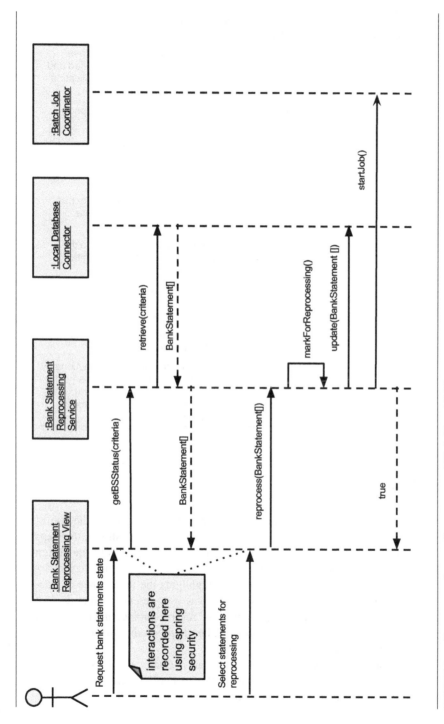

**FIGURE 6.7** Sequence diagram for use case UC-1 (Key: UML)

| Not Addressed | Partially Addressed | Completely Addressed | Design Decisions Made During the Iteration |
|---|---|---|---|
| | | UC-1 | Modules that support the use case and their interfaces were identified and defined based on the Web Application Reference architecture. |
| | | QA-1 | Security logs are handled by Spring Security. |
| | | CON-1 | Spring Security connects to the existing user directory server and uses its information to support authorization and authentication. |
| | | CON-3 | No changes have been made to the module that connects to the data source. |
| | | CON-3 | No changes have been made to the module that connects to the digital signature provider. |
| | | CON-4 | The Web Application Reference architecture that was used specifically supports access from web browsers. |
| | | CRN-1 | The technologies that have been selected are Java related. |
| | | CRN-2 | Integration with the existing functionality was made through the database (using the Database Integration pattern); changes to the existing functionality were not needed. |

## 6.4   Summary

In this chapter, we presented a simple (but real-world) example of the use of ADD in the context of a brownfield system. As this example illustrates, the steps of ADD are followed in exactly the same manner as in the context of the design of greenfield systems. The main difference is that one of the inputs of the design process is the *existing* architecture. This highlights the importance of documenting the architecture: If this information was not present, a great deal of time would need to be spent in understanding and reverse-engineering the code to create an appropriate model of the architecture before proceeding with the design and eventual implementation process.

Design in the context of brownfield systems usually involves more extensive changes than the ones illustrated by this example. Such changes often require refactoring and modification of the existing architecture to support the introduction of new elements and new relationships that result from the design activity. Modifying an existing architecture is oftentimes the most challenging aspect of designing in the context of brownfield systems. In brownfield systems, it is all too common that detailed knowledge of some parts of the system has been lost. Because this process can be complex and some uncertainty exists regarding the consequences of changes, we recommend that you perform an analysis of the proposed design changes before committing them to code.

## 6.5 Further Reading

The Shared Database Integration pattern is discussed in G. Hohpe and B. Woolf, *Enterprise Integration Patterns: Designing, Building and Deploying Messaging Solutions*, Addison Wesley Professional, 2003.

In-depth discussions of software maintenance and evolution can be found in the classic book by F. Brooks, *The Mythical Man Month*, Addison-Wesley, 1995, and also in M. M. Lehman, "On Understanding Laws, Evolution, and Conservation in the Large-Program Life Cycle", *Journal of Systems and Software*, 1:213–221, 2010.

# 7

# Other Design Methods

Over the past two decades, a number of architecture design methods have been proposed and documented. In this chapter we briefly present some of the most well-known methods, which we then relate and compare to ADD. We begin with a "general model" of architecture design, then briefly present five other design methods. We conclude the chapter with a discussion of how ADD differs from these other methods.

## 7.1   A General Model of Software Architecture Design

In their paper "A General Model of Software Architecture Design Derived from Five Industrial Approaches", Hofmeister and her colleagues compared five industrial software architecture design methods and extracted from their commonalities a generic software architecture design approach. The five models they reviewed were ADD 2.0, Siemens 4 views, RUP's 4+1 Views, Business Architecture Process and Organization (BAPO), and Architecture Separation of Concerns (ASC).

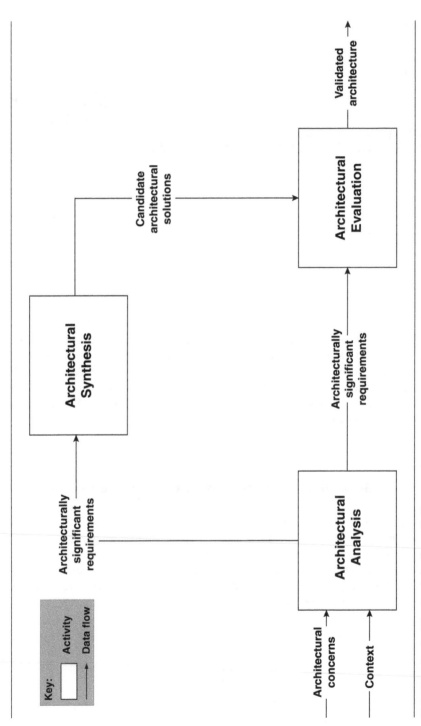

**FIGURE 7.1**   Architectural design activities

The derived general model, shown in Figure 7.1, consists of three main activities that are present in all five models reviewed:

- *Architectural analysis.* In this activity, requirements (called concerns) and the system context are used as inputs to determine a set of architecturally significant requirements (ASRs).
- *Architectural synthesis.* This activity is described as being the core of architecture design. It proposes architecture solutions to a set of ASRs, moving from the problem to the solution space. The results of this activity are candidate architectural solutions, which are partial or complete architecture designs and include information about the rationale.
- *Architectural evaluation.* This activity ensures that the architectural decisions are the right ones. Candidate architectural solutions are measured against ASRs. Several evaluations of different architectural solutions are expected, but the eventual result is the validated architecture.

Hofmeister and her colleagues further explain that these activities do not proceed sequentially, but rather architects proceed in small "leaps" as they move from one activity to another. Progress is driven by an implicit or explicit backlog of smaller needs, issues, problems, and ideas that architects need to address (Figure 7.2).

This general model presented by Hofmeister et al. is not detailed, by intent, because it abstracts the specific techniques found in other design processes, including ADD. Thus the model can represent ADD, but also covers a bigger scope of architecture development, where architectural requirements gathering and analysis are performed using methods such as QAW, architectural synthesis is performed using methods such as the ones presented in the paper, and architectural evaluation is performed using methods such as ATAM.

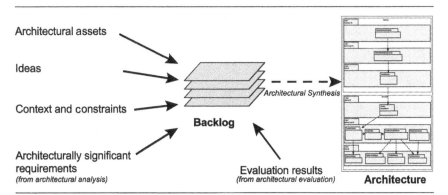

**FIGURE 7.2**    Architecture backlog

## 7.2   Architecture-Centric Design Method

The *Architecture-Centric Design Method (ACDM)* is a software architecture de-velopment method that covers the complete life cycle of the architecture. This iterative method consists of 8 stages, as shown in Figure 7.3.

Stage 3 is focused on design; it is where an initial architectural design is created or refined. For new systems, the first iteration of this process promotes the rapid creation of a "notional" or initial architecture. This iteration proceeds by first establishing the system context and then performing decomposition in an

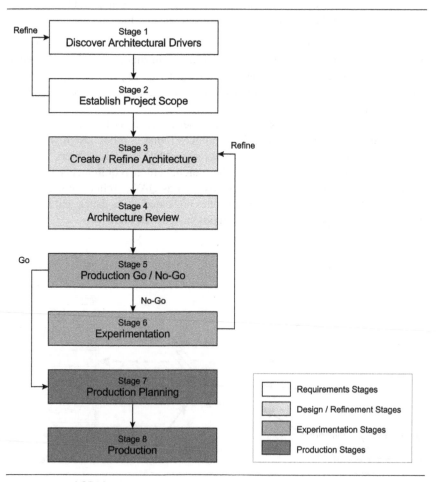

**FIGURE 7.3**   ACDM stages

iterative manner to produce structures. In ACDM, decomposition is driven by quality attribute scenarios and constraints, but functional requirements are also considered. In subsequent iterations, issues uncovered in the architecture review (Stage 4) also serve as inputs. ACDM suggests using patterns to support decomposition and using more than one perspective (static, dynamic) during the process. After decomposition occurs, responsibilities are associated with the elements and interfaces are defined.

ACDM has a broader scope than ADD, as it encompasses the whole architecture development life cycle (requirements, design, evaluation, and documentation) in its 8 stages. Stage 3 of ACDM is the equivalent of ADD. However, ACDM provides less detailed guidance than ADD on how to perform this crucial step. ADD and ACDM can be used together, however. To do so, you can simply use ADD directly in stage 3 of ACDM.

## 7.3 Architecture Activities in the Rational Unified Process

The *Rational Unified Process (RUP)* has been a popular software development process framework for more than a decade. The framework is extensive and the version we reviewed (7.0.1) provides two flavors: one for large projects (used here for discussion) and one for small projects. Every project in RUP is developed iteratively and iterations are performed across four sequential phases:

- *Inception.* In this phase, the project is conceived and feasibility is evaluated.
- *Elaboration.* In this phase, many aspects that are necessary to successfully perform the project are handled. One of these aspects is the design of the architecture.
- *Construction.* In this phase, the system is built iteratively.
- *Transition.* In this phase, the completed system is transitioned from the development environment to the end-user environment.

For RUP, architecture is a fundamental aspect of system creation, and activities are associated with it across the different phases and, in particular, in the inception and elaboration phases. In the inception phase, RUP defines an activity called "perform architectural synthesis", whose goal is to construct and assess an architectural *proof-of-concept* to demonstrate the feasibility of the system. This activity includes tasks such as defining a system context, performing architectural analysis (which actually refers to defining a candidate architecture), constructing an architectural proof-of-concept (a prototype), and evaluating the viability of the proof-of-concept.

The elaboration phase includes two activities associated with software architecture:

- *Define a candidate architecture.* In this activity, an initial sketch of the software architecture is created. This includes defining architecturally significant elements, identifying a set of analysis mechanisms, defining the initial layering and organization of the system, and defining use-case realizations for the current iteration. The key tasks are performing architectural analysis and use case analysis; other tasks include operation analysis and identifying security patterns.

- *Refine the architecture.* This activity is focused on completing the architecture for an iteration. It involves making a transition from analysis activities to design activities by identifying design elements from analysis elements and design mechanisms from analysis mechanisms. In addition, the runtime and deployment architecture is described, along with an implementation model to facilitate the transition between design and implementation. To achieve this, the RUP suggests performing tasks such as identifying design mechanisms, identifying design elements, performing operation analysis, incorporating existing design elements, structuring the implementation model and describing the runtime architecture, describing distribution, and reviewing the architecture.

RUP provides an extensive, detailed process for architectural development. It also makes clear distinctions between analysis, design, and implementation aspects. Initially, the architecture is designed in a conceptual fashion in the analysis tasks, and then it is made concrete in the design and implementation tasks. For example, initially an analysis mechanism such as persistence can be identified. This is refined into a design mechanism such as a DBMS, which is further refined into an implementation mechanism such as a specific Oracle or MySQL database.

The process in RUP is iterative by nature, as several iterations of the architectural activities defined in the inception and elaboration phases can be performed. A nice aspect of the process defined by RUP is that it provides detailed guidance with respect to architectural concerns such as defining the system context and establishing an initial structure for the system both in a logical and a physical way. The architecture process in RUP also has a strong focus on use cases. Even though quality attributes are mentioned (as "supplementary requirements"), they do not drive the architecture design process as much as the use cases. Also, this process explicitly considers the creation of an executable architectural prototype.

Even though the architecture process in RUP is comprehensive, it does not give as much detail as ADD in terms of the concrete steps to perform the design. In this sense, ADD and RUP can be seen as being complementary methods, and ADD can be integrated into RUP (as can other more detailed architecture-based methods such as the QAW, ATAM, and CBAM).

## 7.4 The Process of Software Architecting

In the book *The Process of Software Architecting*, Peter Eeles and Peter Cripps, who are architects at IBM, describe how they approach architecture. Their process covers the entire architecture life cycle and is independent of any software development methodology, but the book makes several references to its use with RUP.

The process described by Eeles and Cripps includes three major activities: "define requirements", "create logical architecture", and "create physical architecture". The last two are the activities where architectural design is performed. According to the authors, the logical architecture is "a stepping stone in getting from the requirements to the solution—a first step that considers the architecture in a largely technology-independent manner. A physical architecture, on the other hand, is more specific—and takes technology into account". The creation of the logical architecture and the physical architecture comprises the same tasks (see Figure 7.4), but in the creation of the physical architecture the focus, not surprisingly, is on its physical aspects.

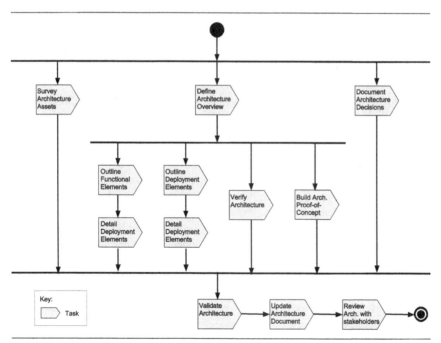

**FIGURE 7.4** Tasks in the "create logical architecture" and "create physical architecture" activities

This process acknowledges the existence of different types of architects: lead, application, infrastructure, and data architects. Also, it makes a distinction between "outlining" tasks, which are associated with the most important architectural elements and are the responsibility of the lead architect, and "detailing" tasks, which are focused on less significant elements and are the responsibility of the other architects, depending on the task. For example, whereas outlining tasks deal with subsystems and components, detailing tasks deal with interfaces and operation signatures.

The method described by Eeles and Cripps also emphasizes two different models: (1) the functional model, which is composed of components with responsibilities and relationships and their collaborations to deliver the required functionality, and (2) the deployment model, which shows the configuration of nodes, communication links between them, and the components that are deployed on the nodes. Both functional and quality attribute requirements influence the functional and deployment models. The authors mention that they adopt the "systems engineering philosophy" of treating software and hardware as peers that collaborate to achieve system qualities.

The following list summarizes the purposes of the tasks in the create logical and physical architecture activities that are related to design. The role that has primary responsibility for the task appears in parentheses, while other types of architects may take a secondary role:

- *Survey architecture assets (lead architect).* Identify reusable architecture assets that can be applied to the system under development.
- *Define architecture overview (lead architect).* Identify and describe the major elements of the system under development from a functional and deployment perspective.
- *Document architecture decisions (lead architect).* Capture key decisions made in shaping the architecture and the rationale behind them. This step includes assessing options and selecting a preferred option.
- *Outline functional elements (application architect).* Identify the major functional elements (subsystems and components) of the system under development.
- *Outline deployment elements (infrastructure architect).* Identify the locations to which the system under development will be deployed and the nodes within each location.
- *Verify architecture (lead architect).* Verify that the architecture work products are consistent and ensure that any concerns that cut across the architecture work products have been addressed consistently.
- *Build architecture proof-of-concept (lead architect).* Synthesize at least one solution (which can be conceptual) that satisfies the architecturally significant requirements to determine whether such a solution, as envisaged by the architects, exists.
- *Detail functional elements (application architect).* Refine the functional elements to the point that they can be handed off to detailed design. This

includes defining component interfaces in a detailed way (e.g., operation signatures, pre and post conditions) using sequence diagrams.

- *Detail deployment elements (infrastructure architect).* Refine the deployment elements to the point they can be handed off to detailed design. This includes assigning components to nodes and defining connections between nodes and locations.

In a spirit that is similar to RUP, the Process of Software Architecting is a framework, and it needs to be adjusted according to the type of project that is being tackled. For instance, the amount of logical architecture that needs to be established can vary; indeed, in some cases, no logical architecture may be created if the system being designed is similar to existing ones. Also, the elaboration phase emphasizes the logical architecture, whereas the construction phase emphasizes the physical architecture. Finally, the logical and physical architectures need not be created sequentially and the process acknowledges that some technology choices may be made early.

The Process of Software Architecting is a comprehensive framework, and this book provides a detailed example of how to execute the different tasks. The tasks related to creating the logical/physical architecture are similar to the steps of ADD combined with the roadmap discussed in Section 3.3. *The Process of Software Architecting,* however, puts less emphasis on guiding iterations by specific scenarios and provides less guidance on how to actually make design decisions.

## 7.5 A Technique for Architecture and Design

In the book *Application Architecture Guide,* second edition, Microsoft proposes a technique for sketching an architecture. This technique consists of five steps that are performed iteratively (Figure 7.5):

1. *Identify architecture objectives.* These goals and constraints shape the design process, provide scope, and help determine when you are finished. Examples include building a prototype, exploring technologies, and developing an architecture. Also, at this point, the consumers for the architecture are identified and the scope, time, and resources that will be dedicated to design activities are established.

2. *Identify key scenarios.* Key scenarios represent issues, architecturally significant use cases, intersections between quality attributes and functionality, or tradeoffs between quality attributes.

3. *Create application overview.* This step refers to creating an overview of what the application will look like when it is complete. At the end of this step, the process suggests "whiteboarding" the architecture—that is, creating an

informal representation of the architecture. This step is divided into the following set of activities:

    a. Determining application type: involves the selection of a reference architecture.

    b. Identifying deployment constraints: involves the selection of a deployment topology.

    c. Identifying important architecture design styles.

    d. Determining relevant technologies: based on the application type and constraints.

4. *Identify key issues.* Key issues are grouped into quality attributes and crosscutting concerns. Crosscutting concerns are features of the design that may apply across all layers, components, and tiers, such as the following:

    a. Authentication and authorization

    b. Caching

    c. Communication

    d. Configuration management (information that must be configurable)

    e. Exception management

    f. Logging and instrumentation

    g. Validation (of input data)

5. *Define candidate solutions.* Candidate architectures include an application type, deployment architecture, architectural style, technology choices, quality attributes, and crosscutting concerns. If a candidate architecture satisfies the requirements and issues, then it becomes a baseline architecture and is refined in further iterations.

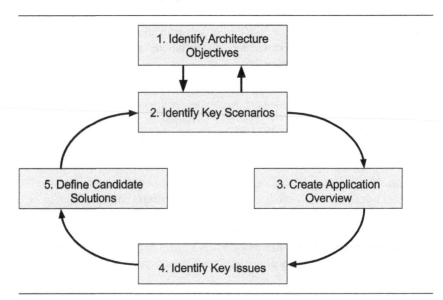

**FIGURE 7.5** Iterative steps of the technique for architecture and design

Besides these five main steps, the technique discussed by the Microsoft team suggests performing reviews of the architecture and representing and communicating the design. This technique is independent of a particular development process and there is only a suggestion that, when using an Agile process, iterations should combine architecture and development activities.

The technique presented by the Microsoft team is not very detailed, but the discussion of this technique is only a small part of Microsoft's book. The rest of the book provides pragmatic and detailed information on the considerations that must be taken into account for different types of applications, including web, rich client, rich internet, and mobile applications, among others. For example, the book devotes a chapter to the specific aspects of the design of the business layer. Although much of the information is technology agnostic, Microsoft has also done an excellent job of showing how its own technologies can be used in this process. In addition, the book provides an extensive discussion of the concerns that must be addressed for a series of reference architectures.

This technique is similar in purpose to ADD but less detailed in terms of how to perform the actual design steps. ADD can be used as an alternative, but it is a good idea to keep Microsoft's book on hand to identify the many specific architectural concerns that you will need to address during design and to leverage all of the practical advice that is provided, particularly if you are designing one of the types of applications discussed in the book. The ideas presented in Microsoft's book inspired us when creating several aspects of this book.

---

## 7.6  Viewpoints and Perspectives Method

The viewpoints and perspectives method is described in the book *Software Systems Architecture: Working with Stakeholders Using Viewpoints and Perspectives,* by Nick Rozanski and Eoin Woods. Two critical concepts, highlighted in the book title, are *viewpoints* and *perspectives,* which the authors define in the following way:

- A viewpoint is a collection of patterns, templates, and conventions for constructing one type of view. It defines the stakeholders whose concerns are reflected in the viewpoint and the guidelines, principles, and template models for constructing its views. The viewpoints defined include functional, information, concurrency, development, deployment, and operational.
- An architectural perspective is a collection of activities, tactics, and guidelines that are used to ensure a system exhibits a set of quality properties that must be considered across the system's architectural views. The primary perspectives that are covered in Rozanski and Woods's book are security, performance and scalability, availability and resilience, and evolution.

Perspectives are orthogonal to viewpoints because a particular perspective can be applied across different viewpoints. For example, the security perspective involves aspects from the functional, information and operational viewpoints.

The architecture is established in the architecture definition process illustrated in Figure 7.6. The steps in this process are outlined here:

1. *Consolidate the inputs.* Understand, validate, and refine the initial inputs.
2. *Identify the scenarios.* Identify a set of scenarios that illustrate the system's most important requirements.
3. *Identify relevant architectural styles.* Identify one or more proven architectural styles that could be used as a basis for the overall organization of the system.
4. *Produce a candidate architecture.* Create a first-cut architecture for the system that reflects its primary concerns (requirements and goals) and that can act as a basis for further architectural evaluation and refinement.
5. *Explore architectural options.* Explore various architectural possibilities for the system and make the key decisions to choose among them.
6. *Evaluate the architecture with stakeholders.* Work through an evaluation of the architecture with your key stakeholders, capture any problems or deficiencies, and gain the stakeholders' acceptance of the architecture.
7. Two steps are performed in parallel at this point:
   A. *Rework the architecture.* Address any concerns that have emerged during the evaluation task.
   B. *Revisit the requirements.* Consider any changes to the system's original requirements that may have to be made in light of architectural evaluations.

This method suggests the creation of a candidate architecture that is obtained from—or at least based on—architectural styles. This candidate architecture is further refined through a series of iterations until it is deemed acceptable after an evaluation is performed.

In comparison with ADD, this method does not provide step-by-step guidance on how to perform steps 4 and 5. One benefit of this approach, however, is that the six viewpoints it defines can be related to general architectural concerns in our approach. Furthermore, tactics and perspectives are related, and the idea of applying perspectives across the different viewpoints is valuable and may be a complement to a scenario-based approach. For example, if you have only one security scenario in your drivers list, you may consider only elements that support this particular scenario. Thinking of a security perspective, however, may be useful in making design decisions concerning security, which may not be directly related to the particular scenario but flow across different areas of concern such as deployment or operation.

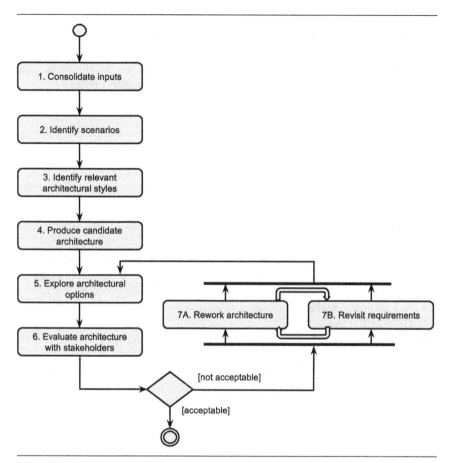

**FIGURE 7.6** Viewpoints and perspectives method steps

## 7.7 Summary

In this chapter, we reviewed a number of design methods and compared them to ADD. As you can see, there are several methods to choose from. So why should you use ADD instead of, or in addition to, these alternatives? Quite simply, ADD is more concrete and specific in its steps and guidance for accomplishing the architecture design activity. Having read this far, you should now be convinced of that.

ADD is focused specifically on design and, as such, provides more detailed guidance to an (aspiring) architect. This is not a weakness of ADD. Many other methods can guide you in the other phases of the architecture life cycle, such as QAW for eliciting and prioritizing architectural requirements, ATAM for analyzing an architecture, the Views and Beyond technique for documenting an architecture. In several parts of this book we have discussed how such methods can be seamlessly integrated into ADD.

In the interest of full disclosure, ADD 3.0 borrows from, benefits from, and owes a debt of gratitude to *all* of the approaches described in this chapter.

---

## 7.8  Further Reading

The architecture design methods discussed in this chapter can be found in the following sources:

- P. Eeles, P. Cripps. *The Process of Software Architecting.* Addison-Wesley Professional, 2009.
- C. Hofmeister, P. Kruchten, R. Nord, H. Obbink, A. Ran, P. America. "A General Model of Software Architecture Design Derived from Five Industrial Approaches", *Journal of Systems and Software*, 80:106–126, 2007.
- A. Lattanze. *Architecting Software Intensive Systems: A Practitioner's Guide.* CRC Press, 2009.
- P. Kruchten. *The Rational Unified Process: An Introduction*, 3rd ed., Addison-Wesley, 2003.
- Microsoft, *Application Architecture Guide,* 2nd ed. Microsoft Press, 2009.
- N. Rozanski, E. Woods. *Software Systems Architecture.* Addison Wesley, 2005.

# 8

# Analysis in the Design Process

While this is a book focused on architectural design, we have always believed that design and analysis are two sides of the same coin. Design is the process of making decisions; analysis is the process of understanding those decisions, so that the design may be evaluated. To reflect this intimate relationship, we now turn our attention to why, when, and how to analyze architectural decisions *during* the design process. We look at various techniques for analysis, discuss when they can be done, and explore their costs and benefits.

## 8.1 Analysis and Design

Analysis is the process of breaking a complex entity into its constituent parts as a means of understanding it. The opposite of analysis is synthesis. Analysis and design are therefore intertwined activities. During the design process, the activity of analysis can refer to several aspects:

- *Studying the inputs to the design process to understand the problem whose solution you are about to design.* This includes giving priority to the drivers as discussed in Section 3.2.2. This type of analysis is performed in steps 1 and 2 of ADD.
- *Studying the alternative design concepts that you identified to solve a design problem so as to select the most appropriate one.* In this situation,

analysis forces you to provide concrete evidence for your choices. This activity is performed in step 4 of ADD and was discussed in Section 3.2.4.

- *Ensuring the decisions made during the design process (or an iteration) are appropriate.* This is the type of analysis that you perform in step 7 of ADD.

The decisions that you make when designing the architecture are not only critical to achieve the quality attribute responses, but frequently the cost associated with correcting them at a later time can be significant, as these decisions may affect many parts of the system. For these reasons, it is necessary to perform analysis *during* the design process, so that problems can be identified, possibly quantified, and corrected quickly. Remember, being too confident and following your gut instincts may not be the best idea (see the sidebar "'I believe' Isn't Good Enough"). Fortunately, if you have followed the recommendations that we have given up to this point, you should be able to conduct analysis either by yourself or with the help of peers by using the preliminary sketches and views that have been produced as you perform the design process.

## "I Believe" Isn't Good Enough

Even if you are following a systematic approach to designing your architecture and using design concepts from well-established sources, and even if you have nice-looking diagrams that represent your structures, nothing really guarantees that the decisions you are making will actually satisfy a particular quality attribute scenario. Certain quality attributes are critical to the success of your system; particularly for these decisions, the rationale of "I believe" is not good enough. Studies of practicing software architects have shown that most follow an "adequacy" approach to making design decisions—that is, they adopt the first decision that appears to meet their needs. All too often, they have no rationale to substantiate those decisions other than their gut instincts, their beliefs, based on their (inevitably limited) experience. Thus important decisions are frequently made after insufficient reasoning, which can add risk to a system.

For drivers that are critical to your system, you owe it to yourself and to your organization to perform a more detailed analysis rather than just trusting your gut instinct, relying on analogy and history, or performing a couple of superficial tests to ensure that your drivers are satisfied. The following options will deepen your analysis and hence support your rationale for the decisions made:

- *Analytic models.* These well-established mathematical models allow you to study quality attributes such as performance or availability. They include Markov and statistical models for availability, and queuing and real-time scheduling theory for performance. Analytic models—particularly those that address performance—are highly mature but may require considerable education and training to be used adequately.

- *Checklists.* Checklists are useful tools that allow you to ensure in a systematic way that certain decisions that need to be taken into account are not forgotten. Checklists are available for particular quality attributes in the public domain— for example, the OWASP checklist guides you in performing black box security testing of web applications. Also, your organization may develop proprietary checklists that are specific to the application domains that you are developing. Tactics-based questionnaires, which we will discuss shortly, are a type of checklist for the most important quality attributes, based on the use of tactics.
- *Thought experiments, reflective questions, and back-of-the-envelope analyses.* Thought experiments are informal analyses performed by a small group of designers in which important scenarios are studied to identify potential problems. For example, you might use a sequence diagram produced inside step 5 of ADD and perform a walk-through of the interaction of the objects that support the scenario modeled in the diagram with a colleague. Reflective questions (discussed in depth in Section 8.5) are questions that challenge the assumptions included in the decision-making process. Back-of-the-envelope analyses are rough calculations that are less precise than analytic models, but can be performed quickly. These calculations, which are frequently based on analogies to other similar systems or on prior experience, are useful to obtain ballpark estimates for desired quality attribute responses. For example, by summing the latencies of a number of processes in a pipeline, you can derive a crude estimate of the end-to-end latency.
- *Prototypes, simulations, and experiments.* Purely conceptual techniques for analyzing a design are sometimes inadequate to accurately understand whether certain design decisions are appropriate, or whether you should favor one particular technology over another. In such situations, the creation of prototypes, simulations, or experiments can be an invaluable option to obtain a better understanding. For example, in the back-of-the-envelope estimate of latency described previously, you may not have taken into account that several of the processes are sharing (and hence competing for) the same resources; thus we cannot simply sum their individual latencies and expect to get accurate results. Prototypes and simulations provide a deeper understanding of system dynamics, but may require a significant effort that needs to be considered in the project plan.

As always, none of these techniques is inherently better than the others. Thought experiments and back-of-the-envelope calculations are inexpensive and can be done early in the design process, but their validity may be questionable. Prototypes, simulations, and experiments typically produce much higher-fidelity results, but at a far greater cost. The choice of which technique to employ depends on the context, the risk involved, and the priorities of your quality attributes.

Even so, applying *any* of these techniques will be helpful in going from "I believe" (that my design is appropriate) to an approach that is backed by documented evidence and argumentation.

## 8.2   Why Analyze?

Analysis and design are two sides of the same coin. Design is (the process of) making decisions. Analysis is (the process of) understanding the consequences—in terms of cost, schedule, and quality—of those decisions. No sensible architect would make any decision, or at least any nontrivial decision, without first attempting to understand the implications of that decision: its near-term effects and possibly its long-term consequences. Architects, of course, make thousands of decisions in the course of designing a large project, and clearly not all of them matter. Furthermore, not all of the decisions that matter are carriers of quality attributes. Some may deal with which vendor to select, or which coding convention to follow, or which programmer to hire or fire, or which IDE to use—important decisions, to be sure, but not ones that are directly linked to a quality attribute outcome.

Of course, some of these decisions *will* affect the achievement of quality attributes. When the architect breaks down the development into a system of layers or modules, or both, this decision will affect how a change ripples through the code base, who needs to talk to who when adding a feature or fixing a bug, how easy or difficult it is to distribute or outsource some of the development, how easy it is to port the software to a different platform, and so forth. When the architect chooses a distributed resource management system, how it determines which services are masters and which are slaves, how it detects failures, and how it detects resource starvation will all affect the availability of the system.

So when and why do we analyze during the design process? First, we analyze *because we can*. An architecture specification, whether it is just a whiteboard sketch or something that has been more formally documented and circulated, is the first artifact supporting an analysis that sheds insight into quality attributes. Yes, we can analyze requirements, but we mainly analyze them for consistency and completeness. Until we translate those requirements into structures resulting from design decisions, we will have little to say about the actual consequences of those decisions, their costs and benefits, and the tradeoffs among them.

Second, and more to the point, we analyze because it is a prudent way of informing decisions and *managing risk*. No design is completely without risk, but we want to ensure that the risks that we take on are commensurate with our stakeholders' expectations and tolerances. For a banking application or a military application, our stakeholders will demand low levels of risk, and they should be willing to pay accordingly for higher levels of assurance. For a startup company, where time to market is of the essence and budgets are tight, we might be prepared to accept far higher levels of risk. As with every important decision in software engineering, the answer is clear: It depends.

Finally, analysis is the key to evaluation. Evaluation is the process of determining the value of something. Companies are evaluated to determine their share price. A company's employees are evaluated annually to determine their raises. In each case, the evaluation is built upon an analysis of the properties of the company or employee.

## 8.3 Analysis Techniques

Different projects will demand different responses to risk. Fortunately we, as architects, have a wide variety of tools at our disposal to analyze architectures. With a bit of planning, we can match our risk tolerance with a set of analysis techniques that both meet our budget and schedule constraints and provide reasonable levels of assurance. The point here is that analysis does not need to be costly or complex. Just asking thoughtful questions is a form of analysis, and that exercise is pretty inexpensive. Building a simple prototype is more expensive, but in the context of a large project this analysis technique may be well worth the additional expense owing to how it explores and mitigates risks, as we saw in Chapter 5.

Examples of (relatively economical, relatively low ceremony) analysis techniques already in widespread use include design reviews and scenario-based analyses, code reviews, pair programming, and Scrum retrospective meetings. Other commonly used, albeit somewhat more costly, analysis techniques include prototypes (throw-away or evolutionary) and simulations.

At the high end of expense and complexity, we can build formal models of our systems and analyze them for properties such as latency or security or safety. When a candidate implementation or a fielded system finally exists, we can perform experiments, including instrumenting running systems and collecting data, ideally from executions of the system that reflect realistic usages.

As indicated in Table 8.1, the cost of these techniques typically increases as you proceed through the software development life cycle. A prototype or experiment is more expensive than a checklist, which is more expensive than an experience-based analogy. This expected cost correlates fairly strongly with the confidence that you can have in the analysis results. Unfortunately, there is no free lunch!

**TABLE 8.1**   Analysis at Different Stages of the Software Life Cycle

| Life-Cycle Stage | Form of Analysis | Cost | Confidence |
| --- | --- | --- | --- |
| Requirements | Experience-based analogy | Low | Low–high |
| Requirements | Back-of-the-envelope analysis | Low | Low–medium |
| Architecture | Thought experiment/ reflective questions | Low | Low–medium |
| Architecture | Checklist-based analysis | Low | Medium |
| Architecture | Tactics-based analysis | Low | Medium |
| Architecture | Scenario-based analysis | Low–medium | Medium |
| Architecture | Analytic model | Low–medium | Medium |
| Architecture | Simulation | Medium | Medium |
| Architecture | Prototype | Medium | Medium–high |
| Implementation | Experiment | Medium–high | Medium–high |
| Fielded system | Instrumentation | Medium–high | High |

## 8.4   Tactics-Based Analysis

Architectural tactics (discussed in Section 2.5.4) have been presented thus far as design primitives. However, because these taxonomies are intended to cover the entire space of architectural design possibilities for managing a quality attribute, we can use them in an analysis setting as well. Specifically, we can use them as guides for interviews or questionnaires. These interviews help you, as an analyst, to gain rapid insight into the architectural approaches taken or not taken.

Consider, for example, the tactics for availability, shown in Figure 8.1.

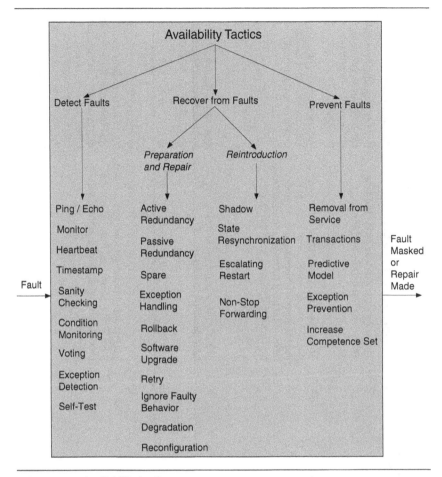

**FIGURE 8.1** Availability tactics

Each of these tactics is a design option for the architect who wants to design a highly available system. Used in hindsight, however, they represent a taxonomy of the entire design space for availability and hence can be a way of gaining insight into the decisions made, and not made, by the architect. To do this, we simply turn each tactic into an interview question. For example, consider the (partial) set of tactics-inspired availability questions in Table 8.2.

TABLE 8.2  Example Tactics-Based Availability Questions

| Tactics Group | Tactics Question | Supported? (Y/N) | Risk | Design Decisions and Location | Rationale and Assumptions |
|---|---|---|---|---|---|
| Detect faults | Does the system use **ping/echo** to detect a failure of a component or connection, or network congestion? | Y | L | The server periodically pings the time servers to see if they are "alive". | It is not possible to modify the time servers take to implement a heartbeat approach. |
| | Does the system use a component to **monitor** the state of health of other parts of the system? A system monitor can detect failure or congestion in the network or other shared resources, such as from a denial-of-service attack. | N | N/A | This was not implemented in the system. We will rely on other techniques to monitor the system. For example, memory consumption or processor load information can be obtained from the OS. | We assume that information beyond what the OS provides is not critical. |
| | Does the system use a **heartbeat**—a periodic message exchange between a system monitor and a process—to detect a failure of a component or connection, or network congestion? | Y | L | The server periodically sends a heartbeat to the clients. | The server does not have to process incoming ping requests from the clients. |
| | Does the system use a **time stamp** to detect incorrect sequences of events in distributed systems? | Y | M | Events sent from the server to the clients have a time stamp, as they have to be processed in the order that they were received. | We want to ensure that clients display an accurate representation of the state of the network, which involves receiving all of the notifications from the server and processing them in the correct order. |

| | Tactics Question | | | Design Decisions and Location | Rationale and Assumptions |
|---|---|---|---|---|---|
| | Does the system use **voting** to check that replicated components are producing the same results? The replicated components may be identical replicas, functionally redundant, or analytically redundant. | N | N/A | This is not required by the system. | N/A |
| | Does the system use **exception detection** to detect a system condition that alters the normal flow of execution—for example, system exceptions, parameter fences, parameter typing, timeouts? | Y | L | Standard Java exception management is used and all exceptions are sent to a log. Timeouts are implemented on the client side, when requests are sent to the server. | The assumption is that exceptions in Java and using timeouts are all that is needed. |
| | Can the system do a **self-test** to test itself for correct operation? | N | N/A | This was not considered in our original design. | The assumption is that monitoring and exception management will provide enough information to test for correct operation. |
| Recover from faults (preparation and repair) | Does the system employ **active redundancy** (hot spare)? In active redundancy, all nodes in a protection group (a group of nodes where one or more nodes are "active", with the remainder serving as redundant spares) receive and process identical inputs in parallel, allowing redundant spares to maintain synchronous state with the active node(s). | Y | H | Active redundancy is used in the application server and the message queue. | Active redundancy was favored over a passive approach to reduce the possibility of losing information that needs to be collected from the time servers because of server failure. This actually exceeds the requirement established in QA-3. Also, we assume there will be no common-mode failure. |

*(continues)*

| Tactics Group | Tactics Question | Supported? (Y/N) | Risk | Design Decisions and Location | Rationale and Assumptions |
|---|---|---|---|---|---|
| | Does the system employ **passive redundancy** (warm spare)? In passive redundancy, only the active members of the protection group process input traffic; one of their duties is to provide the redundant spare(s) with periodic state updates. | N | N/A | Active redundancy was favored. | N/A |
| | Does the system employ **rollback**, so that it can revert to a previously saved good state (the "rollback line") in the event of a fault? | Y | M | Transaction management is supported through the Spring framework. | Spring provides adequate support for the type of transactions required by this system. |

When the questions in Table 8.2 are used in an interview setting, we can record whether each tactic is supported by the system's architecture, according to the opinions of the architect. For example, in the table, the questions have been answered with respect to design decisions made for the FCAPS system presented in Chapter 4. Note that the answers shown in the table are rather succinct because this is an example; more detailed explanations are encouraged in real-world applications. If we are analyzing an existing system we can additionally investigate the following issues:

- Whether there are any obvious risks in the use (or nonuse) of this tactic. If the tactic has been used, we can record here how it is realized in the system (e.g., via custom code, frameworks, or other externally produced components). For example, we might note that the active redundancy tactic has been employed by replicating the application server and other critical components such as the database (as in the case study presented in Chapter 4).
- The specific design decisions made to realize the tactic and where in the code base the implementation (realization) may be found. This information is useful for auditing and architecture reconstruction purposes. Continuing the example from the previous bullet, we might probe how many replicas of the application server have been created and where these replicas are located (e.g., on the same rack in a data center, on different racks, in different data centers).
- Any rationale or assumptions made in the realization of this tactic. For example, we might assume that there will be no common-mode failure, so it is acceptable that the replicas are identical virtual machines, running on identical hardware.

While this interview-based approach might sound simplistic, it can actually be quite powerful and insightful. In your daily activities as an architect, you may not always take the time to step back and consider the bigger picture. A set of interview questions such as those shown in Table 8.2 force you to do just that. This approach is also quite efficient: A typical interview for a single quality attribute takes between 30 and 90 minutes.

A set of tactics-based questionnaires, covering the seven most important system quality attributes—availability, interoperability, modifiability, performance, security, testability, and usability—can be found in Appendix B. In addition, we have included an eighth questionnaire, on DevOps, as an example of how you can combine the other (more fundamental) questionnaires to create a new questionnaire to address a new set of quality concerns.

## 8.5 Reflective Questions

Similar to the tactics-based interviews, a number of researchers have advocated the practice of asking (and answering) reflective questions to augment the design process. The idea behind this process is that we actually think differently when we are problem-solving and when we are reflecting. For this reason, researchers have advocated a separate "reflection" activity in design that both challenges the decisions made and challenges us to examine our biases.

Architects, like all humans, are subject to bias. For example, we are subject to confirmation bias—the tendency to interpret new information in a way that confirms our preconceptions—and we are subject to anchoring bias—the tendency to rely too heavily on the first piece of information that we receive when investigating a problem, using this information to filter and judge any subsequent information. Reflective questions help to uncover such biases in a systematic way, which can lead us to revise our assumptions and hence our designs.

In their research on reflective questions, Razavian et al. have proposed that one can and should reflect on context and requirements (Are the contexts and requirements identified relevant, complete, and accurate?), design problems (Have they been properly and fully articulated?), design solutions (Are they appropriate given the requirements?), and design decisions (Are they principled and justified?). Examples of reflective questions that they propose include the following:

- Which assumptions are made? Do the assumptions affect the design problem? Do the assumptions affect the solution option? Is an assumption acceptable in a decision?
- What are the risks that certain events would happen? How do the risks cause design problems? How do the risks affect the viability of a solution? Is the risk of a decision acceptable? What can be done to mitigate the risks?
- What are the constraints imposed by the contexts? How do the constraints cause design problems? How do the constraints limit the solution options? Can any constraints be relaxed when making a decision?
- What are the contexts and the requirements of this system? What does this context mean? What are the design problems? Which are the important problems that need to be solved? What does this problem mean? Which potential solutions exist for this problem? Are there other problems to follow up in this decision?
- Which contexts can be compromised? Can a problem be framed differently? What are the solution options? Can a solution option be compromised? Are the pros and cons of each solution treated fairly? What is an optimal solution after tradeoff?

Of course, you might not employ all of these questions, and you would not employ this technique for every decision that you make. Used judiciously, however, these kinds of questions can help you to reflect mindfully on the decisions that you are making.

## 8.6 Scenario-Based Design Reviews

Comprehensive scenario-based design reviews, such as the ATAM, have typically been conducted outside the design process. The ATAM is an example of a comprehensive architecture evaluation (see the sidebar "The ATAM").

An ATAM review, as it was initially conceived, was a "milestone" review. When an architect or other key stakeholder believed that there was enough of an architecture or architecture description to analyze, an ATAM meeting could be convened. This might occur when an architectural design had been done but before much, if any, implementation had been completed. More commonly, it occurred when an existing system was in place and some stakeholders wanted an objective evaluation of the risks of the architecture before committing to it, evolving it, acquiring it, and so forth.

---

The ATAM

The *ATAM—Architecture Tradeoff Analysis Method (ATAM)* is an established method for analyzing architectures, driven by scenarios. Its purpose is to assess the consequences of architectural decisions in light of quality attribute requirements and business goals.

The ATAM brings together three groups in an evaluation:

- A trained evaluation team
- An architecture's "decision makers"
- Representatives of the architecture's stakeholders

The ATAM helps stakeholders ask the right questions to discover potentially problematic architectural decisions—that is, risks. These discovered risks can then be made the focus of mitigation activities such as further design, further analysis, prototyping, and implementation. In addition, design tradeoffs are often identified—hence the name of the method. The purpose of the ATAM is *not* to provide precise analyses: This method typically is applied in two 2-day meetings and this (relatively) short time frame does not permit a deep dive into any specific concern. Those kinds of analyses are, however, appropriate as part of the risk mitigation activities that could follow and be guided by an ATAM.

The ATAM can be used throughout the software development life cycle. For example, it can be used in the following circumstances:

- After an architecture has been specified but there is little or no code
- To evaluate potential architectural alternatives
- To evaluate the architecture of an existing system

The outputs of the ATAM evaluation are as follows:

- A concise presentation of the architecture. The architecture is presented in one hour.
- A concise articulation of the business goals for the system under scrutiny. Frequently, the business goals presented in the ATAM are being seen by some of the assembled participants for the first time and these are captured in the outputs.
- A set of prioritized quality attribute requirements, expressed as scenarios.
- A mapping of architectural decisions to quality requirements. For each quality attribute scenario examined, the architectural decisions that help to achieve it are identified and recorded.
- A set of sensitivity and tradeoff points. These architectural decisions have a marked effect on one or more quality attributes.
- A set of risks and non-risks. A *risk* is defined as an architectural decision that may lead to undesirable consequences in light of quality attribute requirements. A *non-risk* is an architectural decision that, upon analysis, is deemed safe. The identified risks form the basis of an architectural risk mitigation plan.
- A set of risk themes. The evaluation team examines the full set of discovered risks to identify overarching themes that reveal systemic weaknesses in the architecture (or perhaps even in the architecture process and team). If left untreated, these weaknesses will threaten the project's ability to meet the business goals.

There are also intangible results of an ATAM-based evaluation: a sense of community developed among the stakeholders, open communication channels between the architect and the stakeholders, a better overall understanding of the architecture and its strengths and weaknesses. While these results are difficult to measure, they are no less important than the others and often are the longest-lasting artifacts.

An ATAM evaluation takes place in four phases. The first phase (phase 0) and the final phase (phase 3) are managerial: setting up the evaluation at the start and reporting results and follow-on activities at the end. The middle phases (phases 1 and 2) are when the actual analysis takes place. The steps enacted in phases 1 and 2 are as follows:

1. Present the ATAM
2. Present the business drivers
3. Present the architecture
4. Identify the architectural approaches
5. Generate a quality attribute utility tree
6. Analyze the architectural approaches
7. Brainstorm and prioritize scenarios
8. Analyze the architectural approaches
9. Present the results

In phase 1, we enact steps 1–6 with a small, internal group of stake-holders—typically just the architect, project manager and perhaps one or two senior developers. In phase 2, we invite a larger group of stakeholders to attend—all the people who attended phase 1 plus external stakehold-ers, such as customer representatives, end-user representatives, quality assurance, operations, and so forth. In phase 2, we review steps 1–6 and enact steps 7–9.

The actual analysis takes place in step 6, where we analyze archi-tectural approaches by asking the architect to map the highest-priority scenarios, one at a time, onto the architectural approaches that have been described. During this step, the analysts ask probing questions, moti-vated by a knowledge of quality attributes, and risks are discovered and documented.

---

The idea of having a separate, distinct evaluation activity once the archi-tecture is "done" fits poorly with the way that most organizations operate today. Today, most software organizations are practicing some form of Agile or iterative development. There is no distinct monolithic "architecture phase" in Agile pro-cesses. Rather, architecture and development are co-created in a series of sprints. For example, as discussed in Chapter 2, many Agile thought leaders are promot-ing practices such as "disciplined agility at scale", the "walking skeleton", and the "scaled Agile framework", all of which embrace the idea that architectures continuously evolve in relatively small increments, addressing the most critical risks. This may be aided by developing a small proof-of-concept or *minimum viable product (MVP)*, or doing strategic prototyping.

To better align with this view of software development, a lightweight scenario-based peer review method, based on the ATAM, has been promoted. A lightweight ATAM evaluation can be conducted in a half-day meeting. It can also be carried out internally, using just project members. Of course, an external review gives more objectivity and may produce better results, but this exercise may be too costly or infeasible due to schedule or intellectual property (IP) constraints. A lightweight ATAM therefore provides a reasonable middle ground between a costly but more objective and comprehensive ATAM and doing no analysis whatsoever, or only doing ad hoc analysis.

An example schedule for a lightweight ATAM evaluation conducted by proj-ect members on their own project is given in Table 8.3.

**TABLE 8.3** A Typical Agenda for a Lightweight ATAM Evaluation

| Step | Time Allotted | Notes |
|---|---|---|
| 1. Present business drivers | 0.25 hour | The participants are expected to understand the system and its business goals and their priorities. Fifteen minutes is allocated for a brief review to ensure that these are fresh in everyone's mind and that there are no surprises. |
| 2. Present architecture | 0.5 hour | All participants are expected to be familiar with the system, so a brief overview of the architecture is presented and 1 or 2 scenarios are traced through the documented architecture views. |
| 3. Identify architectural approaches | 0.25 hour | The architecture approaches for specific quality attribute concerns are identified by the architect. This may be done as a portion of step 2. |
| 4. Generate quality attribute utility tree | 0.5 hour | Scenarios might already exist; if so, use them. A utility tree might already exist; if so, the team reviews it and updates it, if necessary. |
| 5. Analyze architectural approaches | 2.0 hours | This step—mapping the highly ranked scenarios onto the architecture—consumes the bulk of the time and can be expanded or contracted as needed. |
| 6. Present results | 0.5 hour | At the end of the evaluation, the team reviews the existing and newly discovered risks and tradeoffs and discusses priorities. |
| TOTAL | 4 hours | |

A half-day review such as this is similar, in terms of effort, to other quality assurance efforts that are typically conducted in a development project, such as code reviews, inspections, and walk-throughs. For this reason, it is easy to schedule a lightweight ATAM evaluation in a sprint, particularly in those sprints where architectural decisions are being made, challenged, or changed.

## 8.7 Architecture Description Languages

If the application that you are building has stringent quality requirements in the areas of runtime performance (latency, throughput), reliability/availability, safety, or security, then you might consider documenting your design decisions, in the form of architectural structures, in an *architecture description language (ADL)*. ADLs lend themselves to formal, automated analysis, which is precisely why we include them here. ADLs typically employ both a graphical and a (formally defined) textual notation to describe an architecture—primarily the computational (runtime) components and interactions among them—and its properties. The Unified Modeling Language (UML) is the most widely used notation for documenting architectures in industrial practice, though even it is not universally used. Few industrial projects endeavor to describe all, or even most, of their architectures in any ADL.

Some ADLs, such as AADL, strive to be formal models that have precise and decidable semantics. This regimentation means that they can be automatically checked for properties of interest, typically performance, availability, and safety, although in principle other quality attributes can be accommodated. While there is an often a steep learning curve for becoming proficient with the language and the surrounding tool suite, using a formalized ADL offers several benefits. First, an ADL forces you to document your architectural decisions, and hence to explicitly acknowledge when and where your architectural understanding is incomplete or vague. This benefit accrues with any form of documentation—it forces you to be explicit—but is especially true of ADLs. This leads to the second benefit of ADLs: They are typically accompanied by a tool suite that can analyze the architecture description for various properties at the click of a button.

So why are ADLs seldom used outside of academia? A number of possible reasons for this reluctance exist. First, it is not in our common practice. ADLs—even the UML—are typically not taught in computer science or software engineering curricula and are not well supported in most popular IDEs. Second, ADLs are perceived as being challenging to use and not user-friendly, requiring both a large up-front effort and a large continuing effort to maintain. This point is, perhaps, the most significant one: Architects and programmers generally do not want to maintain a second, parallel base of knowledge about their systems. For some systems, this may be the right choice. For others—typically those with stringent and uncompromising quality attribute requirements—having a separate and separately analyzable representation of the design might be the most prudent course of action. In civil engineering, by way of contrast, no project may be approved for construction without first being represented in a separate analyzable document.

## 8.8 Summary

No one would consider fielding code that they had not tested—yet architects and programmers regularly commit to (implement) architectural decisions that have not been analyzed. Why the dichotomy? Surely, if testing code is important, then "testing" the design decisions you have made is an order of magnitude more important, as these decisions often have long-term, system-wide, and significant impacts.

The most important message of this chapter is that design and analysis are not really separate activities. Every important design decision that you make should be analyzed. A variety of techniques can be applied to do this continuously, in a relatively disruption-free manner, as part of the process of designing and evolving a system.

The interesting questions are not whether to analyze, but rather how much to analyze and when. Analysis is inherent in doing good design, and it should be a continuous process.

## 8.9   Further Reading

The sets of architectural tactics used here have been documented in L. Bass, P. Clements, and R. Kazman, *Software Architecture in Practice* (3rd ed.), Addison-Wesley, 2012. The availability tactics were first created in J. Scott and R. Kazman, "Realizing and Refining Architectural Tactics: Availability", CMU/ SEI-2009-TR-006, 2009.

The idea of reflective questions was first introduced in M. Razavian, A. Tang, R. Capilla, and P. Lago, "In Two Minds: How Reflections Influence Software Architecture Design Thinking", VU University Amsterdam, Tech. Rep. 2015-001, April 2015. The idea that software designers satisfice—that is, they look for a "good enough", as opposed to an optimal, solution—has been discussed in A. Tang and H. van Vliet, "Software Designers Satisfice", *European Conference on Software Architecture (ECSA 2015)*, 2015.

The ATAM was comprehensively described in P. Clements, R. Kazman, and M. Klein, *Evaluating Software Architectures: Methods and Case Studies*, Addison-Wesley, 2001. The lightweight ATAM was first presented in L. Bass, P. Clements, and R. Kazman, *Software Architecture in Practice* (3rd ed.), Addison-Wesley, 2012. In addition, ATAM-style peer reviews have been described in F. Bachmann, "Give the Stakeholders What They Want: Design Peer Reviews the ATAM Style", *Crosstalk*, November/December 2011.

Architecture description languages have a history almost as long as the history of software architecture itself. The most widely used ADL in practice is AADL (Architecture Analysis and Design Language), which is described in P. Feiler and D. Gluch, *Model-Based Engineering with AADL: An Introduction to the SAE Architecture Analysis & Design Language*, Addison-Wesley, 2013. An overview of, and analysis of industrial requirements for, ADLs can be found in I. Malavolta, P. Lago, H. Muccini, P. Pelliccione, and A. Tang, "What Industry Needs from Architectural Languages: A Survey", *IEEE Transactions on Software Engineering*, 39(6):869–891, June 2013.

# 9

# The Architecture Design Process in the Organization

Chapter 1 introduced a set of software architecture life-cycle activities—things like collecting requirements, designing the architecture, and evaluating and implementing the architecture. We called these "life-cycle activities" because we recognize that not all organizations do all of them; those that do them might do them in different ways, and might embed them into different life-cycle models and organizational contexts. This chapter takes a closer look at those aspects of software development and considers how architecture design fits in with them.

## 9.1 Architecture Design and the Development Life Cycle

Two important phases that occur in most development projects, as illustrated in Figure 9.1, are *pre-sales* and *development and operations*.

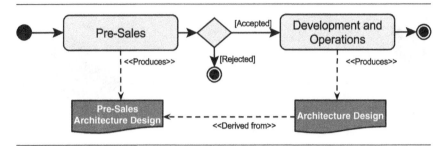

**FIGURE 9.1** The two major phases of project development

- During the pre-sales phase, the scope of the project is established and a business case is established. Although we call this phase "pre-sales", it occurs in every organization, whether they engage in "sales" or not. One frequent and important product of this phase is an estimation of the cost and duration of the project. This estimation is used by the customers (or funders) to decide if they want to pursue the project.
- The development and operations phase occurs when the pre-sales proposal has been accepted by the customer. Development can be performed following different methodologies including Agile, RUP, or TSP. Once the system (or part of it) is developed, it is put into operation. Newer approaches such as DevOps intend to reduce the gap that is usually present between development and operation.

Architectural design plays an important role in these two major phases, as we will now discuss.

### 9.1.1 Architecture Design During Pre-Sales

In many types of development projects, but particularly in the context of custom software development, organizations typically need to provide an initial estimate of the time and cost of the project during the pre-sales phase. Frequently the pre-sales activities must be performed in a short time period, and the information that is available to inform this process is always limited. For example, typically only high-level requirements or features (rather than detailed use cases) are available at this phase.

The problem with limited information is that the estimate that is produced frequently has a lot of uncertainty, as illustrated by the *cone of uncertainty* depicted in Figure 9.2. The cone of uncertainty refers to the uncertainty surrounding estimates in a project, typically those of cost and schedule, but also risk. All of these estimates get better as a project progresses, and the cone narrows. When the project is done, uncertainty is zero. The issue for any development methodology is how to narrow the cone of uncertainty earlier in the project's life cycle.

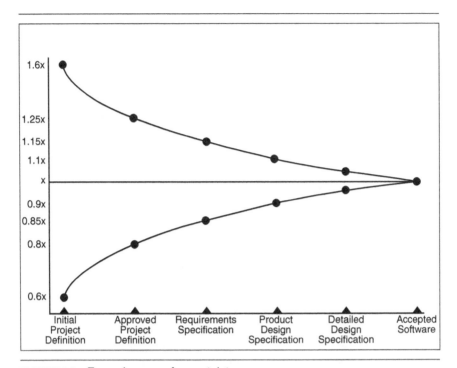

**FIGURE 9.2** Example cone of uncertainty

Architectural practices can be applied in the pre-sales phase to help reduce the cone of uncertainty:

- Architectural drivers can be identified in the pre-sales phase. Even if it may be complicated to describe detailed quality attribute scenarios at this point, the most important quality attributes with initial measures and constraints should be identified.
- ADD can be used to produce an initial architecture that is then used as the basis for early cost and schedule estimates.
- Sketches of this initial architecture are useful for communication with the customer. They are also useful as a basis to perform lightweight evaluations of this initial design.

Generating an initial architecture allows estimation to be performed using the "standard components" technique. Standard components are a type of proxy; they include web pages, business rules, and reports, among other things. When estimating with standard components, companies typically build historic databases that contain, for example, measurements and size data for components that have been built into previously developed systems. To estimate with standard components, you need to identify the components that will be required for the problem that you are trying to solve, and then use historical data (or some other technique such as Wideband Delphi) to estimate the size of these components. The total size can then be translated into effort, and these estimates can be rolled up to produce a project-level time and cost estimate.

Identifying the components that are required to create estimates with this technique can be achieved in a short time frame through the use of ADD. This approach is similar to what we just recommended for the design of greenfield systems:

- The goal of your first design iteration should be to address the concern of establishing an initial overall structure for the application. The reference architecture, if you employ one, dictates the types of standard components that will be used in the estimation. At this point, the most relevant technologies to use in the project can also be selected, particularly if your historical data is tied to specific technologies.
- The goal of your second design iteration should be to identify components to support all of the functionality that needs to be considered for the estimation. As opposed to what we discussed for the design of greenfield systems, when designing to produce an estimate, you need to consider more than just primary functionality. To identify the standard components, you need to consider *all* of the important functional requirements that are part of the scope and map them to the structure that you defined in the first iteration. Doing so ensures you will have a more accurate estimation.

This technique will help you estimate costs and schedule for meeting the most important functional requirements. At this point, however, you will likely not have taken quality attributes into account. As a consequence, you should perform a few more iterations focusing on where you will make design decisions to address the driving quality attributes. If the time available to perform the pre-sales process is limited, you will not be able to design it in much detail, so the decisions that you should take here are the ones that will have a significant impact in the estimate. Examples include identifying redundant hardware or additional standard components to address quality attributes such as performance, availability, and security.

When this technique is used in the pre-sales process, an initial architecture design is produced—the pre-sales architecture design (see Figure 9.1). If the project proposal is accepted by the customer and the project proceeds, this initial architecture can become one of the bases for a contract. This architecture should be used as a starting point in the subsequent architecture design activities that are performed during the Development and Operation phase of the project. In this case, the roadmap for designing brownfield systems (discussed in Section 3.3.3) can be used.

The preliminary documentation produced for this initial architecture can also be included as part of the technical proposal that is provided to the customer. Finally, this initial architecture design can be evaluated, preferably before estimation occurs. This can be performed using a technique such as the lightweight ATAM presented in Section 8.6.

## 9.1.2   Architecture Design During Development and Operation

The development of a software system can be performed using different methodologies. Architectural design, however, is performed independently of the chosen development methodology. For this reason, a design method such as ADD can be used in conjunction with different development methodologies. We now discuss the relationship between architectural design and some development methodologies that are commonly used in industry.

### 9.1.2.1   Agile Methods

The relationship between software architecture and agility has been the subject of some debate over the past decade. Although we believe, and much research has shown, that architectural practices and Agile practices are actually well aligned, this position has not always been universally accepted.

Agile practices, according to the original Agile Manifesto emphasize, "Individuals and interactions over processes and tools, working software over comprehensive documentation, customer collaboration over contract negotiation, and responding to change over following a plan". None of these values is inherently in conflict with architectural practices. So why has the belief arisen—at least in some circles—that the two sets of practices are somehow incompatible? The crux of the matter is the one principle on which Agile practices and architectural practices differ.

The original creators of the Agile Manifesto described 12 principles behind the manifesto. While 11 of these are fully compatible with architectural practices, one of them is not: "The best architectures, requirements, and designs emerge from self-organizing teams". While this principle may have held true for small and perhaps even medium-sized projects, we are unaware of any cases where it has been successful in large projects, particularly those with complex requirements and distributed development. The heart of the problem is this: Software architecture design is "up-front" work. You could always just start a project by coding and doing minimal or no up-front analysis or design. This is what we call the *emergent approach*, as shown in Figure 9.3b. In some cases—small systems, throw-away prototypes, systems where you have little idea of the customer's requirements—this may, in fact, be the optimal decision. At the opposite extreme, you could attempt to collect all the requirements up front, and from that synthesize the ideal architecture, which you would then implement, test, and deploy. This so-called *Big Design Up Front* approach (BDUF; Figure 9.3a) is usually associated with the classic Waterfall model of software development. The Waterfall model has fallen out of favor over the past decade due to its complexity and rigidity, which led to many well-documented cases of cost overruns, schedule overruns, and customer dissatisfaction. With respect to architectural design, the downside of the BDUF approach is that it can end up producing an extensively documented but untested design that may not be appropriate. This occurs because problems in the design are often discovered late and may require a lot of rework, or the original design may end up being ignored and the true architecture is not documented.

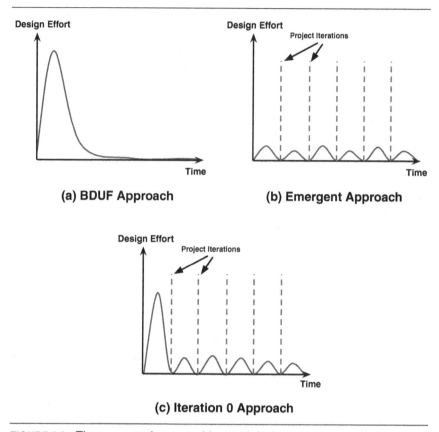

**FIGURE 9.3** Three approaches to architectural design

Clearly, neither of these extremes makes sense for most real-world projects, where some (but not all) of the requirements are well understood up front but there is also a risk of doing too much too soon and hence becoming locked in to a solution that will inevitably need to be modified, at significant cost. So the truly interesting question is this: How much up-front work, in terms of requirements analysis, risk mitigation, and architecture, should a project do? Boehm and Turner have presented evidence arguing that there is no single right answer to this question, but that you can find a "sweet spot" for any given project. The "right" amount of project work depends on several factors, with the most dominant being project size, but other important factors include requirements complexity, requirements volatility (related to the precedentedness of the domain), and degree of distribution of development.

So how do architects achieve the right amount of agility? How do they find the right balance between up-front work and technical debt leading to rework?

For small, simple projects, no up-front work on architecture is justifiable. It is easy and relatively inexpensive to turn on a dime and refactor. In projects where there is some understanding of the requirements, begin by performing a few ADD iterations. These design iterations can focus on choosing the major architectural patterns (including a reference architecture, if one is appropriate) and frameworks. This is the *iteration 0* approach depicted in Figure 9.3c. This will help to structure the project, define work assignments and team formation, and address the most critical quality attributes. If and when requirements change—particularly if these are driving quality attribute requirements—adopt a practice of Agile experimentation, where spikes are used to address new requirements. A *spike* is a time-boxed task that is created to answer a technical question or gather information; it is not intended to lead to a finished product. Spikes are developed in a separate branch and, if successful, merged into the main branch of the code. In this way, emerging requirements can be welcomed and managed without being too disruptive to the overall process of development.

Agile architecture practices, however, help to tame some of the complexity, narrowing the cone of uncertainty and hence reducing project risk. A reference architecture defines families of technology components and their relationships. It guides integration and indicates where abstraction should be built into the architecture, to help reduce rework when a new technology (from within a family) replaces an existing one. Agile spikes allow prototypes to be built quickly and to "fail fast", thereby guiding the eventual selection of technologies to be included on the main development branch.

### 9.1.2.2 Rational Unified Process

The Rational Unified Process (RUP) is a software development process framework that puts a strong emphasis on architecture. In the RUP (which we also discussed in Section 7.3), development projects are divided in four major phases, which are carried out sequentially; within these phases, a number of iterations are performed. The four phases of the RUP are as follows:

- *Inception.* In this first phase, the goal is to achieve concurrence among project stakeholders. During this phase the scope of the project and a business architecture are defined. Also, a candidate architecture is established. This phase is the equivalent to the pre-sales phase discussed previously.
- *Elaboration.* In the second phase, the goal is to baseline the architecture of the system and to produce architectural prototypes.
- *Construction.* In the third phase, the goal is to incrementally develop the system from the architecture that was defined in the previous phase.
- *Transition.* In the fourth phase, the goal is to ensure that the system is ready for delivery. The system is transitioned from the development environment to its final operation environment.

We could argue that, from the elaboration phase until the end of the project, RUP intrinsically follows the iteration 0 approach described earlier. RUP also provides some guidance with respect to architectural design, although this guidance is far less detailed than that offered by ADD. As a consequence, ADD can be used as a complement to the RUP. ADD iterations can be performed during inception to establish the candidate architecture by following the approach described in Section 9.1.1. Furthermore, during the elaboration phase, the initial architecture is taken as a starting point for performing additional design iterations until an architecture that can be baselined is produced. During construction, additional ADD iterations may be performed as part of the development iterations.

### 9.1.2.3   Team Software Process

The *Team Software Process (TSP)* is a development process that strongly emphasizes quality and measurement. A TSP software project proceeds through a series of development cycles, where each cycle begins with a planning process called a launch and ends with a closing process called a postmortem. Within each development cycle, activities belonging to different phases can be performed. These phases include requirements (REQ), high-level design (HLD), implementation (IMPL), and testing (TEST). The REQ phase of TSP focuses on producing a complete system requirements specification (SRS) document. The main goal of the HLD phase is to produce a high-level design that will guide product implementation. This high-level design must define the components (i.e., modules) that constitute the system and that have to be designed and developed independently following the *Personal Software Process (PSP)* in the IMPL phase. Finally, the TEST phase focuses on performing integration and system testing and on preparing the delivery of the system. Note that the life-cycle model of a particular project (Waterfall, incremental) is defined by the phases that are performed in each development cycle: An iterative project will typically include activities from all four phases in a single development cycle.

The TSP does not give full consideration to software architecture development. For instance, none of the roles defined in the TSP is that of software architect. There is also no emphasis on quality attributes in the REQ phase. Furthermore, the process script for the HLD phase (see Table 9.1) does not provide detailed guidance on how to design the system architecture. These issues can, however, be addressed by introducing ADD, and other architectural practices, into TSP.

ADD can be used in the context of TSP in a straightforward way. In step 1 of the HLD script, ADD can be used to produce the overall product design concept, similar to what was discussed for the pre-sales process. Furthermore, in each development cycle, one or more ADD iterations can be performed (steps 4 and 5 of the HLD script). Also, the HLD phase should consider a separation between architectural design and element interaction design (discussed in Section 2.2.2). A TSP development cycle can involve a few ADD iterations followed by the element interaction design activities that include identification of elements and their interfaces. These interfaces are later used in the development phase (IMPL) for performing detailed design and development of the elements.

**TABLE 9.1**  Summary of TSP High-Level Design (HLD) Script Steps

| Step | Activities | Summary |
|---|---|---|
| 1 | Structural design | An overall product design concept is produced. It includes the system architectural components and the product components, principal functions, and interfaces. |
| 2 | Development strategy | A development strategy is established. The strategy includes the sequence of component development and integration and the reuse and testing strategies. |
| 3 | High-level design strategy | In this step, a decision is made about whether to design the system in a single design cycle or in multiple cycles (focusing, for example, on one layer at a time). |
| 4 | First cycle design | The requirements are reviewed and the class definitions, relationships, and transition diagrams are produced. |
| 5 | Subsequent design cycles | Design issues from previous cycles are assessed and the current design is reviewed. Additional class definitions, relationships, and transition diagrams are produced. |
| 6 | Integration and system test strategies | Strategies for testing are established. |
| 7 | System design specification (SDS) | A design document is produced. |
| 8 | Design walkthrough | A walk-through of the high-level design is performed with different stakeholders. |
| 9 | Design inspection | The materials produced as a result of this phase are inspected. |
| 10 | SDS baseline | The design specification is put into a baseline. |
| 11 | Postmortem | A postmortem of the phase is performed. |

#### 9.1.2.4  DevOps

*DevOps* is a natural outgrowth of the Agile mindset. DevOps refers to a set of practices that help achieve continuous delivery of software. Such practices are intended to reduce the time between making a change to a system and the change being placed into normal production, while ensuring high quality. This term intentionally blurs the distinction between "development" and "operations". While DevOps is not inherently tied to architectural practices, if architects do not consider DevOps as they design, build, and evolve the system, then critical activities such as continuous build integration, automated test execution, high availability, and scalable performance will be more challenging and less efficient. By embracing DevOps, small iterations are supported and encouraged, creating an environment where

Agile spikes are easy to create, deploy, and test, thereby providing crucial feedback to the architect.

For example, a tightly coupled architecture can become a barrier to continuous integration because even small changes may require a rebuild of the entire system, which limits the number of builds possible in a day. To fully automate testing, the system needs to provide architectural (system-wide) test capabilities such as interfaces to record, play back, and control system state. To support high availability, the system must be self-monitoring, requiring architectural capabilities such as self-test, ping/echo, heartbeat, monitor, hot spares, and so forth.

In large-scale systems, DevOps can be achieved only with architectural support. Any ad hoc or manual process would put the growth and success of such a system at risk. Adopting the DevOps approach requires a small change in the mindset of an architect. Instead of just designing the system, you now need to think about the design of the entire deployment pipeline. Is the pipeline easy to change, and can these changes be deployed at the click of a button? Is the pipeline easy to scale? Is it easy to test? Fortunately, there are good answers to all of these questions, and they do not require a distinct mindset or strategy. ADD can help design a system to achieve DevOps goals, in exactly the same ways and employing exactly the same design primitives as in design for any other driver. The different aspects that need to be considered to allow DevOps to be performed successfully can be included as part of the system drivers, either as architectural concerns or as quality attributes. The design concepts that help us to achieve modifiability or testability or scalability or high availability in a system can also be applied to the deployment pipeline. To slightly misquote Gertrude Stein, "Architecture is architecture is architecture".

## 9.2   Organizational Aspects

In addition to the choice of a specific development method and the introduction of a design method such as ADD into this method, other aspects of the design process can be supported by a software development organization to facilitate design activities. Here we briefly discuss some of these aspects.

### 9.2.1   Designing as an Individual or as a Team

In large and complex projects, it seems straightforward that an architecture team should be responsible for performing the design. Even in smaller projects, however, you may find that having more than one person participate in the design process yields important advantages. You can decide if only one person is the architect and the others are observers (as in the practice of pair programming) or if the group actively collaborates on design decisions (although even here we recommend that you have one lead architect).

There are various benefits from this approach:

- Two (or more) heads can be better than one, particularly if the design problem that you are trying to solve is different from ones that you have addressed before.
- Different people can have different areas of expertise that are useful in the design of the architecture. For example, you might have distinct software and infrastructure architects, or people who specialize in different domains or different types of design concepts.
- Design decisions are reflected upon and reviewed as they are being made and, as a consequence, can be corrected immediately.
- Less experienced people can participate in the design process, which can be an excellent mentoring practice.

You should, however, be aware of certain difficulties with this approach:

- Design by committee can be complicated if agreement is not achieved in a reasonable time frame. The search for consensus can lead to "analysis paralysis".
- The cost of design increases and, in many cases, the time for design also increases.
- Managing the logistics can be complex, because this approach requires the regular availability of the group of people.
- You may encounter personality and political conflicts, resulting in resentment or hurt feelings or in design decisions being heavily influenced by the person who shouts longest and loudest ("design by bullying").

### 9.2.2 Using a Design Concepts Catalog in Your Organization

Design concepts are used in the design process to satisfy drivers (see Section 2.5). In general, drivers can be seen as recurring design problems. Whether it is the concern of structuring an application, allocating functionality, or satisfying a particular quality attribute, these drivers have most certainly been addressed in other systems previously. Furthermore, people have taken the time to document ways to address these design problems or to develop components that serve this purpose. As we saw in Section 3.4, the selection of design concepts is one of the most challenging aspects of the design process. This problem is exacerbated by the fact that information is scattered in many places: Architects usually need to consult several pattern and tactics catalogs and do extensive research to find the design concepts that can be considered and used.

One possible way to resolve this issue is the creation of *design concepts catalogs*. These catalogs group collections of design concepts for particular application domains. Such catalogs are intended to facilitate the identification and selection of design concepts when performing design. They are also useful in enhancing consistency in the designs across the organization. For example, designers may be required to use the technologies in a particular catalog as much as possible because this facilitates estimation, reduces learning curves, and may lead to opportunities for reuse. Catalogs can also be useful for training purposes.

An example of a design concepts catalog appears in Appendix A. This catalog is oriented toward the design of enterprise applications. A similar catalog for the Big Data domain could be created from the technology families and specific technologies illustrated in Figure 2.10 (Section 2.5.5).

The creation of these catalogs involves considerable effort and, once created, they should be maintained as new design concepts, and particularly new technologies, are introduced or removed in the organization. This effort is worthwhile, however, as these catalogs are a valuable organizational asset.

## 9.3  Summary

In this chapter we discussed how ADD can be used in relation to several organizational aspects. ADD can be used from the project's inception, when a pre-sales proposal is developed, to facilitate estimation using standard components. As the project evolves, ADD can be used in conjunction with any modern software development life-cycle method. In general, ADD is a valuable complement to life-cycle methods that do not provide detailed guidance on how to perform architectural design.

We also briefly reviewed some related concerns, such as the composition of the design team and the development of organizational assets, such as a design concepts catalog, that are useful during the design process.

## 9.4  Further Reading

Organizational structure and its influences on software architecture are addressed in the field of enterprise architecture management. Enterprise architecture frameworks are discussed in F. Ahlemann et al. (Eds.), *Strategic Enterprise Architecture Management: Challenges, Best Practices, and Future Developments*, Springer-Verlag Berlin Heidelberg, 2012.

A nice set of articles looking at the relationship between architecture and Agile methods can be found in the April 2010 *IEEE Software* magazine special issue on this topic.

A number of studies have looked at how architecture and agility methods complement and support each other, such as S. Bellomo, I. Gorton, and

R. Kazman, "Insights from 15 Years of ATAM Data: Towards Agile Architecture", *IEEE Software*, September/October 2015, and S. Bellomo, R. Nord, and I. Ozkaya, "A Study of Enabling Factors for Rapid Fielding: Combined Practices to Balance Speed and Stability", *Proceedings of ICSE 2013*, 982–991, 2013.

Barry Boehm and Richard Turner have taken an empirical look at the topic of the relationship between agility and "discipline" (not just architecture) in their book *Balancing Agility and Discipline: A Guide for the Perplexed* (Boston: Addison-Wesley, 2004).

The practice of creating architectural "spikes" as a means of resolving uncertainty in Agile sprints is discussed in T. C. N. Graham, R. Kazman, and C. Walmsley, "Agility and Experimentation: Practical Techniques for Resolving Architectural Tradeoffs", *Proceedings of the 29th International Conference on Software Engineering (ICSE 29)*, (Minneapolis, MN), May 2007. A general discussion of spikes can be found at https://www.scrumalliance.org/community/articles/2013/march/spikes-and-the-effort-to-grief-ratio.

Many practitioners and researchers have thought deeply about how Agile methods and architectural practices fit together. Some of the best examples of this thinking can be found in the following sources:

- S. Brown. *Software Architecture for the Developers.* LeanPub, 2013.
- J. Bloomberg. *The Agile Architecture Revolution.* Wiley CIO, 2013.
- Dean Leffingwell. "Scaled Agile Framework". http://scaledagileframework.com/
- A. Cockburn. "Walking Skeleton". http://alistair.cockburn.us/Walking+skeleton
- "Manifesto for Agile Software Development". http://agilemanifesto.org/
- Scott Ambler and Mark Lines. "Scaling Agile Software Development: Disciplined Agility at Scale". http://disciplinedagileconsortium.org/Resources/Documents/ScalingAgileSoftwareDevelopment.pdf

An extensive treatment of estimation techniques, including estimation using standard components, is given in S. McConnell, *Software Estimation: Demystifying the Black Art*, Microsoft Press, 2006.

An overview of the Team Software Process can be found in W. Humphrey, *The Team Software Process[SM] (TSP[SM])*, Technical Report CMU/SEI-2000-TR-023, November 2000. Extensive details about TSP can be found in the different books written by Humphrey about this process.

The integration of ADD 2.0 (as well as other architecture development methods) with RUP, is discussed in R. Kazman, P. Kruchten, R. Nord, and J. Tomayko, "Integrating Software-Architecture-Centric Methods into the Rational Unified Process", Technical Report CMU/SEI-2004-TR-011, July 2004.

There are now several excellent books on the topic of DevOps, such as L. Bass, I. Weber, and L. Zhu, *DevOps: A Software Architect's Perspective,* Addison-Wesley, 2015. A set of architectural tactics for DevOps was described in H-M Chen, R. Kazman, S. Haziyev, V. Kropov, and D. Chtchourov,

"Architectural Support for DevOps in a Neo-Metropolis BDaaS Platform", *IEEE 34th Symposium on Reliable Distributed Systems Workshop (SRDSW),* Montreal, Canada, September 2015.

Considerable attention has been given to the problem of architecture knowledge representation and management. For a good overview of this area, see P. Kruchten, P. Lago, and H. Van Vliet, "Building Up and Reasoning About Architectural Knowledge", in *Quality of Software Architectures,* Springer, 2006. For a perspective on tools for architecture knowledge management, see A. Tang, P. Avgeriou, A. Jansen, R. Capilla, and M. Ali Babar, "A Comparative Study of Architecture Knowledge Management Tools", *Journal of Systems and Software,* 83(3):352–370, 2010.

# 10

# Final Words

In this chapter we reflect, once again, on the nature of design and why we need methods for design. This is, after all, the major point of this book! And we leave you with a few words about where to go with the information and skills that you have gleaned from reading this book.

## 10.1 On the Need for Methods

Given that you have prevailed and reached this final chapter, we can assume that you are committed to being a *professional* software architect. Being a professional means that you can perform (at least) adequately and repeatedly in all sorts of contexts. To achieve this level of performance, you need *methods*.

We all need methods when we are performing complex tasks that have serious consequences if we get them wrong. Consider this: Jet pilots and surgeons are two of the most highly trained groups of professionals in the world, and yet they use checklists and standardized procedures for every important task that they perform. Why? Because the consequences of making a mistake are serious. You probably will not be designing the architectures for systems that have life-and-death consequences. Even so, the systems that you do design, particularly if they are large and complex, may very well have consequences for the health and well-being of your organization. If you are designing a throwaway prototype or a trivial system, perhaps an explicit architecture design step may be omitted. If you are designing the *n*th variant of a system that you have created over and over in the past, perhaps architecture design is little more than a cut-and-paste from your prior experiences.

But if the system you are charged with creating or evolving is nontrivial and if there is *risk* associated with its creation, then you owe it to yourself, you owe it to your organization, and you owe it to your profession to do the best job that you can in this most critical step in the software development life cycle. To achieve that goal, you need a method. Methods help to ensure uniformity, consistency, and completeness. Methods help you take the right steps and ask the right questions.

Of course, no method can substitute for proper training and education. No one would trust a novice pilot at the controls of a 787 or a first-year medical student wielding a scalpel in an operating theater, armed only with a method or a checklist. A method, however, is a key to producing high-quality results repeatedly. And this is, after all, what we all desire as software engineering professionals.

Fred Books, writing about the design process, said:

> Any systematization of the design process is a great step forward compared to "Let's just start coding, or building". It provides clear steps for planning a design project. It furnishes clearly definable milestones for planning a schedule and for judging progress. It suggests project organization and staffing. It helps communication within the design team, giving everyone a single vocabulary for the activities. It wonderfully helps communication between the team and its manager, and between the manager and other stakeholders. It is readily teachable to novices. It tells novices facing their first design assignments where to begin.

Design is just too important to be left to chance. And there needs to be a better way of getting good at design than "shoot yourself in the foot repeatedly". As the Nobel Prize–winning scientist Herbert Simon wrote in 1969, "Design . . . is the core of all professional training; it is the principal mark that distinguishes the professions from the sciences. Schools of engineering, as well as schools of architecture, business, education, law, and medicine, are all centrally concerned with the process of design". Simon went on to say that lack of professional competence is caused by the relative neglect of design in universities' curricula. This trend is, we are happy to note, gradually reversing, but nearly 50 years later it is still a cause for concern.

In this book we have provided you with a road-tested method—ADD 3.0—for doing architectural design. Methods are useful in that they provide guidance for the novice and reassurance for the expert. Like any good method, ADD 3.0 has a set of steps, and these steps have been updated somewhat from prior versions of ADD. But just as important, we have focused on the broader architecture life cycle and shown how some changes to the design process can help make your life as an architect better, and provide you with better outcomes. For example, we have expanded the set of inputs that you need to think about to include things like design purpose and architectural concerns. This broader view helps you create an architecture that not only meets your customer's requirements, but also is aligned with the business needs of your team and your organization. In addition, we have shown that design can and should be guided by a "design concepts catalog"—a corpus of reusable architectural knowledge consisting of reference architectures, patterns, tactics, and externally developed components such as frameworks and technology families. By cataloging these concepts, design can be made more predictable and repeatable. Finally, we have argued that design should be documented, perhaps informally in sketches, and should be accompanied by a consistent practice of analyzing the decisions made.

If we are to conceive of ourselves as software engineers, we need to take the title of "engineer" seriously. No mechanical or electrical or structural engineer would commit significant resources to a design that was not based on sound principles and components, or that was not analyzed and documented. We think that software engineering in general, and software architecture specifically, should strive for similar goals. We are not "artistes", for whom creativity is paramount; we are engineers, so predictability and repeatability should be our most cherished goal.

## 10.2  Next Steps

Where should you go from here? We see four answers to this question. One answer focuses on what you can do as an individual to hone your skills and experience as an architect. The second answer revolves around how you might engage your colleagues to think more consciously about architecture design. The third answer is where your organization can go with a more explicit commitment to architecture design. And the fourth answer is about how you can contribute to your community, and to the larger community of software architects.

Our advice to you, as an individual, about how to proceed is simple: *practice*. Like any other complex skill worth having, your skill as an architect will not come immediately, but your confidence should increase steadily. "Fake it till you make it" is the best advice that we can give. Having a method that you can consult, and a ready supply of common design concepts, gives you a solid foundation on which to "fake it" and learn.

To help you practice your skills and to engage your colleagues, we have developed an architecture game. This game, which is called "Smart Decisions", can be found at http://www.smartdecisionsgame.com. It simulates the architecture design process using ADD 3.0 and promotes learning about it in a fun, pressure-free way. The game is currently focused on the Big Data Analytics application domain, similar to the extended design example in Chapter 5, but it can be easily adapted to other application domains.

You might also think about next steps to be taken in your organization. You can be an agent for change. Even if your company does not "believe in" architecture, you can still practice many of the ideas embodied in this book and in ADD. Ensure that your requirements are clear by insisting on response goals for your requirements. Even when facing tight deadlines and schedule pressures, try to get agreement on the major architectural design concepts being employed. Do quick, informal design reviews with colleagues, huddled around a whiteboard, and ask yourself reflective questions. None of these "next steps" needs to be daunting or hugely time-consuming. And we believe—and our industrial experience has shown—that they will be self-reinforcing. Better designs will lead to better outcomes, which will lead you and your group and your organization to want to do more of the same.

Finally, you can contribute to your local software engineering community, and even to the worldwide community of software architects. You could, for example, play the architecture game in a local software engineering meetup and then share your experiences. You could contribute case studies about your successes and failures as an architect with real-world projects. We strongly believe that example is the best way to teach and while we have provided three case studies in this book, more is always better. Self-publishing is easy in today's web.

Happy architecting!

---

## 10.3   Further Reading

The long quotation by Fred Books in this chapter comes from his thought-provoking book *The Design of Design: Essays from a Computer Scientist,* Pearson, 2010.

Many of the ideas in this chapter, in this book, and in the field of software architecture in general can be traced back to Herbert Simon's seminal book on the science of design: *The Sciences of the Artificial*, MIT Press, 1969.

# A Design Concepts
# Catalog

This chapter presents an excerpt from a catalog that groups design concepts that are associated with the domain of enterprise applications, such as the one presented in the case study in Chapter 4. As opposed to traditional catalogs that list just a single type of design concept, such as pattern catalogs, the catalog presented here groups different varieties of related design concepts. In this case, the catalog includes a selection of reference architectures, deployment patterns, design patterns, tactics, and externally developed components (frameworks). Also, the design concepts that are included in this catalog are gathered from different sources, reflecting what occurs in real-life design. The design concepts are presented in a very succinct way, and the reader looking for more detail should refer to the original sources using the references provided at the end of the chapter.

## A.1  Reference Architectures

Reference architectures provide a blueprint for structuring an application (see Section 2.5.1). This section is based on the catalog in the *Microsoft Application Architecture Guide*.

## A.1.1 Web Applications

This web application is typically initiated from a web browser that communicates with a server using the HTTP protocol. The bulk of the application resides on the server, and its architecture is typically composed of three layers: the presentation, business, and data layers. The presentation layer contains modules that are responsible for managing user interaction. The business layer contains modules that handle aspects related to the business logic. The data layer contains modules that manage data that is stored either locally or remotely. In addition, certain functionality that is common to modules across the layers is organized as cross-cutting concerns. This cross-cutting functionality includes aspects related to security, logging, and exception management. Figure A.1 presents the components associated with the modules in web applications.

The following table summarizes the responsibilities of the components present in this reference architecture:

| Component Name | Responsibility |
| --- | --- |
| Browser | A web browser running on the client machine. |
| User interface | These components are responsible for receiving user interactions and presenting information to the users. They contain UI elements such as buttons and text fields. |
| UI process logic | These components are responsible for managing the control flow of the application's use cases. They are responsible for other aspects such as data validation, orchestrating interactions with the business logic, and providing data coming from the business layer to the user interface components. |
| Application facade | This component is optional. It provides a simplified interface (a facade) to the business logic components. |
| Business workflow | These components are responsible for managing (long-running) business processes, which may involve the execution of multiple use cases. |
| Business logic | These components are responsible for retrieving and processing application data and applying business rules on this data. |
| Business entities | These components represent the entities from the business domain and their associated business logic. |
| Data access | These components encapsulate persistence mechanisms and provide common operations used to retrieve and store information. |
| Helpers and utilities | These components contain functionality common to other modules in the data layer but not specific to any of them. |
| Service agents | These components abstract communication mechanisms used to transfer data to external services. |
| Security | These components include cross-cutting functionality that handles security aspects such as authorization and authentication. |

| Component Name | Responsibility |
|---|---|
| Operation management | These components include cross-cutting functionality such as exception management, logging, and instrumentation and validation. |
| Communication | These components include cross-cutting functionality that handles communication mechanisms across layers and physical tiers. |

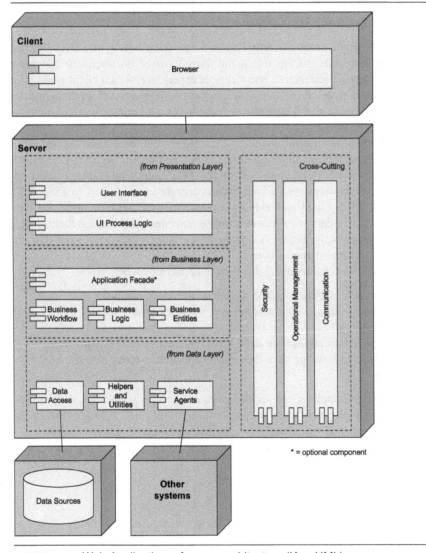

**FIGURE A.1** Web Application reference architecture (Key: UML)

You should consider using this type of application when:

- You do not require a rich user interface.
- You do not want to deploy the application by installing anything on the client machine
- You require portability of the user interface.
- Your application needs to be accessible over the Internet.
- You want to use a minimum of client-side resources.

## A.1.2   Rich Client Applications

Rich client applications are installed and run on a user's machine. Because the application runs on the user's machine, its user interface can provide a high-performance, interactive, and rich user experience. A rich client application may operate in stand-alone, connected, occasionally connected, or disconnected mode. When connected, it typically communicates with remote services provided by other applications.

Rich client application modules are structured in three main layers or in a cross-cutting grouping, similar to a web application (see Section A.1.1). Rich client applications can be "thin" or "thick." Thin-client applications consist primarily of presentation logic, which obtains user data and sends it to a server for processing. Thick-client applications contain business and data logic and typically connect to a data storage server only to exchange information that needs to be persisted remotely. Figure A.2 presents the components associated with the modules in rich client applications.

You should consider using this type of application when:

- You want to deploy your application on the users' machines.
- You want your application to support intermittent or no network connectivity.
- You want your application to be highly interactive and responsible.
- You want to leverage the user's machine resources (such as a graphics card).

Since these applications are deployed on the user's machine, they are less portable and deployment and updating is more complicated. A range of technologies to facilitate their installation are available, however.

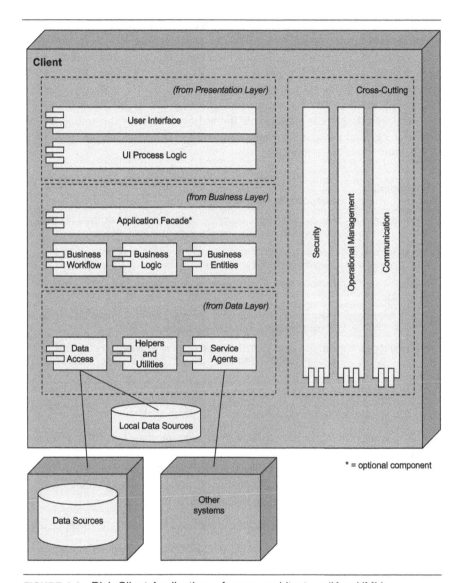

**FIGURE A.2**   Rich Client Application reference architecture (Key: UML)

## A.1.3   Rich Internet Applications

Rich Internet applications (RIAs) typically run inside a browser and may be developed using code that is executed by the browser such as Asynchronous Java-Script and XML (AJAX). RIAs may also run inside a browser plug-in, such as Silverlight. These applications are more complex than standard web applications and support rich user interaction and business logic. They are, however, typically restricted with respect to accessing local resources because of security concerns.

Typical RIAs are structured using the same three layers and modules found in web applications (see Section A.1.1). In RIAs, some business logic may be executed on the client machine, and some data may be stored locally. Like rich client applications, RIAs may range from relatively thin to quite thick clients.

The following table summarizes the responsibilities of the components of this reference architecture (shown in Figure A.3) that are not present in the Web Application reference architecture:

| Component Name | Responsibility |
| --- | --- |
| Presentation | Responsible for managing user interaction (represents both UI components and UI process logic components). |
| Rich UI engine | Responsible for rendering user interface elements inside the plug-in execution container. |
| Business processing | Responsible for managing business logic on the client side. |
| Service interfaces | Responsible for exposing services that are consumed by the components that run on the browser. |
| Message types | Responsible for managing the types of messages that are exchanged between the client part and the server part of the application. |

You should consider using this type of application when:

- You want your application to have a rich user interface but still run inside a browser.
- You want to perform some of the processing on the client side.
- You want to deploy and update your application in a simple manner, without having to perform installations on the user machine.

However, there are some limitations associated with this type of application:

- Access to local resources can be limited, because the application may run in a sandbox.
- Loading time is non-negligible.
- Plug-in execution environments may not be available in all platforms.

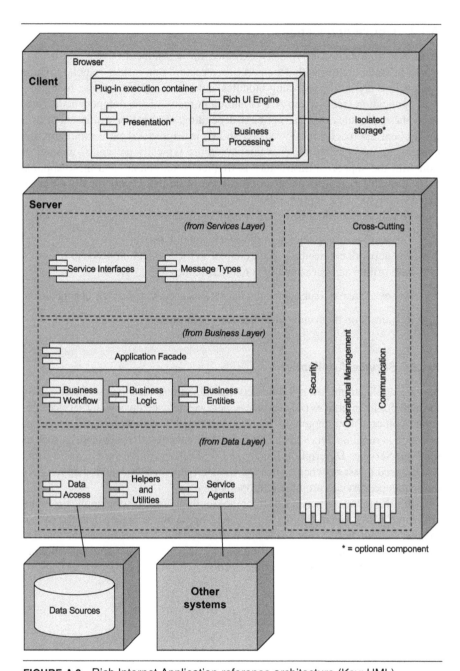

**FIGURE A.3**  Rich Internet Application reference architecture (Key: UML)

### A.1.4 Mobile Applications

A mobile application is typically executed on a handheld device and usually works in collaboration with a support infrastructure that resides remotely. These applications are structured using modules and layers similar to those found in a web application (see Section A.1.1), although many of the components derived from these modules may be optional depending on whether a thin-client or a thick-client approach is followed. As shown in Figure A.4, at a minimum, the components responsible for user interaction are typically present. Communication with the support infrastructure is frequently unreliable, and these applications normally include some type of local data store that is periodically synchronized with data in the support infrastructure.

You should consider using this type of application when:

- You want your application to run in a handheld device.
- The network connectivity is unreliable, so the application needs to run in both offline and occasionally connected modes.

However, there is a substantial limitation associated with this type of application:

- Resources on the handheld device may be limited.

### A.1.5 Service Applications

Service applications are non-interactive applications that expose functionality through public interfaces (i.e., services). Services may be invoked by service consumer components remotely or from the same machine in which the service application is running. Services can be defined using a description language such as the Web Services Description Language (WSDL); operations are invoked using XML-based message schemas that are transferred over a transport channel. As a consequence, services promote interoperability.

Similar to the other types of reference architectures, service applications are structured using layers (Figure A.5). These applications are not interactive, so the presentation layer is not needed. It is replaced by a service layer that contains components responsible for exposing the services and exchanging information, similar to the server part of RIAs (see Section A.1.3).

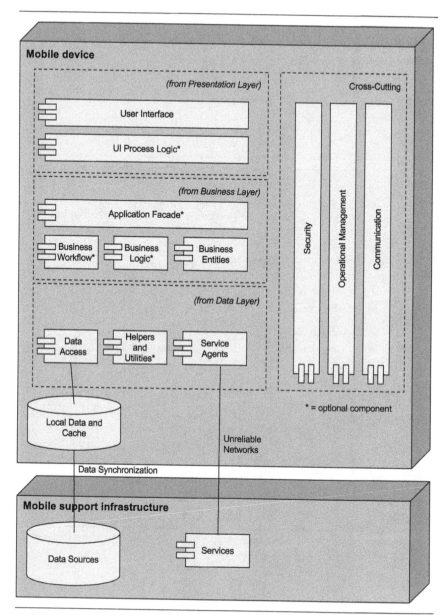

**FIGURE A.4**   Mobile Application reference architecture (Key: UML)

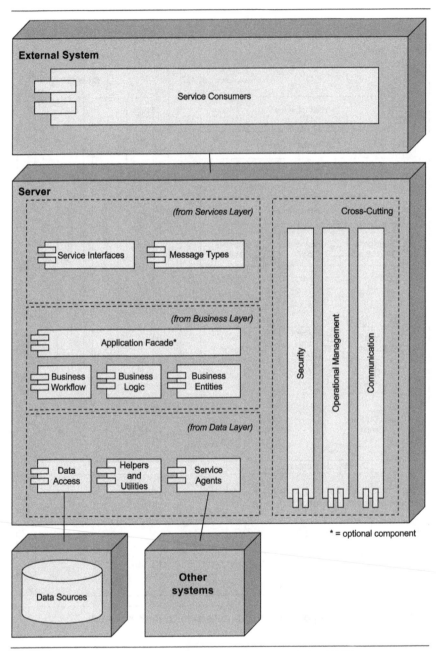

**FIGURE A.5** Service Application reference architecture (Key: UML)

You should consider using this type of application when:

- Your application is not used by humans but rather by other systems and, as a consequence, does not have a user interface.
- Your application and the clients should be loosely coupled.

Except in cases where services are consumed by applications that reside in the same machine, network connectivity is required for the clients to communicate with the service application.

## A.2 Deployment Patterns

Deployment patterns provide guidance on how to structure the system from a physical standpoint (see Section 2.5.3). Good decisions with respect to the deployment of the software system are essential to achieve important quality attributes such as performance, usability, availability, and security. This section is a summary from the catalog included in the *Microsoft Application Architecture Guide*.

### A.2.1 Nondistributed Deployment

In nondistributed deployment, all of the components from the modules in the different layers reside on a single server except for data storage functionality (Figure A.6). Because the components communicate locally, this may improve performance due to the lack of network communication delays. However, performance may be affected by other aspects of the system, such as resource contention. Also, this type of application must support the peak usage of the largest consumers of system resources. Scalability and maintainability may be negatively affected because the same physical hardware is shared by all of the components.

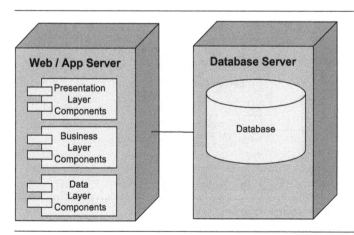

**FIGURE A.6** Nondistributed deployment example (Key: UML)

## A.2.2 Distributed Deployment

In a distributed deployment, the components of the application reside on separate physical tiers (Figure A.7). Typically, the components associated with specific layers are deployed in different tiers. Tiers can be configured differently to best meet the requirements of the components that it hosts.

Distributed deployment facilitates scalability but the addition of tiers also brings additional costs, network latency, complexity, and deployment effort. More tiers may also be added to promote security. Different security policies may be applied according to the particular tier, and firewalls may be placed between the tiers. The following subsections describe various alternatives of distributed deployment that can be used in conjunction with the reference architectures from Section A.1.

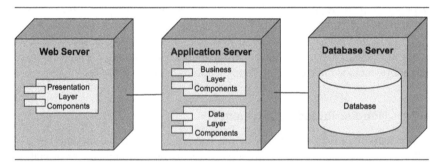

**FIGURE A.7**  Distributed deployment example (Key: UML)

### Two-Tier Deployment (Client-Server)
Two-tier deployment is the most basic layout for distributed deployment. The client and the server are usually deployed on different physical tiers, as shown in Figure A.8.

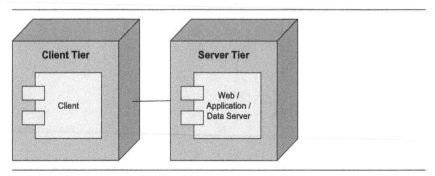

**FIGURE A.8**  Two-tier deployment pattern (Key: UML)

**Three-Tier Deployment**

In three-tier deployment, the application is deployed in a tier that is separate from the one that hosts the database, as shown in Figure A.9. This is a very common physical layout for web applications.

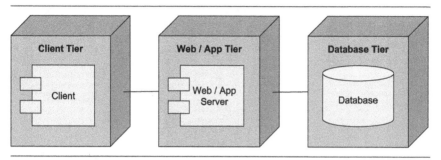

**FIGURE A.9** Three-tier deployment pattern (Key: UML)

**Four-Tier Deployment**

In four-tier deployment, shown in Figure A.10, the web server and the application server are deployed in different tiers. This separation is usually done to improve security, as the web server may reside in a publicly accessible network while the application resides in a protected network. Additionally, firewalls may be placed between the tiers.

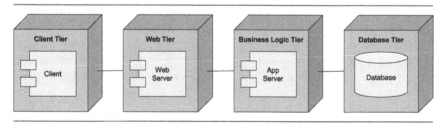

**FIGURE A.10** Four-tier deployment pattern (Key: UML)

## A.2.3 Performance Patterns: Load-Balanced Cluster

In the Load-Balanced Cluster pattern, the application is deployed on multiple servers that share the workload, as shown in Figure A.11. Client requests are received by a load balancer, which redirects them to the various servers according to their current load. The different application servers can process several requests concurrently, which results in performance improvements.

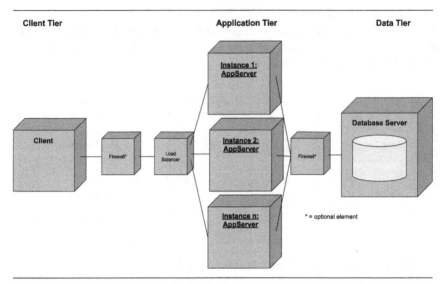

**FIGURE A.11** Load-balanced cluster deployment pattern (Key: UML)

## A.3 Architectural Design Patterns

This section includes architectural design patterns (see Section 2.5.2) used in the case study in Chapter 4. The patterns presented here are based on the book *Pattern-Oriented Software Architecture: A Pattern Language for Distributed Computing, Volume 4*. The numbers in parentheses [e.g., Domain Model (182)] indicate the page in the book where the pattern is documented.

Note that we are using a home-grown notation for the patterns here, which is common in the patterns community. We define the symbols in a legend accompanying the first diagram (Layers) and use these symbols throughout this section.

### A.3.1 Structural Patterns

These patterns are used to structure the system but they provide less detail than the reference architectures.

| Name | Layers |
|---|---|
| Problem and context | When transforming a Domain Model (182) into a set of modules that can be allocated to teams, [...] we need to support several concerns: the independent development of the modules, the independent evolution of the modules, the interaction among the modules. |
| Solution | Define two or more layers for the software under development, where each layer has a distinct and specific responsibility. To make the layering more effective, the interactions between the layers should be highly constrained. The strictest layering, as shown below, allows only unidirectional dependencies and forbids layer-bridging. |
| Structure | |
| Consequences and related patterns | Typically, each self-contained and coherent responsibility within a layer is realized as a separate domain object. Domain objects are the containers (modules) that can be developed and evolved independently. |

| Name | Domain Object |
|---|---|
| Problem and context | When realizing a Domain Model (182) in terms of Layers (185), a key concern is to decouple self-contained and cohesive application responsibilities. |
| Solution | Encapsulate each distinct, nontrivial piece of application functionality in a self-contained building block called a domain object. |

*continues*

| Name | Domain Object |
|------|---------------|
| Structure | 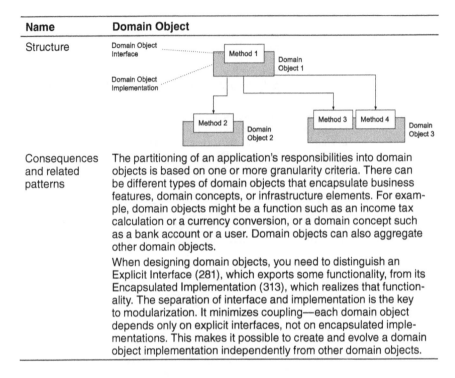 |

| Consequences and related patterns | The partitioning of an application's responsibilities into domain objects is based on one or more granularity criteria. There can be different types of domain objects that encapsulate business features, domain concepts, or infrastructure elements. For example, domain objects might be a function such as an income tax calculation or a currency conversion, or a domain concept such as a bank account or a user. Domain objects can also aggregate other domain objects. |
|  | When designing domain objects, you need to distinguish an Explicit Interface (281), which exports some functionality, from its Encapsulated Implementation (313), which realizes that functionality. The separation of interface and implementation is the key to modularization. It minimizes coupling—each domain object depends only on explicit interfaces, not on encapsulated implementations. This makes it possible to create and evolve a domain object implementation independently from other domain objects. |

## A.3.2 Interface Partitioning

| Name | Explicit Interface |
|------|---------------------|
| Problem and context | When designing Layers (185) and their constituent Domain Objects (208), an important concern is how to properly create component (module) interfaces. |
|  | A module is a self-contained unit of functionality (and a self-contained unit of deployment) with a published interface. Clients can build upon existing modules as building blocks when providing their own functionality. Direct access to the module's implementation might make clients dependent on the module's internals, which ultimately increases coupling and erodes the ability of the application to evolve. |
| Solution | Separate the explicit interface of a module from its implementation. Export the explicit interface to the clients of the module, but keep its implementation private. |

| Name | Explicit Interface |
| --- | --- |
| Structure | 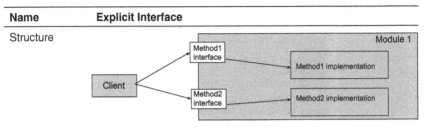 |

| | |
| --- | --- |
| Consequences and related patterns | A call from the client through an explicit interface will be forwarded to the implementation, but the client code will depend only on the public interface, not on the implementation.<br><br>An explicit interface therefore enforces the separation of the component's interface from its implementation. This separation means that a component's implementation may be modified and the clients that use it will be unaffected, so long as the interfaces are unchanged. |

| Name | Proxy |
| --- | --- |
| Problem and context | When specifying an Explicit Interface (281), we often want to avoid accessing services of a component implementation directly, as these services may change or even be unknown until execution time.<br><br>Most modern software systems consist of cooperating components, some of which you create and others that you do not. Your components access and use the services provided by other components. It may be impractical or even impossible to access the services of a component directly—for example, because the implementation resides on a remote server. |
| Solution | Encapsulate all the details of interacting with the component within a surrogate—called the proxy—and let clients communicate via the proxy rather than directly with the subject component. |
| Structure | 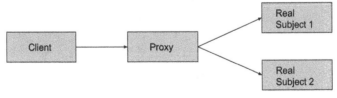 |
| Consequences and related patterns | A proxy frees both the client and the subjects from implementing component-specific housekeeping functionality. It is also transparent to clients whether they are connected with the real subject component or its proxy, because both publish an identical interface. The drawbacks of a proxy are additional execution time added to each client interaction (although, unless your application is highly sensitive to latency, this additional overhead is likely inconsequential). |

## A.3.3 Concurrency

| Name | Half-Sync/Half-Async |
| --- | --- |
| Problem and context | When developing concurrent software, a critical concern is to ensure that concurrent programming is relatively straightforward without sacrificing runtime efficiency. |
| | Concurrent software typically performs both asynchronous and synchronous processing of service requests. Asynchrony is used to process low-level service requests (such as events) efficiently, whereas synchronous processing is used to simplify the processing of application services. To benefit from both programming models, it is essential to coordinate both kinds of processing. |
| Solution | Decompose the services of concurrent software into two separate streams or "layers"—synchronous and asynchronous—and add a queueing "layer" to mediate communication between them. |
| Structure | |

| | |
| --- | --- |
| Consequences and related patterns | This pattern allows you to process complex service requests, such as domain functionality or database queries, synchronously in separate threads. Similarly, lower-level system services, such as protocol handlers that respond to hardware interrupts, are handled asynchronously. In cases where services in the synchronous layer need to communicate with services in the asynchronous layer, they may exchange messages via the queueing layer. |
| | The Half-Sync/Half-Async arrangement employs Layers (185) to keep the three distinct execution and communication models encapsulated and hence independent from one another. |

## A.3.4 Database Access

| Name | Data Mapper (Data Access Object [DAO]) |
|---|---|
| Problem and context | When designing a Database Access Layer (538), we need to insulate applications from the details of how data is represented in persistent storage, such as the specific SQL queries to use. |
| | Object-oriented applications and relational databases use different abstractions for representing data. However, many applications need to transfer data between these two "worlds." It is desirable to keep the object-oriented domain model ignorant of the relational database schema. In this way, changes to one domain model will be less likely to ripple to the other. |
| Solution | Introduce a data mapper for each type of persistent application object. The responsibility of this mapper is to transfer data from the objects to the database, and vice versa. |
| Structure | |
| Consequences and related patterns | A data mapper is a mediator that moves data between an object-oriented domain model and a relational database. A client can use the data mapper to store or retrieve application data in the database. The data mapper performs any needed data transformations and maintains consistency between the two representations. |
| | When a data mapper is used, in-memory objects do not even need to know that a database is present. Hence, they require no SQL code and can have complete ignorance of the database schema. In addition, the relational database schema and the object-oriented domain model can evolve independently. This provides an additional benefit that accrues to any abstraction interface: It simplifies unit testing, by allowing mappers to databases to be replaced by mock objects that support in-memory testing. |
| | The data mapper makes application objects simpler and reduces their external dependencies, making them easier to evolve. There are two potential drawbacks to the Data Mapper pattern, however: (1) Changes in either the application object model or the database schema may require changes to a data mapper; and (2) the additional level of indirection introduces overhead, and hence latency, to every data access, which might be problematic for systems with hard real-time deadlines, for example. |

## A.4 Tactics

Tactics were presented in Section 2.5.4. Here we present a summarized catalog of tactics for seven commonly encountered quality attributes. This catalog comes from the book *Software Architecture in Practice*.

### A.4.1 Availability Tactics

Figure A.12 summarizes the tactics to achieve availability.

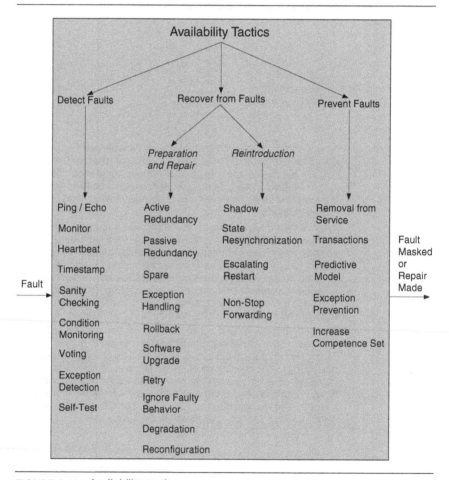

**FIGURE A.12** Availability tactics

**Detect Faults**

- *Ping/echo*: An asynchronous request/response message pair exchanged between nodes is used to determine reachability and the round-trip delay through the associated network path.
- *Monitor*: A component is used to monitor the state of health of other parts of the system. A system monitor can detect failure or congestion in the network or other shared resources, such as from a denial-of-service attack.
- *Heartbeat*: A periodic message exchange occurs between a system monitor and a process being monitored.
- *Timestamp*: Detect incorrect sequences of events, primarily in distributed message-passing systems.
- *Sanity checking*: Check the validity or reasonableness of a component's operations or outputs; typically based on a knowledge of the internal design, the state of the system, or the nature of the information under scrutiny.
- *Condition monitoring*: Check conditions in a process or device, or validates assumptions made during the design.
- *Voting*: Check that replicated components are producing the same results. Comes in various flavors, such as replication, functional redundancy, analytic redundancy.
- *Exception detection*: Detect a system condition that alters the normal flow of execution, such as a system exception, parameter fence, parameter typing, or timeout.
- *Self-test*: Procedure for a component to test itself for correct operation.

**Recover from Faults (Preparation and Repair)**

- *Active redundancy (hot spare)*: All nodes in a protection group receive and process identical inputs in parallel, allowing redundant spare(s) to maintain synchronous state with the active node(s).
- *Passive redundancy (warm spare)*: Only the active members of the protection group process input traffic; one of their duties is to provide the redundant spare(s) with periodic state updates.
- *Spare (cold spare)*: Redundant spares of a protection group remain out of service until a failover occurs, at which point a power-on-reset procedure is initiated on the redundant spare prior to its being placed in service.
- *Exception handling*: Deal with the exception by reporting it or handling it, potentially masking the fault by correcting the cause of the exception and retrying.
- *Rollback*: Revert to a previous known good state, referred to as the "rollback line."
- *Software upgrade*: Perform in-service upgrades to executable code images in a non-service-affecting manner.
- *Retry*: When a failure is transient, retrying the operation may lead to success.

- *Ignore faulty behavior:* Ignore messages sent from a source when it is determined that those messages are spurious.
- *Degradation:* Maintain the most critical system functions in the presence of component failures, dropping less critical functions.
- *Reconfiguration:* Reassign responsibilities to the resources that continue to function, while maintaining as much functionality as possible.

### Recover from Faults (Reintroduction)

- *Shadow:* Operate a previously failed or in-service upgraded component in a "shadow mode" for a predefined time prior to reverting the component back to an active role.
- *State resynchronization:* Passive redundancy; state information is sent from active to standby components, in this partner tactic to active redundancy.
- *Escalating restart:* Recover from faults by varying the granularity of the component(s) restarted and minimizing the level of service affected.
- *Non-stop forwarding:* Functionality is split into supervisory and data variants. If a supervisor fails, a router continues forwarding packets along known routes while protocol information is recovered and validated.

### Prevent Faults

- *Removal from service:* Temporarily place a system component in an out-of-service state for the purpose of mitigating potential system failures.
- *Transactions:* Bundle state updates so that asynchronous messages exchanged between distributed components are atomic, consistent, isolated, and durable.
- *Predictive model:* Monitor the state of health of a process to ensure that the system is operating within nominal parameters; take corrective action when conditions are detected that are predictive of likely future faults.
- *Exception prevention:* Prevent system exceptions from occurring by masking a fault, or prevent them via smart pointers, abstract data types, and wrappers.
- *Increase competence set:* Design a component to handle more cases— faults—as part of its normal operation.

### A.4.2 Interoperability Tactics

Figure A.13 summarizes the tactics to achieve interoperability.

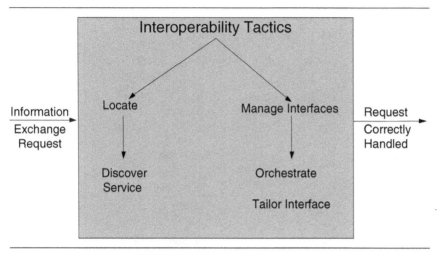

**FIGURE A.13**  Interoperability tactics

## Locate

- *Discover service*: Locate a service by searching a known directory service. There may be multiple levels of indirection in this location process—that is, a known location may point to another location that in turn can be searched for the service.

## Manage Interfaces

- *Orchestrate*: Use a control mechanism to coordinate, manage, and sequence the invocation of services. Orchestration is used when systems must interact in a complex fashion to accomplish a complex task.
- *Tailor interface*: Add or remove capabilities to an interface such as translation, buffering, or data smoothing.

## A.4.3  Modifiability Tactics

Figure A.14 summarizes the tactics to achieve modifiability.

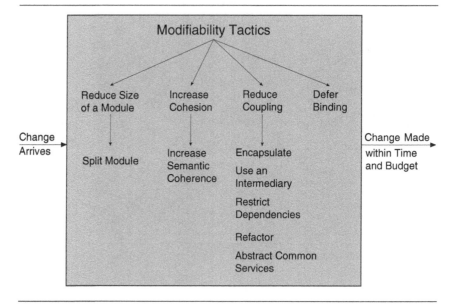

**FIGURE A.14**   Modifiability tactics

### Reduce Size of a Module

- *Split module*: If the module being modified includes a great deal of capability, the modification costs will likely be high. Refining the module into several smaller modules should reduce the average cost of future changes.

### Increase Cohesion

- *Increase semantic coherence*: If the responsibilities A and B in a module do not serve the same purpose, they should be placed in different modules. This may involve creating a new module or moving a responsibility to an existing module.

### Reduce Coupling

- *Encapsulate*: Encapsulation introduces an explicit interface to a module. This interface includes an API and its associated responsibilities, such as "perform a syntactic transformation on an input parameter to an internal representation."
- *Use an intermediary*: Given a dependency between responsibility A and responsibility B (for example, carrying out A first requires carrying out B), the dependency can be broken by using an intermediary.

- *Restrict dependencies*: Restrict the modules that a given module interacts with or depends on.
- *Refactor*: Refactoring is undertaken when two modules are affected by the same change because they are (at least partial) duplicates of each other.
- *Abstract common services*: When two modules provide not quite the same but similar services, it may be cost-effective to implement the services just once in a more general (abstract) form.

### Defer Binding

- *Defer binding*: Allow decisions to be bound after development time.

### A.4.4   Performance Tactics

Figure A.15 summarizes the tactics to achieve performance.

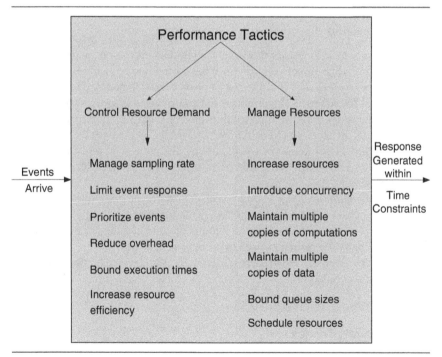

**FIGURE A.15**   Performance tactics

### Control Resource Demand

- *Manage sampling rate*: If it is possible to reduce the sampling frequency at which a stream of data is captured, then demand can be reduced, albeit typically with some loss of fidelity.
- *Limit event response*: Process events only up to a set maximum rate, thereby ensuring more predictable processing when the events are actually processed.
- *Prioritize events*: If not all events are equally important, you can impose a priority scheme that ranks events according to how important it is to service them.
- *Reduce overhead*: The use of intermediaries (important for modifiability) increases the resources consumed in processing an event stream; removing them improves latency.
- *Bound execution times*: Place a limit on how much execution time is used to respond to an event.
- *Increase resource efficiency*: Improving the algorithms used in critical areas will decrease latency.

### Manage Resources

- *Increase resources*: Faster processors, additional processors, additional memory, and faster networks all have the potential to reduce latency.
- *Increase concurrency*: If requests can be processed in parallel, the blocked time can be reduced. Concurrency can be introduced by processing different streams of events on different threads or by creating additional threads to process different sets of activities.
- *Maintain multiple copies of computations*: The purpose of replicas is to reduce the contention that would occur if all computations took place on a single server.
- *Maintain multiple copies of data*: Keep copies of data (with one potentially being a subset of the other) on storage with different access speeds.
- *Bound queue sizes*: Control the maximum number of queued arrivals and consequently the resources used to process the arrivals.
- *Schedule resources*: When there is contention for a resource, the resource must be scheduled.

### A.4.5    Security Tactics

Figure A.16 summarizes the tactics to achieve security.

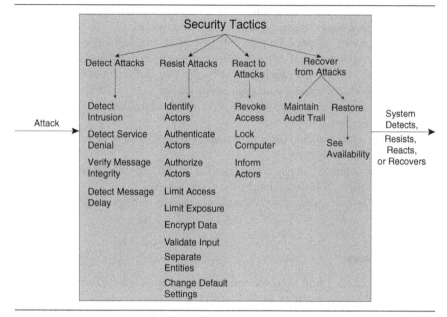

**FIGURE A.16**   Security tactics

## Detect Attacks

- *Detect intrusion*: Compare network traffic or service request patterns within a system to a set of signatures or known patterns of malicious behavior stored in a database.
- *Detect service denial*: Compare the pattern or signature of network traffic coming into a system to historic profiles of known denial-of-service attacks.
- *Verify message integrity*: Use techniques such as checksums or hash values to verify the integrity of messages, resource files, deployment files, and configuration files.
- *Detect message delay*: By checking the time that it takes to deliver a message, it is possible to detect suspicious timing behavior.

## Resist Attacks

- *Identify actors*: Identify the source of any external input to the system.
- *Authenticate actors*: Ensure that an actor (user or a remote computer) is actually who or what it purports to be.
- *Authorize actors*: Ensure that an authenticated actor has the rights to access and modify either data or services.

- *Limit access*: Control what and who may access which parts of a system, such as processors, memory, and network connections.
- *Limit exposure*: Reduce the probability of a successful attack, or restrict the amount of potential damage—for example, by concealing facts about a system ("security by obscurity") or by dividing and distributing critical resources ("don't put all your eggs in one basket").
- *Encrypt data*: Apply some form of encryption to data and to communication.
- *Validate input*: Validate input from a user or an external system before accepting it in the system.
- *Separate entities*: Use physical separation on different servers attached to different networks, virtual machines, or an "air gap."
- *Change default settings*: Force the user to change settings assigned by default.

### React to Attacks

- *Revoke access*: Limit access to sensitive resources, even for normally legitimate users and uses, if an attack is suspected.
- *Lock computer*: Limit access to a resource if there are repeated failed attempts to access it.
- *Inform actors*: Notify operators, other personnel, or cooperating systems when an attack is suspected or detected.

### Recover from Attacks

In addition to the availability tactics for recovery of failed resources, an audit may be performed to recover from attacks.

- *Maintain Audit Trail*: Keep a record of user and system actions and their effects, to help trace the actions of, and to identify, an attacker.

### A.4.6 Testability Tactics

Figure A.17 summarizes the tactics to achieve testability.

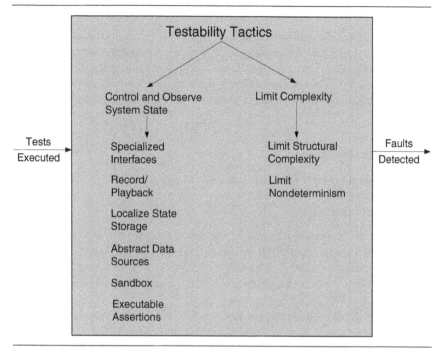

**FIGURE A.17**   Testability tactics

### Control and Observe System State

- *Specialized interfaces*: Control or capture variable values for a component either through a test harness or through normal execution.
- *Record/playback*: Capture information crossing an interface and use it as input for further testing.
- *Localize state storage*: To start a system, subsystem, or module in an arbitrary state for a test, it is most convenient if that state is stored in a single place.
- *Abstract data sources*: Abstracting the interfaces lets you substitute test data more easily.
- *Sandbox*: Isolate the system from the real world to enable experimentation that is unconstrained by the worry about having to undo the consequences of the experiment.
- *Executable assertions*: Assertions are (usually) hand-coded and placed at desired locations to indicate when and where a program is in a faulty state.

### Limit Complexity

- *Limit structural complexity*: Avoid or resolve cyclic dependencies between components, isolate and encapsulate dependencies on the external environment, and reduce dependencies between components in general.
- *Limit nondeterminism*: Find all the sources of non-determinism, such as unconstrained parallelism, and weed them out as far as possible.

### A.4.7   Usability Tactics

Figure A.18 summarizes the tactics to achieve usability.

### Support User Initiative

- *Cancel*: The system must listen for the cancel request; the command being canceled must be terminated; resources used must be freed; and collaborating components must be informed.
- *Pause/resume*: Temporarily free resources so that they may be reallocated to other tasks.
- *Undo*: Maintain a sufficient amount of information about system state so that an earlier state may be restored at the user's request.
- *Aggregate*: Aggregate lower-level objects into a group, so that a user operation may be applied to the group, freeing the user from the drudgery.

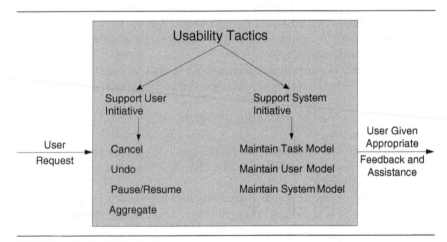

**FIGURE A.18**   Usability tactics

### Support System Initiative

- *Maintain task model*: Determine the context so the system can have some idea of what the user is attempting and provide assistance.
- *Maintain user model*: Explicitly represent the user's knowledge of the system, the user's behavior in terms of expected response time, and other characteristics of the system.
- *Maintain system model*: The system maintains an explicit model of itself. This tactic is used to determine expected system behavior so that appropriate feedback can be given to the user.

## A.5 Externally Developed Components

Externally developed components, including frameworks, were discussed in Section 2.5.5. Here we present a small sample of Java frameworks used in the case study in Chapter 4. Each framework is described very briefly and is associated with particular technology families, patterns, and tactics. Full details for the different frameworks can be found by visiting the URL that is provided.

### A.5.1 Spring Framework

| Framework Name | Spring Framework |
| --- | --- |
| Technology family | Dependency injection and aspect-oriented programming (AOP) container |
| Language | Java |
| URL | http://projects.spring.io/spring-framework/ |
| Purpose | The application framework allows the objects that form an application to be connected. It also supports different concerns through AOP. |
| Overview | The Spring container connects standard Java objects, or POJOs (Plain Old Java Objects), by using information from an XML file called "Application Context" or annotations in the Java code. This is the "Inversion of Control and Dependency Injection" pattern, since object dependencies are injected by the container. |
| | The framework supports several aspects using AOP which are introduced as proxies between the Java objects when the container connects them. Supported aspects include: |
| | - Security |
| | - Transaction management |
| | - Publishing object interfaces so the objects can be accessed remotely—for example, via Web Services |

*(continues)*

| Framework Name | Spring Framework |
|---|---|

Structure

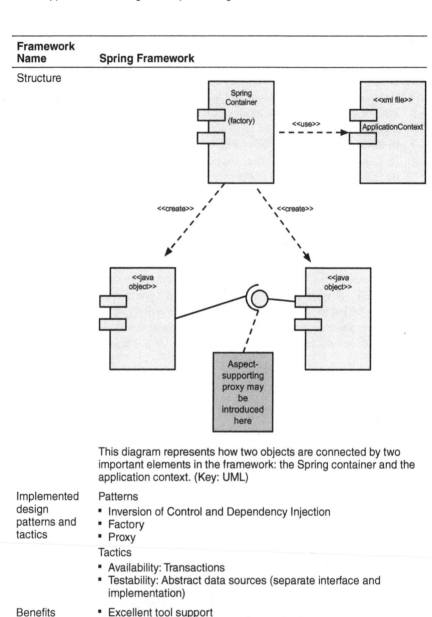

This diagram represents how two objects are connected by two important elements in the framework: the Spring container and the application context. (Key: UML)

| Implemented design patterns and tactics | Patterns<br>• Inversion of Control and Dependency Injection<br>• Factory<br>• Proxy<br><br>Tactics<br>• Availability: Transactions<br>• Testability: Abstract data sources (separate interface and implementation) |
|---|---|
| Benefits | • Excellent tool support<br>• Simple integration with other frameworks such as web UI (Spring MVC, JSF), and persistence (JPA, Hibernate, iBatis) and integration (JMS) |
| Limitations | • Apache License 2.0<br>• Complex framework |

## A.5.2   Swing Framework

| Framework Name | Swing Framework |
|---|---|
| Technology family | Local user interface |
| Language | Java |
| URL | http://docs.oracle.com/javase/tutorial/uiswing/index.html |
| Purpose | Framework to support the creation of portable local (non-web) user interfaces. |
| Overview | The Swing framework provides a library of user interface components, including JFrame (windows), JMenu, JTree, JButton, JList, and JTable, among others. These components are built around the Model View Controller and Observer patterns.<br><br>Components such as JTables are views and controllers, and each has a corresponding model class (e.g., TableModel).<br><br>Components allow observers (called "listeners") to be registered to manage different events. For example, JButtons allow ActionListeners to be registered as observers so that when the button is clicked, a callback method (`actionPerformed`) is invoked. |
| Structure | |

JComponent    *    JFrame
children

JButton
addActionListener(ActionListener al)

JTable    JTree    TreeModel
model

*  listeners
ActionListener
actionPerformed(ActionEvent evt)

This diagram represents a small fraction of the framework's classes (Key: UML)

| Implemented design patterns and tactics | Patterns:<br>• Model View Controller<br>• Observer<br>• Others such as Composite and Iterator |
| Benefits | • Portable (can run on any operating system)<br>• Part of Java API<br>• Good tool support |
| Limitations | • Slower than using native UI elements<br>• Not the same look and feel as native UI elements |

## A.5.3   Hibernate Framework

| Framework Name | Hibernate |
| --- | --- |
| Technology family | Object-oriented to relational mapper |
| Language | Java |
| URL | http://hibernate.org/ |
| Purpose | Simplify persistence of objects in a relational database. |
| Overview | Hibernate allows objects to be easily persisted in a relational database (and it supports different database engines). Object-relational mapping rules are described declaratively in an XML file called `hibernate.cfg` or using annotations in the classes whose objects need to be persisted. |
| | Hibernate supports transactions and provides a query language called HQL (Hibernate Query Language) that is used to retrieve objects from the database. Hibernate utilizes multilevel caching schemes to improve performance. It also provides mechanisms to allow lazy acquisition of dependent objects to improve performance and reduce resource consumption. These mechanisms are configured declaratively in the configuration files. |
| Structure | |
| | This diagram represents an entity that is persisted to a database by the Hibernate runtime using the information in the configuration file (Key: UML) |
| Implemented design patterns and tactics | Patterns:<br>• Data Mapper<br>• Resource Cache<br>• Lazy Acquisition<br>Tactics:<br>• Availability: Transactions<br>• Performance: Maintain multiple copies of data (cache) |

| Framework Name | Hibernate |
|---|---|
| Benefits | ▪ Greatly simplifies the persistence of objects in relational database |
| Limitations | ▪ Complex API<br>▪ Slower than JDBC (Java Database Connectivity)<br>▪ Difficult to map to legacy database schemas |

### A.5.4 Java Web Start Framework

| Framework Name | Java Web Start Framework |
|---|---|
| Technology family | Deployment mechanism |
| Language | Java |
| URL | http://docs.oracle.com/javase/tutorial/deployment/webstart/ |
| Purpose | Provide a platform-independent, secure, and robust deployment technology. |
| Overview | By using a web browser, end users can start standard (non-applet) Java applications, and Java Web Start ensures they are running the latest version. To launch an application, users click a link on a page. If this is the first time the application is used, Java Web Start downloads the application. If the application has been previously used, Java Web Start verifies that the local copy is the latest version and launches it or downloads the newest version. |
| Structure | Not available |
| Implemented design patterns and tactics | Tactics:<br>▪ Security: Limit access (sandbox)<br>▪ Performance: Maintain multiple copies of data (cache) |
| Benefits | ▪ Applications run in a sandbox but can read and write to local files.<br>▪ Because the application is cached, once it has been downloaded startup time is greatly reduced. |
| Limitations | ▪ First launch may take some time |

## A.6  Summary

In this appendix we presented a design concepts catalog for the application domain of enterprise applications. Catalogs such as this one can become useful organizational assets, and we can readily imagine catalogs for other application domains such as Big Data (which we employ in Chapter 5) or mobile development.

The catalog presented here is not intended to be exhaustive, as it contains only the design concepts used in the Chapter 4 case study. A real catalog, however, would contain a larger number of design concepts with more detailed descriptions and would be a valuable asset in a software development organization.

## A.7  Further Reading

Reference architectures and deployment patterns are taken from Microsoft, *Application Architecture Guide* (2nd ed.), October 2009.

The tactics catalog is derived primarily from L. Bass, P. Clements, and R. Kazman, *Software Architecture in Practice* (3rd ed.), 2012. Some of these tactics were earlier described in: F. Bachmann, L. Bass, and R. Nord, "Modifiability Tactics", SEI/CMU Technical Report CMU/SEI-2007-TR-002, 2007, and J. Scott and R. Kazman, "Realizing and Refining Architectural Tactics: Availability", CMU/SEI-2009-TR-006, 2009.

The architectural patterns are taken from R. Buschmann, K. Henney, and D. Schmidt, *Pattern-Oriented Software Architecture*, Volume 4, Wiley, 2007.

The Spring framework is discussed in C. Walls, *Spring in Action* (4th ed.), Manning Publications, 2014.

The Swing framework is discussed in J. Elliot, R. Eckstein, D. Wood, and B. Cole, *Java Swing* (2nd ed.), O'Reilly Media, 2002.

The Hibernate framework is discussed in C. Bauer and G. King, *Java Persistence with Hibernate*, Manning Publications, 2015.

# B

# Tactics-Based
# Questionnaires

This appendix provides a set of tactics-based questionnaires for the seven most important quality attributes: availability, interoperability, modifiability, performance, security, testability, and usability. How do we know that these are the seven most important ones? This decision was based on an analysis of the quality attributes that were elicited from stakeholders in more than 15 years of SEI ATAM data.

In addition to these "top seven", we include a tactics-based questionnaire for DevOps, which is a combination of tactics from modifiability, availability, performance, and testability, to illustrate how simple it is to tailor such questionnaires for your own use.

## B.1   Using the Questionnaires

These questionnaires could be used by an analyst, who poses each question, in turn, to the architect and records the responses, as a means of conducting a lightweight architecture review. Alternatively, the questionnaires could be employed as a set of reflective questions, that you could, on your own, use to examine your architecture.

In either case, to use these questionnaires, simply follow these four steps:

1. For each tactics question, fill the "Supported" column with Y if the tactic is supported in the architecture and with N otherwise. The tactic name in the "Tactics Question" column appears in **bold.**
2. If the answer in the "Supported" column is Y, then in the "Design Decisions and Location" column describe the specific design decisions made to support the tactic and enumerate where these decisions are manifested (located) in the architecture. For example, indicate which code modules, frameworks, or packages implement this tactic.
3. In the "Risk" column, indicate the anticipated/experienced difficulty or risk of implementing the tactic using a (H = high, M = medium, L = low) scale. For example, a tactic that was of medium difficulty or risk to implement (or which is anticipated to be of medium difficulty, if it has not yet been implemented) would be labeled M.
4. In the "Rationale" column, describe the rationale for the design decisions made (including a decision to *not* use this tactic). Briefly explain the implications of this decision. For example, you might explain the rationale and implications of the decision in terms of the effort on cost, schedule, evolution, and so forth.

## B.2 Availability

| # | Tactics Group | Tactics Question | Supported? (Y/N) | Risk | Design Decisions and Location | Rationale and Assumptions |
|---|---|---|---|---|---|---|
| 1 | Detect faults | Does the system use **ping/echo** to detect a failure of a component or connection, or network congestion? | | | | |
| 2 | | Does the system use a component to **monitor** the state of health of other parts of the system? A system monitor can detect failure or congestion in the network or other shared resources, such as from a denial-of-service attack. | | | | |
| 3 | | Does the system use a **heartbeat**—a periodic message exchange between a system monitor and a process—to detect a failure of a component or connection, or network congestion? | | | | |
| 4 | | Does the system use a **time stamp** (as in section A.4.1) to detect incorrect sequences of events in distributed systems? | | | | |

| # | Tactics Group | Tactics Question | Supported? (Y/N) | Risk | Design Decisions and Location | Rationale and Assumptions |
|---|---|---|---|---|---|---|
| 5 | | Does the system do any **sanity checking:** checking the validity or reasonableness of a component's operations or outputs? | | | | |
| 6 | | Does the system do **condition monitoring,** checking conditions in a process or device, or validating assumptions made during the design? | | | | |
| 7 | | Does the system use **voting** to check that replicated components are producing the same results? The replicated components may be identical replicas, functionally redundant, or analytically redundant. | | | | |
| 8 | | Do you use **exception detection** to detect a system condition that alters the normal flow of execution (e.g., system exception, parameter fence, parameter typing, timeout)? | | | | |
| 9 | | Can the system do a **self-test** to test itself for correct operation? | | | | |
| 10 | Recover from faults (preparation and repair) | Does the system employ **active redundancy** (hot spare)? In active redundancy, all nodes in a protection group (a group of nodes where one or more nodes are "active", with the remainder serving as redundant spares) receive and process identical inputs in parallel, allowing redundant spares to maintain synchronous state with the active node(s). | | | | |
| 11 | | Does the system employ **passive redundancy** (warm spare)? In passive redundancy, only the active members of the protection group process input traffic; one of their duties is to provide the redundant spare(s) with periodic state updates. | | | | |

*(continues)*

| # | Tactics Group | Tactics Question | Supported? (Y/N) | Risk | Design Decisions and Location | Rationale and Assumptions |
|---|---|---|---|---|---|---|
| 12 | | Does the system employ **spares** (cold spares)? Here redundant spares of a protection group remain out of service until a failover occurs, at which point a power-on-reset procedure is initiated on the redundant spare prior to its being placed in service. | | | | |
| 13 | | Does the system employ **exception handling** to deal with faults? Typically the handling involves either reporting the fault or handling it, potentially masking the fault by correcting the cause of the exception and retrying. | | | | |
| 14 | | Does the system employ **rollback**, so that it can revert to a previously saved good state (the "rollback line") in the event of a fault? | | | | |
| 15 | | Can the system perform in-service **software upgrades** to executable code images in a non-service-affecting manner? | | | | |
| 16 | | Does the system systematically **retry** in cases where the component or connection failure may be transient? | | | | |
| 17 | | Can the system simply **ignore faulty behavior** (e.g., ignore messages sent from a source when it is determined that those messages are spurious)? | | | | |
| 18 | | Does the system have a policy of **degradation** when resources are compromised, maintaining the most critical system functions in the presence of component failures, and dropping less critical functions? | | | | |

| # | Tactics Group | Tactics Question | Supported? (Y/N) | Risk | Design Decisions and Location | Rationale and Assumptions |
|---|---|---|---|---|---|---|
| 19 | | Does the system have consistent policies and mechanisms for **reconfiguration** after failures, reassigning responsibilities to the resources left functioning, while maintaining as much functionality as possible? | | | | |
| 20 | Recover from faults (reintroduction) | Can the system operate a previously failed or in-service upgraded component in a "**shadow mode**" for a predefined time prior to reverting the component back to an active role? | | | | |
| 21 | | If the system uses active or passive redundancy, does it also employ **state resynchronization**, to send state information from active to standby components? | | | | |
| 22 | | Does the system employ **escalating restart**— that is, does it recover from faults by varying the granularity of the component(s) restarted and minimizing the level of service affected? | | | | |
| 23 | | Can message processing and routing portions of the system employ **nonstop** (as in section A.4.1) **forwarding**, where functionality is split into supervisory and data planes? In this case, if a supervisor fails, a router continues forwarding packets along known routes while protocol information is recovered and validated. | | | | |
| 24 | Prevent faults | Can the system **remove components from service**, temporarily placing a system component in an out-of-service state, for the purpose of mitigating potential system failures? | | | | |

*(continues)*

| # | Tactics Group | Tactics Question | Supported? (Y/N) | Risk | Design Decisions and Location | Rationale and Assumptions |
|---|---|---|---|---|---|---|
| 25 | | Does the system employ **transactions**—bundling state updates so that asynchronous messages exchanged between distributed components are *atomic, consistent, isolated*, and *durable*? | | | | |
| 26 | | Does the system use a **predictive model** to monitor the state of health of a component to ensure that the system is operating within nominal parameters? When conditions are detected that are predictive of likely future faults, the model initiates corrective action. | | | | |
| 27 | | Does the system **prevent exceptions** from occurring by, for example, masking a fault, using smart pointers, abstract data types, or wrappers? | | | | |
| 28 | | Has the system been designed to **increase its competence set**, for example by designing a component to handle more cases—faults—as part of its normal operation? | | | | |

## B.3   Interoperability

| # | Tactics Group | Tactics Question | Supported? (Y/N) | Risk | Design Decisions and Location | Rationale and Assumptions |
|---|---|---|---|---|---|---|
| 1 | Locate | Does the system have a way to **discover services** (typically through a directory service)? | | | | |
| 2 | Manage interfaces | Does the system have a way to **orchestrate** the activities of services? That is, does it have a control mechanism to coordinate, manage, and sequence the invocation of services? | | | | |

| # | Tactics Group | Tactics Question | Supported? (Y/N) | Risk | Design Decisions and Location | Rationale and Assumptions |
|---|---|---|---|---|---|---|
| 3 | | Does the system have a way to **tailor interfaces**? For example, can it add or remove capabilities to an interface such as translation, buffering, or data smoothing? | | | | |

# B.4 Modifiability

| # | Tactics Group | Tactics Question | Supported? (Y/N) | Risk | Design Decisions and Location | Rationale and Assumptions |
|---|---|---|---|---|---|---|
| 1 | Reduce size of a module | Do you make modules simpler by **splitting the module**? For example, if you have a large, complex module, can you split it into two (or more) smaller, simpler modules? | | | | |
| 2 | Increase cohesion | Does the system consistently support **increasing semantic coherence**? For example, if responsibilities in a module do not serve the same purpose, they should be placed in different modules. This may involve creating a new module or moving a responsibility to an existing module. | | | | |
| 3 | Reduce coupling | Does the system consistently **encapsulate** functionality? This typically involves isolating the functionality under scrutiny and introducing an explicit interface to it. | | | | |

*(continues)*

| # | Tactics Group | Tactics Question | Supported? (Y/N) | Risk | Design Decisions and Location | Rationale and Assumptions |
|---|---|---|---|---|---|---|
| 4 | | Does the system consistently **use an intermediary** to keep modules from being too tightly coupled? For example, if A calls concrete functionality C, you might introduce an abstraction B that mediates between A and C. | | | | |
| 5 | | Do you **restrict dependencies** between modules in a systematic way? Or is any system module free to interact with any other module? | | | | |
| 6 | | When two or more unrelated modules change together—that is, when they are regularly affected by the same changes—do you regularly **refactor** the functionality to isolate the shared functionality as common code in a distinct module? | | | | |
| 7 | | Does the system **abstract common services**, in cases where you are providing several similar services? For example, this technique is often used when you want your system to be portable across operating systems, hardware, or other environment variations. | | | | |
| 8 | Defer binding | Does the system regularly **defer binding** of important functionality so that it can be replaced later in the life cycle, perhaps even by end users? For example, do you use plug-ins, add-ons, or user scripting to extend the functionality of the system? | | | | |

# B.5  Performance

| # | Tactics Group | Tactics Question | Supported? (Y/N) | Risk | Design Decisions and Location | Rationale and Assumptions |
|---|---|---|---|---|---|---|
| 1 | Control resource demand | If your inputs are a continuous stream of data, does the system **manage the sampling rate**? That is, is it possible to sample the data at varying rates (with concomitant changes in accuracy/fidelity)? | | | | |
| 2 | | Does the system monitor and **limit its event response**? Does the system limit the number of events it responds to in a time period, to ensure predictable responses for the events that are actually serviced? | | | | |
| 3 | | Given that you may have more requests for service than available resources, does the system **prioritize events**? | | | | |
| 4 | | Does the system **reduce the overhead** of responding to service requests by, for example, removing intermediaries or co-locating resources? | | | | |
| 5 | | Does the system monitor and **bound execution time**? More generally, do you bound the amount of any resource (e.g., memory, CPU, storage, bandwidth, connections, locks) expended in response to requests for services? | | | | |
| 6 | | Do you **increase resource efficiency**? For example, do you regularly improve the efficiency of algorithms in critical areas, to decrease latency and improve throughput? | | | | |

*(continues)*

| # | Tactics Group | Tactics Question | Supported? (Y/N) | Risk | Design Decisions and Location | Rationale and Assumptions |
|---|---|---|---|---|---|---|
| 7 | Manage resources | Can the system seamlessly **increase resources** (e.g., CPU, memory, network bandwidth)? | | | | |
| 8 | | Can the system **introduce concurrency**? For example, does it support the seamless addition of parallel processing streams so that more requests for services can be processed concurrently? | | | | |
| 9 | | Does the system **maintain multiple copies of data** (e.g., by replicating databases or using caches) to decrease contention for frequently accessed data? | | | | |
| 10 | | Does the system **maintain multiple copies of computations** (e.g., by keeping a pool of servers in a server farm) to decrease contention for frequently accessed computational resources? | | | | |
| 11 | | Does the system **bound queue sizes**? That is, do you limit the number of events placed in a queue, waiting for services? | | | | |
| 12 | | Does the system **schedule resources**, particularly scarce resources, so that they may be allocated according to an explicit scheduling policy? | | | | |

# B.6  Security

| # | Tactics Group | Tactics Question | Supported? (Y/N) | Risk | Design Decisions and Location | Rationale and Assumptions |
|---|---|---|---|---|---|---|
| 1 | Detecting attacks | Does the system support the **detection of intrusions**? An example is comparing network traffic or service request patterns within a system to a set of signatures or known patterns of malicious behavior stored in a database. | | | | |
| 2 | | Does the system support the **detection of denial-of-service attacks**? An example is the comparison of the pattern or signature of network traffic coming into a system to historic profiles of known denial-of-service attacks. | | | | |
| 3 | | Does the system support the **verification of message integrity**? An example is the use of techniques such as checksums or hash values to verify the integrity of messages, resource files, deployment files, and configuration files. | | | | |
| 4 | | Does the system support the **detection of message delays**? An example is checking the time that it takes to deliver a message. | | | | |
| 5 | Resisting attacks | Does the system support the **identification of actors**? An example is identifying the source of any external input to the system. | | | | |
| 6 | | Does the system support the **authentication of actors**? An example is ensuring that an actor (a user or a remote computer) is actually who or what it purports to be. | | | | |

*(continues)*

| # | Tactics Group | Tactics Question | Supported? (Y/N) | Risk | Design Decisions and Location | Rationale and Assumptions |
|---|---|---|---|---|---|---|
| 7 | | Does the system support the **authorization of actors**? An example is ensuring that an authenticated actor has the rights to access and modify either data or services. | | | | |
| 8 | | Does the system support **limiting access**? An example is controlling what and who may access which parts of a system, such as processors, memory, and network connections. | | | | |
| 9 | | Does the system support **limiting exposure**? An example is reducing the probability of a successful attack, or restricting the amount of potential damage, by concealing facts about a system ("security by obscurity") or dividing and distributing critical resources ("don't put all your eggs in one basket"). | | | | |
| 10 | | Does the system support **data encryption**? An example is to apply some form of encryption to data and to communication. | | | | |
| 11 | | Does the system **validate input** in a consistent, system-wide way? An example is the use of a security framework or validation class to perform actions such as filtering, canonicalization, and escaping of external input. | | | | |

| # | Tactics Group | Tactics Question | Supported? (Y/N) | Risk | Design Decisions and Location | Rationale and Assumptions |
|---|---|---|---|---|---|---|
| 12 | | Does the system design consider the **separation of entities**? An example is the physical separation of different servers attached to different networks, the use of virtual machines, or an "air gap". | | | | |
| 13 | | Does the system support **changes in the default settings**? An example is forcing the user to change settings assigned by default. | | | | |
| 14 | Reacting to attacks | Does the system support **revoking access**? An example is limiting access to sensitive resources, even for normally legitimate users and uses, if an attack is suspected. | | | | |
| 15 | | Does the system support **locking access**? An example is limiting access to a resource if there are repeated failed attempts to access it. | | | | |
| 16 | | Does the system support **informing actors**? An example is notifying operators, other personnel, or cooperating systems when an attack is suspected or detected. | | | | |
| 17 | Recovering from attacks | Does the system support **maintaining an audit trail**? An example is keeping a record of user and system actions and their effects, to help trace the actions of, and to identify, an attacker | | | | |

## B.7 Testability

| # | Tactics Group | Tactics Question | Supported? (Y/N) | Risk | Design Decisions and Location | Rationale and Assumptions |
|---|---|---|---|---|---|---|
| 1 | Control and observe system state | Does the system or the system components provide **specialized interfaces** to facilitate testing and monitoring? | | | | |
| 2 | | Does the system provide mechanisms that allow information that crosses an interface to be recorded so that it can be used later for testing purposes (**record/playback**)? | | | | |
| 3 | | Is the state of the system, subsystem, or modules stored in a single place to facilitate testing (**localized state storage**)? | | | | |
| 4 | | Can you **abstract data sources**—for example, by abstracting interfaces? Abstracting the interfaces lets you substitute test data more easily. | | | | |
| 5 | | Can the system be executed in isolation (a **sandbox**) to experiment or test it without worrying about having to undo the consequences of the experiment? | | | | |
| 6 | | Are **executable assertions** used in the system code to indicate when and where a program is in a faulty state? | | | | |
| 7 | Limit complexity | Is the system designed in such a way that **structural complexity is limited**? Examples include avoiding cyclic dependencies, reducing dependencies, and using techniques such as dependency injection. | | | | |

| # | Tactics Group | Tactics Question | Supported? (Y/N) | Risk | Design Decisions and Location | Rationale and Assumptions |
|---|---|---|---|---|---|---|
| 8 | | Does the system include few or no (i.e., **limited) sources of nondeterminism**? This helps to limit the behavioral complexity that comes with unconstrained parallelism, which in turn simplifies testing. | | | | |

## B.8   Usability

| # | Tactics Group | Tactics Question | Supported? (Y/N) | Risk | Design Decisions and Location | Rationale and Assumptions |
|---|---|---|---|---|---|---|
| 1 | Supporting user initiative | Does the system support operation **canceling**? | | | | |
| 2 | | Does the system support operation **undoing**? | | | | |
| 3 | | Does the system support operations to be **paused** and later resumed? Examples are pausing the download of a file in a web browser and allowing the user to retry an incomplete (and failed) download. | | | | |
| 4 | | Does the system support operations to be applied to groups of objects (**aggregation**)? For example, does it allow you to see the cumulative size of a number of files that are selected in a file browser window? | | | | |

*(continues)*

| # | Tactics Group | Tactics Question | Supported? (Y/N) | Risk | Design Decisions and Location | Rationale and Assumptions |
|---|---|---|---|---|---|---|
| 5 | Support system initiative | Does the system provide assistance to the user based on the tasks that he or she is performing (by **maintaining a task model**)? Examples include:<br>• Validation of input data<br>• Drawing user attention to changes in the UI<br>• Maintaining UI consistency<br>• Adding toolbars and menus to help users find functionality provided by the UI<br>• Using wizards or other techniques to guide users in performing key user scenarios | | | | |
| 6 | | Does the system support adjustments to the UI with respect to the class of users (by **maintaining a user model**)? Examples include supporting UI customization (including localization) and supporting accessibility. | | | | |
| 7 | | Does the system provide appropriate feedback to the user based on the system characteristics (by **maintaining a system model**)? Examples include:<br>• Avoiding blocking the user while handling long-running requests<br>• Providing feedback on action progress (i.e., progress bars)<br>• Displaying user-friendly errors without exposing sensitive data by managing exceptions<br>• Adjusting the UI with respect to screen size and resolution | | | | |

# B.9 DevOps

| # | Tactics Group | Tactics Question | Supported? (Y/N) | Risk | Design Decisions and Location | Rationale and Assumptions |
|---|---|---|---|---|---|---|
| 1 | Testability: control and observe system state | Does the system or the system components provide **specialized interfaces** to facilitate testing and monitoring? | | | | |
| 2 | | Does the system provide mechanisms that allow information that crosses an interface to be recorded so that it can be used later for testing purposes (**record/playback**)? | | | | |
| 3 | | Can the system be executed in isolation (a **sandbox**) to experiment or test it without worrying about having to undo the consequences of the experiment? | | | | |
| 4 | Performance: manage resources | Can the system seamlessly **increase resources** (e.g., CPU, memory, network bandwidth)? | | | | |
| 5 | | Can the system **introduce concurrency**? For example, does it support the seamless addition of parallel processing streams so that more requests for services can be processed concurrently? | | | | |
| 6 | | Does the system **maintain multiple copies of data** (e.g., by replicating databases or using caches) to decrease contention for frequently accessed data? | | | | |

*(continues)*

| # | Tactics Group | Tactics Question | Supported? (Y/N) | Risk | Design Decisions and Location | Rationale and Assumptions |
|---|---|---|---|---|---|---|
| 7 | | Does the system **maintain multiple copies of computations** (e.g., by keeping a pool of servers in a server farm) to decrease contention for frequently accessed computational resources? | | | | |
| 8 | | Does the system **schedule resources**, particularly scarce resources, so that they may be allocated according to an explicit scheduling policy? | | | | |
| 9 | Performance: control resource demand | Does the system **reduce overhead** of responding to service requests by, for example, removing intermediaries or co-locating resources? | | | | |
| 10 | | If your inputs are a continuous stream of data, does the system **manage the sampling rate**? That is, is it possible for you to sample the data at varying rates (with concomitant changes in accuracy/fidelity)? | | | | |
| 11 | | Does the system monitor and **limit its event response**? That is, does the system limit the number of events it responds to in a time period, to ensure predictable responses for the events that are actually serviced? | | | | |
| 12 | | Given that you may have more requests for service than available resources, does the system **prioritize events**? | | | | |

| # | Tactics Group | Tactics Question | Supported? (Y/N) | Risk | Design Decisions and Location | Rationale and Assumptions |
|---|---|---|---|---|---|---|
| 13 | Modifiability: reduce coupling | Does the system consistently **encapsulate** functionality? This typically involves isolating the functionality under scrutiny and introducing an explicit interface to it. | | | | |
| 14 | | Does the system **abstract common services**, in cases where you are providing several similar services? For example, this technique is often used when you want your system to be portable across operating systems, hardware, or other environment variations. | | | | |
| 15 | Modifiability: defer binding | Does the system regularly **defer binding** of important functionality so that it can be replaced later in the life cycle, perhaps even by end users? For example, do you use plug-ins, add-ons, or user scripting to extend the functionality of the system? | | | | |
| 16 | Availability: detect faults | Does the system use a component to **monitor** the state of health of other parts of the system? A system monitor can detect failure or congestion in the network or other shared resources, such as from a denial-of-service attack. | | | | |
| 17 | | Do you use **exception detection** to detect a system condition that alters the normal flow of execution (e.g., system exception, parameter fence, parameter typing, timeout)? | | | | |

*(continues)*

266 Appendix B—Tactics-Based Questionnaires

| # | Tactics Group | Tactics Question | Supported? (Y/N) | Risk | Design Decisions and Location | Rationale and Assumptions |
|---|---|---|---|---|---|---|
| 18 | | Does the system use **voting** to check that replicated components are producing the same results? The replicated components may be identical replicas, functionally redundant, or analytically redundant. | | | | |
| 19 | Availability: recover from faults (preparation and repair) | Does the system employ **rollback**, so that it can revert to a previously saved good state (the "rollback line") in the event of a fault? | | | | |
| 20 | | Does the system employ **active redundancy** (hot spare)? In active redundancy, all nodes in a protection group (a group of nodes where one or more nodes are "active", with the remainder serving as redundant spares) receive and process identical inputs in parallel, allowing redundant spares to maintain synchronous state with the active node(s). | | | | |
| 21 | | Does the system have consistent policies and mechanisms for **reconfiguration** after failures, reassigning responsibilities to the resources left functioning, while maintaining as much functionality as possible? | | | | |
| 22 | | Does the system employ **exception handling** to deal with faults? Typically, the handling involves either reporting the fault or handling it, potentially masking the fault by correcting the cause of the exception and retrying. | | | | |

## B.10 Further Reading

The tactics catalog from which the questionnaires are derived can be found in L. Bass, P. Clements, and R. Kazman, *Software Architecture in Practice* (3rd ed.), 2012.

An analysis of quality attribute data from SEI ATAMs, showing which qualities are the most common in practice, can be found in I. Ozkaya, L. Bass, R. Sangwan, and R. Nord, "Making Practical Use of Quality Attribute Information", *IEEE Software*, March/April 2008, and in a later study by S. Bellomo, I. Gorton, and R. Kazman, "Insights from 15 Years of ATAM Data: Towards Agile Architecture", *IEEE Software*, 32:5, 38-45, September/October 2015.

The set of DevOps tactics was developed and presented in H-M Chen, R. Kazman, S. Haziyev, V. Kropov, and D. Chtchourov, "Architectural Support for DevOps in a Neo-Metropolis BDaaS Platform", *IEEE 34th Symposium on Reliable Distributed Systems Workshop (SRDSW)*, Montreal, Canada, September 2015.

# Glossary

**Active Reviews for Intermediate Design (ARID) method** A method in which the architecture design (or part of it) is presented to a group of reviewers—typically the engineers who will use the design. After the presentation, a set of scenarios is selected. The reviewers attempt to use the elements in the architecture to satisfy the scenarios. The reviewers are asked to write code or pseudocode or to create sequence diagrams for the purpose of identifying interfaces. This method can be used in preparation for element interaction design.

**ADD** *See* Attribute Driven Design method.

**ADL** *See* Architecture Description Language.

**Analysis** The process of breaking a complex entity into its constituent parts as a means of understanding it. Analysis is used at different moments in the design process; for example, the inputs are analyzed to make design decisions and the resulting architecture is also analyzed to gauge if it is appropriate to satisfy its associated drivers.

**Application framework** A reusable software element, constructed out of patterns and tactics, that provides generic functionality addressing recurring domain and quality attribute concerns across a broad range of applications. Also called a framework.

**Architectural concern** An additional aspect that needs to be considered as part of architectural design but that is not expressed as a traditional requirement. Examples include general concerns, such as creating an overall system structure, and more specific concerns, such as managing exceptions or generating logs. Other architectural concerns include internal requirements, which are seldom expressed by customers, and issues resulting from analysis activities, such as architectural evaluations.

**Architectural design** The activity of making decisions to translate ideas from the world of needs (architectural drivers) to the world of solutions, in terms of structures.

**Architectural drivers** The design purpose, architecturally significant requirements, and architectural concerns that serve as an input to the design process. These considerations are critical to the success of the system and, as such, they drive and shape the architecture.

**Architectural evaluation** A technique to analyze and assess the value of architectural decisions.

**Architectural pattern** *See* Patterns (Architectural and Design).

**Architecturally significant requirement (ASR)** A system requirement that has a particular importance with respect to the software architecture. ASRs include quality attributes, primary functional requirements, and constraints.

**Architecture Description Language (ADL)** A notation to document an architecture. ADLs typically employ both a graphical notation and a (formally defined) textual notation to describe an architecture—primarily the computational (runtime) components and interactions among them—and its properties.

**Architecture Tradeoff Analysis Method (ATAM)** An established method for analyzing architectures, driven by scenarios. Its purpose is to assess the consequences of architectural decisions in light of quality attribute requirements and business goals.

**ARID** *See* Active Reviews for Intermediate Design method.

**ASR** *See* Architecturally significant requirement.

**ATAM** *See* Architecture Tradeoff Analysis Method.

**Attribute-Driven Design (ADD) method** An iterative architecture design method that takes drivers as inputs and produces an architecture. In each iteration, structures are produced by refining elements identified in previous iterations. These structures are created primarily from design concepts, which are selected and instantiated to address a subset of the drivers that are selected for the iteration.

**Big Design Up Front (BDUF)** The (now largely discredited) practice of attempting to do all of the architectural design at the beginning of a project. It is usually associated with a waterfall software development life cycle.

**Brownfield development** Software development that builds upon an existing asset. Contrast with greenfield development.

**Constraint** A decision over which the architect has little or no control. It may be either technical or organizational.

**Cost Benefit Analysis Method (CBAM)** A method that associates costs, benefits, and schedule implications with strategies chosen to make improvements in an architecture. This method is used to rank the strategies, as a means of finding an optimal set of strategies to implement in the next iteration.

**Design concept**   The building blocks from which the structures that make up the architecture are created. Different types of design concepts exist, including reference architectures, deployment patterns, architectural patterns, tactics, technology families, and externally developed components (such as frameworks).

**Design concepts catalog**   A collection of design concepts for a particular application domain.

**Design decision**   A decision that is made during the design process, including the selection of a design concept and the instantiation of the selected design concept.

**Design iteration**   A group of design decisions through which a subset of the drivers is transformed into structures. One or more design iterations are performed within a design round.

**Design pattern**   *See* Patterns (Architectural and Design).

**Design purpose**   The reason why the architecture design is performed. For example, the design may be performed for estimation during pre-sales, prototyping, or development purposes.

**Design round**   The architecture design activities performed within a development cycle if an iterative development model is used, or the entire set of architecture design activities if a waterfall model is used.

**Deployment pattern**   A pattern that provides a model for how to physically structure the system to deploy it.

**Development cycle**   The development of a project increment (i.e., a project iteration).

**DevOps**   A portmanteau word, combining "development" and "operations". DevOps stands in contrast to earlier forms of running a software project, in which development teams developed software and then "tossed it over the wall" to operations. In DevOps, the two teams work closely together and adopt processes, tools, and architectures to make it easier to rapidly modify, build, test, release, and monitor software.

**Element (in definition of software architecture)**   One of the parts that compose the structures of the architecture. Elements may exist at runtime or development time or they may exist physically. Elements are connected by relations.

**Element interaction design**   The identification of the modules and their associated interfaces to support the nonprimary use cases. This is typically performed using sequence diagrams according to the decisions made during architectural design.

**Element internals design**   The internal design of the elements identified as part of element interaction design, so as to satisfy the element's interface.

**Externally developed component**   A design concept that is concrete in nature and that is not built as part of the system development, but rather is acquired and reused. Such components include application frameworks, products, and platforms.

**Greenfield development**   Software development that begins with little or no legacy code base to build upon.

**Instantiation**   The process of adapting a design concept to the particular problem being addressed. It involves creating elements and relations, and associating responsibilities with the elements, from the selected design concept. Instantiation can also refer to configuration when design concepts are externally developed components.

**Interface**   The externally visible properties of elements that establish a contractual specification that allows elements to collaborate and exchange information, via relations.

**Marketecture**   A single-page, typically informal, representation of a software system architecture. This representation is aimed primarily at nontechnical people, and is used to present a system vision.

**Minimum viable product (MVP)**   An evolutionary prototype with *only* those core features that allow the product to be deployed. It emphasizes hypothesis testing by fielding the product with real users and collecting usage data that then helps to confirm or reject the hypothesis.

**Patterns (architectural and design)**   Conceptual solutions to recurring design problems that exist in a defined context. When they are used to address an architectural driver, they are "architectural patterns"; when their use has just a local influence—for example, when used to perform element internals design—they are "design patterns".

**Platform**   A complete infrastructure upon which to build and execute applications.

**Pre-sales**   A phase in project development in which the scope of the project, a business case, and an initial plan are established. This phase is used by the customers (or funders) to decide whether they want to pursue the project.

**Primary functional requirements**   Functionality is the ability of the system to do the work for which it was intended. Primary functionality is usually defined as functionality that is critical to achieve the business goals that motivate the development of the system.

**Product**   A self-contained functional piece of software that can be integrated into the system that is being designed and that requires only minor configuration or coding. Also called a software package.

**Proof of concept (PoC)**    A prototype that is used to quickly evaluate a technology, thereby determining whether it can satisfy critical architecture scenarios, usually related to quality attributes such as performance and scalability.

**QAW**    *See* Quality Attribute Workshop.

**Quality attribute**    A measurable or testable property of a system that is used to indicate how well the system satisfies the needs of its stakeholders. Quality attributes are orthogonal to functionality.

**Quality attribute scenario**    *See* Scenario.

**Quality Attribute Workshop (QAW)**    A facilitated brainstorming session involving a group of system stakeholders in eliciting, specifying, prioritizing, and achieving consensus on quality attributes.

**Rationale**    A line of reasoning and justification that led to a design decision.

**Refactoring**    Changing the system's architecture or code, without affecting its functionality, to achieve different quality attribute responses.

**Reference Architecture**    Blueprints that provide an overall logical structure for types of applications, consisting of a reference model that is mapped onto one or more architectural patterns. It has been proven in business and technical contexts, and typically comes with a set of supporting artifacts that facilitates its use.

**Relation (in definition of software architecture)**    One of the parts that compose the structures of an architecture. Relations may exist at runtime or development time or they may exist physically. Relations connect elements.

**Scenario**    A technique to specify quality attributes that describes a stimulus received by the system and a measurable response to this stimulus. Scenarios are testable, falsifiable hypotheses about the quality attribute behavior of the system under consideration. Completely developed scenarios are described using six parts, but less elaborate ("raw") scenarios can also be described.

**Sketch of a view**    A preliminary type of documentation that is created as part of the design process. The sketch can be refined to become a full-fledged view, typically after the design activity has finished.

**Software architecture**    "The set of structures needed to reason about the system, which comprise software elements, relations among them, and properties of both".

**Spike**    A time-boxed task that is created to answer a technical question or gather information.

**Structure**    A coherent set of software elements, relations, and properties. Structures are represented in views.

**Tactic**    A proven design strategy that influences the control of a quality attribute response.

**Technical debt**   The decisions—often called "hacks"—made in a software project that trade off short-term gains, such as ease of implementation, at the cost of long-term sustainability of the system. By taking such shortcuts, the software base "goes into debt".

**Technology family**   A group of technologies with common functional purposes.

**View**   A representation of an architectural structure. A view usually includes a graphical representation of the structure and additional information that complements the information presented in the diagram.

# About the Authors

**Humberto Cervantes** is a professor at Universidad Autónoma Metropolitana Iztapalapa in Mexico City. His primary research interest is software architecture and, more specifically, the development of methods and tools to aid in the design process. He is active in promoting the adoption of these methods and tools in the software industry. Since 2006, Cervantes has been a consultant for software development companies in topics related to software architecture. He has authored numerous research papers and popularization articles, and has also coauthored one of the few books in Spanish on the topic of software architecture.

Cervantes received a master's degree and a Ph.D. from Université Joseph Fourier in Grenoble, France. He holds the Software Architecture Professional and ATAM Evaluator certificates from SEI. Besides software engineering, Cervantes enjoys spending time with his family and friends, exercising, and traveling.

**Rick Kazman** is a professor at the University of Hawaii and a research scientist at the Software Engineering Institute of Carnegie Mellon University. His primary research interests are software architecture, design and analysis tools, software visualization, and software engineering economics. Kazman has created several highly influential methods and tools for architecture analysis, including SAAM (Software Architecture Analysis Method), ATAM (Architecture Tradeoff Analysis Method), CBAM (Cost–Benefit Analysis Method), and the Dali and Titan tools. He is the author of more than one hundred fifty peer-reviewed papers, and is coauthor of several books, including *Software Architecture in Practice, Third Edition* (Addison-Wesley, 2013), *Evaluating Software Architectures* (Addison-Wesley, 2002), and *Ultra-Large-Scale Systems* (Software Engineering Institute, 2006).

Kazman received a B.A. (English/music) and M.Math. (computer science) from the University of Waterloo, an M.A. (English) from York University, and a Ph.D. (computational linguistics) from Carnegie Mellon University. How he ever became a software engineering researcher is anybody's guess. When not architecting or writing about architecture, Kazman may be found cycling, playing the piano, practicing Tae Kwon Do and Jiu Jitsu, or (more often) flying back and forth between Hawaii and Pittsburgh.

# Index

# Learn More About Software Architecture from the SEI

## SATURN and the SEI Architecture Curriculum

**SATURN Conference**

The Software Engineering Institute (SEI) Architecture Technology User Network (SATURN) Conference is designed for practitioners who are responsible for producing robust software architectures and those who view software architecture as a critical element of achieving their business goals.

As the premier architecture conference for senior engineers, SATURN offers keynotes and sessions on both essential skills and cutting-edge methods for software architects.

**To learn more about SATURN, see www.sei.cmu.edu/saturn.**

**SEI Architecture Curriculum**

Based on decades of experience architecting software-reliant systems and supported by four widely acclaimed books, this curriculum equips software professionals with state-of-the-art practices, so they can efficiently design, evolve, and maintain software-reliant systems that meet their intended business goals.

**To learn more about this curriculum, see www.sei.cmu. edu/training/find/courses.**